Margy Le

# *Illustrated Dictionary*

# *of Art Terms*

**B.T. Batsford Ltd   London**

Revised and edited for the English edition by Henry Malt

First published by North Light, an imprint of
Writer's Digest Books, 9933 Alliance Road,
Cincinnati, Ohio 45242

Published in Britain by
B.T. Batsford Ltd
4 Fitzhardinge Street
London W1H 0AH

Typeset by Tek-Art Ltd, Kent and
printed in Great Britain by
Anchor Brendon Ltd
Tiptree, Essex

First US Printing 1984
First Printing in Britain 1987

ISBN 0 7134 5333 8 (cased)
ISBN 0 7134 5334 6 (limp)

# ACKNOWLEDGMENTS
## (by Henry Malt)

Many people have, knowingly or unknowingly, helped with the research for this book. My first debt must, however, be to Margy Lee Elspass who compiled the original work. This delights by its simplicity and I hope I have retained her freshness of style and unprejudiced approach.

Most of the UK manufacturers provided catalogues and information about their products, to which I hope I have done justice short of listing all their products which they do perfectly well themselves.

Oliver Green of the London Transport Museum provided an immense amount of information which forms the basis of one particular entry and gave the initiative for much additional research on twentieth-century British illustration.

Acknowledgments for copyright of paintings reproduced are as follows: ADAGP 1987 for Braque, Chagall, Schwitters, Duchamp, Kandinsky and Bonnard; ADAGP, Paris and COSMOPRESS, Geneva 1987 for Klee; DACS 1987 for the works of Matisse, Mondrian, Picasso, Lichtenstein and Roualt; The Tate Gallery for Bacon, Bomberg, Cézanne, Collier, Constable, Cotman, Crome, Degas, De Wint, Gainsborough, Gaugin, Girtin, Hockney, Kline, Malevich, Manet, Modigliani, Monet, Munch, Piper, Pollock, Reynolds, Rodin, Seurat, Spencer, Turner and Whistler. *Regatta at Argenteuil*, Auguste Renoir, is from the National Gallery of Art, Washington; Ailsa Mellon Bruce Collection. *Child in a straw hat*, Mary Cassatt, is from the National Gallery of Art, Washington; collection of Mr & Mrs Paul Mellon.

Finally, my family put up with frequent interruptions as I disappeared in mid-meal or conversation in order to write up a new idea.

# PREFACE (*by Henry Malt*)

The purpose of any specialized dictionary is to enable the user to understand and practise the topic in question. If the subject is technical, jargon, rules and formulae are explained and that, more or less, is an end of it. But what of art? The word itself defies definition, yet how often have we heard someone say, 'that's not art!'; so if not, what is? There are grave dangers in rigid definition.

The original on which this book is based was written for American college students. It contains much that will not translate, much that is obvious, but a great deal of clarity and simplicity which I have tried to retain. I have tried to make it a book for the practising artist who wants clarification of a name or a term or a quick explanation of a topic discovered elsewhere. I have kept the entries as short as possible, for there are many other books which will explain specific subjects more comprehensively than there is space to do here.

As with every dictionary, a certain amount of cross-referencing is required. This helps retain the simplicity of the individual entries and may also introduce new subjects, but I apologize now to those who prefer everything in one place.

Included in the listings are several short biographies of individual artists. It has not been possible to be exhaustive and those who have been included are here because they are particularly influential or represent a particular school, style or period. A list of noteworthy Western artists is on p. 216.

It is the purpose of this book to cover a lot of ground in a small space. If it provides some enlightenment and stimulates additional research, it has served its purpose. You may also find that consulting it for one topic will introduce others; and if, each time you use it, you find something you did not previously know, it will have succeeded completely.

# A

**A** — Symbol on tube of paint indicating a standard degree of colour permanence

**AA** — Symbol on tube of paint indicating the highest degree of colour permanence

**abbozzo** — Sketch or rough drawing; first draft of a work of art; underpainting

**absorbent ground** — A ground or base on a surface to be painted that absorbs the liquid from the paint

**abstract art** — An art form in which the essence of a subject is stated in a brief or simplified manner, with emphasis on design and little or no attempt to represent forms or subject matter realistically. *See also* **design elements**; **nonrepresentational art**

**abstract expressionism** — A style of non-geometric abstract art that started in the 1940s and became popular in the 1950s; paintings were usually large and forceful. Among others, Wassily Kandinsky, Arshile Gorky, Jackson Pollock, Willem DeKooning, and Mark Rothko are classified in this style. *See also* **action painting; nonobjective art**

**Abstraction-Creation Group** — An international school of painters and sculptors of the 1930s who were dependent on geometric shapes and forms; Piet Mondrian was the major figure

**academician** — 1. An elected member of an academy. 2. One who follows the principles of the conservative academic tradition

**academy (art)** — 1. A learned group accepted as authoritative in its area of art. 2. A school in which art is taught

**academy blue** — Pigment; a mixture of viridian and ultramarine blue

**academy board** — A cardboard once used by students in oil painting, replaced by canvas board

**academy figure** — A nude figure (life drawing or painting), about half life-size, used for instruction and not considered a work of art

**acanthus** — A plant with thorny leaves seen on capitals of Corinthian columns and elsewhere as a decorative motif

**accent** — To emphasize by drawing attention to an area of a picture. This is usually accomplished by stressing in a limited area one or more of the design elements such as value or colour contrasts, texture, etc. *See also* **design elements**

**accent colour** — A small amount of contrasting colour used against another colour; for example, orange accent in a predominantly blue area

**acetate** — A strong, transparent, or semitransparent sheet of plastic, available in various thicknesses and used in covers for artwork, in colour separation, in retouching, and in animation drawing. *See also* **cel; frisket**

**acetate, prefixed or prepared** — A clear, treated plastic that can be painted on either side with watercolours, inks, or dyes without crawling or peeling of colours; used for overlays in graphic arts and in colour separation of art or photography

**acetic acid** — In graphics, a liquid used to clean a plate just before the mordant is applied

**acetone** — A flammable, volatile solvent, mildly toxic, often used in the restoration and cleaning of old paintings. Its most common form is nail varnish remover

**achromatic** — Without colour, as in white, black, and any grey made from the mixture of black and white

**acid bath** — In the etching process, an acid or acid mixture in which a plate is immersed to be bitten or etched

**acid-free** — Said of art paper with a 7 pH (ideal); above 8.5 pH or below 6.5 pH is not considered acid-free

**acid-resist substance** — An acid resistant substance used to block the action of acid in **etching**

**Acra** — Pigment; a violet colour with a decided reddish-pink cast when reduced; permanent

**Acra red** — Pigment; a medium bright red; permanent

**acrolith** — A statue made of more than one material

**acrylic flow improver** — A medium used with acrylic paint to improve its flow without the loss of colour strength

**acrylic inks** — A variety of toxic, flammable synthetic inks used in silk-screen process on acetate and acrylic sheets such as Perspex

**acrylic paints** — Paints based on a synthetic plastic medium. Initially water-soluble, but set hard very quickly. Very popular when first introduced, but less so as the disadvantages became apparent. Requiring quick work, they produce bright, light-proof and non-fading colours. Colour ranges are generally restricted. Trade names include Cryla, Liquitex. Some of the disadvantages were overcome by alkyd

**acrylic retarder** — A medium added to acrylics to slow drying time

**acrylic sheets** — Crystal-clear sheets of plexiglass plastic, generally known as Perspex, that can be carved, sawn, cemented, or moulded

**acrylic varnish** — *See* **picture varnish**

**acrylic varnish remover** — A solution used to remove acrylic varnish

**action lines** — In cartooning, extraneous lines used to suggest action or movement

**action painting** — Imageless, spontaneous painting, marked by drips, splashes, and spatters; represented by Jackson Pollock, Mark Toby, Franz Kline, and others. *See also* **abstract expressionism**

action painting by
Franz Kline (*Meryon*)

3

**action pose** — Attitude or pose that suggests movement

**Ada school** — Named for Ada, thought to be a sister of Charlemagne, who patronized a group of ivory sculptors and manuscript illuminators in late eighth and early ninth centuries

**additive colour mixing** — White light is the product of three primary colours, red, yellow and blue. In additive mixing, variations of colour are produced by the introduction of a new light source or by reflecting individual primaries separately. In a simple example, a blue light and a yellow light shone onto a white surface will appear green. In painting this effect is exploited by pointillism, where individual dots of colour are placed close together so as to be indistinguishable by the eye at a normal viewing distance. See also **subtractive colour mixing**

**adjacent colours** — *See* **analogous colours**

**adjustable triangle** — A triangle that has one adjustable arm that can be clamped at different angles, with a protractor between the adjustable arm and the main area of the triangle

**advancing colours** — Colours that appear to move forward or closer to the viewer, usually red, yellow, and orange

adjustable triangle

**adventure strip** — A realistically treated cartoon strip that deals with a continuing adventure story; usually syndicated in newspapers

**advertising agency** — A group of writers, artists, and marketing experts who create advertisements, sales campaigns, marketing surveys and tests, seminars, displays, package designs, audiovisuals, and similar promotions for clients

**advertising director** — The person responsible for the overall appearance and placing of an advertisement, including design, copy and media

**adz, adze** — In sculpture and woodcarving, a cutting tool used to rough-shape wood

**Aegean painting** — Painting of Crete, Mycenae, and the Cyclades, 2600-1200 BC; colourful, stylized, but with a strong feeling for naturalism

**aerial perspective** — In painting, achievement of an effect of atmosphere and apparent distance by receding values and indistinctness of colour

**aerugo** — *See* **patina**

4

**aesthetic** — Pertaining to the beautiful, refined, tasteful, and artistic

**aestheticism** — A doctrine whereby art exists solely for its own sake; the nineteenth-century aesthetic movement

**aes ustum** — *See* **patina**

**African art** — Ceremonial sculpture, masks, and crafts derived from African tribal cultures

**afterimage** — An illusory optical image that continues after its source is removed; often tends toward the complementary colour of the original image

**agate** — In printing, a small-size type, approximately 5½-point

**agate line** — A unit of measurement for depth of a column of printed advertising, in which fourteen agate lines equal one column inch

**agent** — A business representative for an artist

**agglutinant** — An adhesive used as a binder in watercolour paints, pastels, and some inks

**'air'** — A term used to indicate 1. atmosphere in a landscape or waterscape; 2. space in a painting around objects or portraits; 3. open, unprinted space in printed material

**airbrush** — A miniature precision spray gun attached to an air compressor, carbon dioxide tank, or other means of air pressure; used by commercial artists to create a smooth application of paint or gradations in value and colour; frequently used in photo retouching and sometimes in illustration and other types of painting

abcdefghijklmnopqrstuvwxyz
ABCDEFGHIJKLMNOPQRSTUVWXYZ

agate type –
5½ point Baskerville

airbrush

**airbrush lithography** — A lithography technique in which the airbrush is used to draw directly on the stone or plate

**air eraser** — A tool similar to the airbrush; uses an abrasive in a fine, controlled spray to erase ink or paint; sometimes used to blend highlights and shadows in drawings or paintings

**alabaster** — A whitish semitranslucent gypsum that can be carved and cut into sculpture

**à la colle** — *See* **distemper**

**à la poupée** — In intaglio, a means of printing several colours at one time by applying each colour to the plate separately with a pad of felt

**album leaves** — (oriental) A collection of small paintings in album form, usually six, eight, or ten

**alcohol** — A flammable, anhydrous (without water) solvent used mainly to thin lacquers and shellac

**Alexandrian blue** — Pigment. *See* **Egyptian blue**; close to cobalt blue

**Alexandrian style** — A soft and sentimental style developed by Hellenistic artists of the third to first centuries BC (Ptolemaic period)

**alizarin** — Organic pigment developed from coal tar

**alizarin blue** — Pigment; a clear transparent lake generally used in printing inks and for semipermanent artwork; close to indigo on the colour chart

**alizarin brown** — Pigment; a reddish transparent brown, permanent; close to burnt sienna on the colour chart

**alizarin carmine** — An obsolete name for alizarin crimson

**alizarin crimson** — Pigment; a deep transparent red; mixes well with blue to create a true purple; permanent

**alizarin crimson, golden** — Pigment; a warmer, less bluish alizarin; some artists prefer it for skin tones; permanent

**alizarin green** — Pigment; a clear transparent lake generally used in printing inks and for semipermanent artwork

**alizarin violet** — Pigment; a clear transparent lake; not permanent; close to magenta on the colour chart

**alizarin yellow** — Pigment; a brownish transparent yellow, semipermanent

**alkyd colours** — Artists' paints similar to oils but with a faster drying time, distributed by Winsor and Newton; can be used with any medium used with oil paints

**alla prima painting** — (Italian, *the first time*) Method of direct painting (usually in oil) often in one sitting, with minimal or no underpainting

**alligatoring** — *See* **crackle**

**Almohad style** — An art style introduced into Spain by the Almohads, a Moroccan Berber Moslem dynasty, in the twelfth and thirteenth centuries

**alto-rilievo** — (Italian *high relief*) In sculpture, a type of relief where the design projects almost entirely away from the surface

**Amarna art** — Egyptian, during the time of Akhenaten, a religious reformer (1375-1358 BC); a more natural than stylistic art, based on expressing the truth

**Amberlith** — A transparent, amber-coloured masking film used in making mechanicals and in the film processes of photolithography

**American Gothic** — A hard-edge, realistic type of painting associated with the American painter, Grant Wood; title of a popular painting by that artist

**American Indian prints** — Geometric patterns often in horizontal or vertical stripes

**American Ten, the** — A group of American impressionists founded in 1898 by J. Alden Weir; the artists involved did not gain the kind of recognition achieved by their counterparts in France; prominent in this movement were William Merritt Chase, Childe Hassam, Ernest Lawson, and John Twactman

**amorphous** — Lacking a definite shape or form

**A.N.A.** — Associate member of the National Academy of Design

**anaglyph** — Sculpture or decoration (such as a cameo) in relief

**analogous colours** — Colours that are closely related, such as blue, blue green, and green; three or four colours that are adjacent (touch) on the colour wheel

**anatomy** — The study of body structure, human or animal – muscles, bones, etc; the visual appearance of the form

**Anglo-Saxon art** — An art style of the fifth to eleventh centuries in England, characterized by interlaced motifs. *See* **arabesque**

**angular perspective** — *See* **two-point perspective**

**aniline colours** — Colours made from coal tars; a disparaging term for synthetic dyes and pigments that are not sufficiently light-fast for artists' use

**animate** — To cause to appear lifelike and to have movement, as in animated cartoons

**animated cartoons** — In motion pictures, a series of successive still cartoons projected one after the other so rapidly that there is an appearance of movement

**animator** — In an animation studio, the artist who draws the cels that give the character movement

**animation paper** — Two- or three-ply paper available in rolls, used for animation drawings

**ankh** — The Egyptian Cross; the symbol of life; modern symbolism includes two meanings: everlasting life and love

**ansate cross** — Same as **ankh**

**anthemion** — A decorative design of honeysuckle or palm leaves

**anti-cerne** — A white space in the form of a line between two areas of colour in a picture; frequently used by the Fauve artists; the opposite of a black line

**antimony colours** — Pigments; bright orange and vermilion, now generally replaced by cadmiums

**antimony white** — Similar to titanium white, but darkens from sulphur fumes; permanent

**antimony yellow** — Pigment; Naples yellow, name obsolete

**antiques** — Plaster casts of classical sculptures used in drawing classes to study form

**antiquing** — Using a glaze of burnt or raw umber over a work of art to create an appearance of age

**Antwerp blue** — Pigment; a reduced Prussian blue, transparent, not permanent

**Antwerp red** — Pigment; light earth red, permanent; between Venetian red and cadmium red light on the colour chart

**Antwerp school** — Early sixteenth-century Flemish painters who were influenced by the Italian Renaissance; Quentin Massys was one of the prominent artists.

**apex** — The highest point or summit

**appliqué** — In design, one material cut out and applied to another

**aqua fortis** — (Latin, *nitric acid*) In etching, the mordant or solution used to etch the plates, diluted for use with one to five parts water

**aquagraph** — A monoprint made by painting with a water medium on a metal, glass, or plastic plate and pulling one print from that plate; additional colours can be printed by aligning the paper to the plate design

**aquarelle** — (French) Transparent watercolour

**aquarelle brush** — A particular style of watercolour brush, used flat for large areas and on the edge for fine lines

ankh

8

**aquatint** — An intaglio printing process in which tones can be etched, rather than just lines, and rich darks as well as transparent tints can be produced; often resembles a wash drawing

**aquatint mezzotint** — In etching, a plate is first bitten in a solid aquatint, then a design is worked on top of the aquatint with a scraper and burnisher, producing a result similar to a mezzotint

**A.R.A.** — (British) Associate of the Royal Academy of Art

**arabesque** — An interlaced ornamental design, floral and/or geometric

**arc** — A portion or section of a curved line

**Arches (D'Arches)** — Trade name of a popular 100 percent rag watercolour paper made in France; available in weights of 72, 90, 140, 300, 400 and 550 pounds, as well as different textures – hot press (smooth), cold press (medium rough), and rough. Now generally available in the UK

arabesque

**archival mounting** — The use of acid-free mount boards to ensure that there is no damage to the work mounted. Also referred to as museum mounting

**armature** — In sculpture, a skeleton of wire or other durable material on which the artist builds his work in clay, plaster, etc.

**armature wire** — Wire used to build an armature, available in different diameters

**Armory Show, the** — In 1913, innovative and avant-garde artists from America and Europe held a show at the 69th Regiment Armory in New York City; the public derided the works, but nonetheless the impact on American art was lasting. 'The Armory Show' has become a historical benchmark in America, separating earlier modes of art from 'modern art'

figure armature

**Arnaudon's green** — Pigment; a chromium oxide green, now obsolete

**art** — One of the most misused terms in the English language and for which everyone has their own definition. Strictly, it refers to any human skill, but is frequently used qualitatively to imply excellence

**art appreciation** — The understanding of and regard for the arts

**Art Brut** — (French, *art in the raw*) Jean Dubuffet (early 1900s) patterned his art after the primitive work of children and the insane, which he found to have directness and vitality

**art buyer** — The person who is a link between an agency and freelance artists; buys artwork for the agency

**Art Deco** — A geometric, sleek, elegant style of decorative art popular in the 1920s and 1930s, and embracing painting, buildings and general artefacts

**art director** — Person with overall responsibility for a project involving several artists

**art engagé** — (French, *art involved in life*) Art with a social or political significance

**artgum** — An eraser that crumbles as it erases, not scratching or discolouring artwork

**artist's bridge** — A tool used to balance the hand and keep it clear of the working surface while drawing or painting delicate pasages. *See also* **mahlstick**

**artists' colours** — Generally used to refer to a manufacturer's highest grade, using the best pigments

**artist's proof** — One of the first proofs from a limited edition of prints, for the artist's own copyright use; marked as artist's proof (A.P.) and not numbered; may draw a premium price. May have E.A. (*épreuve d' artiste*) instead of A.P.

**art nouveau** — (French, *The New Art*) Art movement popular in the 1890s and early 1900s in Europe and America; a busy, decorative style characterized by flowing vines and flat shapes (as seen in Tiffany glass) and undulating line (seen in Toulouse-Lautrec posters). Aubrey Beardsley and Gustav Klimt are among the other noted artists associated with the movement, but its beginnings are attributed to William Morris. It is also known as Jugendstil and Yellow Book style

**Arts & Crafts Movement** — British design movement of the late nineteenth century founded by William Morris in which utilitarian objects were given new value as works of art. To an extent deriving from the pre-Raphaelite Brotherhood, the movement also paved the way for art nouveau

**Arts Council** — The chief regulatory and grant-awarding body for the arts in the UK

**Art Students League** — An art institute in New York City, founded in 1875; subjects taught are: drawing, painting, graphics, sculpture, illustration, anatomy, colour, composition, design, portraiture, and mural painting

**artwork** — A general term applied to any artistic production, but generally graphic design used for printing

**ascender** — The part of a lowercase letter that projects above the main line, as in d, f, h, k, l, t

**asphaltum** — 1. In etching, a liquid used on plates as a soft ground and on the backs of plates to protect them from the mordant. 2. In lithography, used to process the drawing chemically. 3. An old oil colour, destructive to paintings

**assemblage** — The combination of objets trouvés to form a three-dimensional structure which, if it were two-dimensional, would be collage

**Asturian art** — A ninth-century Gothic style with Moorish derivation used in Spanish churches in the Asturias region

**asymmetry** — An informal balance arrived at by the informal distribution of elements. Balance similar to that of a steelyard scale: an arm is suspended off centre and the object to be weighed is hung from the short arm, while a smaller weight is moved outward on the long arm until a balance is reached. May be compared also to a seesaw with one child weighing more than the other, where the heavier weight is moved closer to the centre to achieve balance

**atectonic** — In sculpture, describes shapes or forms that tend to reach out into open space

**atelier** — (French, *artist's studio, workshop*)

**atlantes** — In sculpture, supporting columns carved in the form of heroic men. *See also* **caryatid**

**atmospheric perspective** — *See* **aerial perspective**

**atomizer** — A device for spraying a mist of thin liquid, such as a fixative, on artwork

**attribution** — Ascribing a work of art to a particular artist by means of deduction from style, brushwork, materials or any other means. In sale catalogues 'attributed to' is often a means of inflating the value of a piece of otherwise doubtful provenance!

**au premier coup painting** — (French, *at first blow*). *See* **alla prima painting**

**Auerbach, Frank** — 1931-    , naturalized British painter of what are often quintessentially English subjects with a modern interpretation. Auerbach works with immensely thick pigments and frequently incorporates solid objects into his pictures

**aureole** — The halo, or nimbus, painted around the head of a holy person, as seen in medieval and Renaissance art

**aureolin yellow** — Pigment; a cobalt yellow, bright, transparent, and durable; close to cadmium yellow light on the colour chart

**aurora yellow** — Pigment; a bright yellow between a cadmium yellow light and a cadmium yellow medium, transparent and durable

**autographic ink** — A greasy ink used in lithography

**autography** — In graphic arts, the process by which a pen and greasy ink drawing is transferred from paper to stone; in lithography, reproduction of a print on autographic paper

**automatic drawing** — *See* **automatism**

**automatism** — A surrealist technique of closing the eyes and letting the hand draw without conscious direction; sometimes called *automatic drawing*

**Autone prints** — Trademark, in commercial art, for colour- or metallic-based photoprints. Also the tradename of a tinted photographic paper

**autoportrait** — (French, *self-portrait*)

**avant-garde** — (French, *vanguard*) A term applied to art that is considered ahead of its time, innovative, and experimental

**Avignon school** — Late fifteenth- and early sixteenth-century school of painting centered around Avignon, France, influenced by Italian and Flemish styles

**A.W.S.** — Abbreviation for American Watercolor Society

**axis** — 1. A real or imaginary area in a picture that serves as a fulcrum in visually balancing the elements of the composition. 2. An imaginary

line to which elements of a work of art are referred
for measurement

**axonometric projection** — In mechanical
drawing, includes isometric, dimetric, and
trimetric projection; used to represent three-
dimensional objects, not for an illusion of reality,
but to show dimensions and other geometric
information. *See also* **oblique projection,
isometric projection**

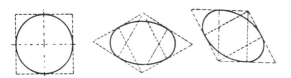

isometric drawings of
a circle

**azo yellow light** — Pigment; a cool yellow, durable
acrylic

**azo yellow medium** — Pigment; a medium yellow
between cadmium yellow light and cadmium
yellow medium, durable acrylic

**azo yellow orange** — Pigment; similar to cadmium
yellow, deep, durable acrylic

**azure blue** — Pigment; a medium blue colour
coming from copper carbonate

**azure cobalt** — Pigment; a mixture of cobalt blue
and viridian, permanent

**azurite** — Pigment; from a clear dark blue mineral,
permanent, used in watercolours; now replaced
by more easily obtainable blues

**azzuro** — Pigment; ultramarine blue, name
obsolete

13

# B

**B** — Symbol on tube of paint indicating a colour of a less than permanent quality, but fairly durable

**backing board** — Any heavy cardboard or similar material used for mounting pictures or to protect the back of a stretched canvas. *See also* **chipboard**

**backing-up** — In printing, a term meaning to print on both sides of a sheet of paper, as the pages of a book

**backlight** — Light coming from behind a subject

**Backstein Gothic** — An architectural term used to describe the fourteenth-century German variant of Gothic structures wherein brick was used in place of stone

**backup** — 1. Paper or cardboard glued to the back of artwork to prevent curled edges. 2. The printing on the second side of a printed page. 3. The process of filling in the back of a thin copper electroplate, making it solid

**Bacon, Francis** — 1909-      , English artist in the modern style, best known for his middle-period paintings featuring sometimes violent brushwork on a heavy impasto. His more recent work has become more painterly, but no less exotic

**badger blender** — A soft-hair artist's brush similar to a shaving brush, used dry, flattened, and spread out to blend areas of colour; also called a *sweetener*

badger blender

**baguette moulding** — A simple strip of moulding used for framing

**balance** — In composition, a visually favourable distribution of elements

**ball-flower** — In architectural decoration, three or four petals with a ball shape in the middle

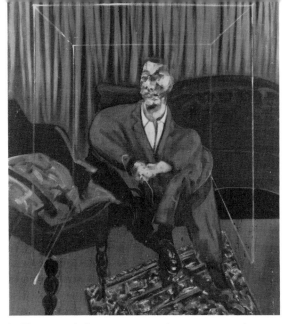

**Francis Bacon**
*Seated Figure*

**balloon** — 1. In cartooning, the writing inside a
balloon shape. 2. In watercolour, an accidental
puddle that has dried in a noticeable balloon
shape

**balsa wood** — A soft wood used for carving and
crafts, although, technically, a hardwood

**bamboo brush** — An oriental brush with a handle
of bamboo. *See also* **calligraphy brush; fude;
hake**

**bamboo pen** — A Japanese pen made from a
piece of bamboo, used for drawing and
calligraphy; a versatile instrument that can
produce a range of fine to heavy lines

**band** — In design work, a running motif

**banderole** — In design work, a narrow, forked
streamer, sometimes inscribed

**banding wheel** — A small turntable for banding
pottery with coloured glaze

**Barbizon School** — A group of French naturalist
painters who left Paris and gathered in the village
of Barbizon in the mid-1880s and sought a fresh
approach to nature by painting on the site; led by
Theodore Rousseau and Charles François
Daubigny, other members were François Millet,
Narcisse-Virgile Diaz, and Constant Troyon

**barbola paste** — A putty-like paste which can be
used for modelling or applied to a flat surface to
create an embossed effect

15

**baren**— A round, smooth, flat pad used to lift an impression by hand from a wood or linoleum block; the traditional Japanese type is covered with bamboo, but barens are now available in wood, nylon, and other synthetics

**baroque** — 1. A style of European art dating from the latter part of the sixteenth to the early eighteenth centuries. Although centered in Rome, where the sculptural work of Bernini and the paintings of Cortona are dominant examples, the style also flourished in other areas. The Flemish painter Rubens is classified as high baroque. Sometimes derided for being flamboyant and overly decorative, baroque should not be confused with rococo, a style that overlapped and followed it. 2. Used as an adjective, baroque was, until the nineteenth century, synonymous with the absurd or irregular, but such meaning is no longer credited

**bars** — In commercial art, especially textile design, a set of parallel bars used to mask an area for a stripe to be made with an airbrush

**barium yellow**— A pale yellow similar to sulphur, permanent

**baryta green** — Pigment; manganese green derived from barium oxide; name obsolete

**baryta white** — An artificial barium sulphate used as a base for certain inert pigments; obsolete name for blanc fixe

**B.A.T.** — *See* **bon à tirer**

**Bateau-lavoir, Groupe du** — (French, *the group of the floating wash house*) A group of international artists located in Montmartre, Paris, from 1908 to the beginning of World War I; title derived from a tenement building occupied by Picasso. Cubism was a leading pursuit; important names were Delaunay, Gris, Leger, and Modigliani

**b and w** — Abbreviation of black and white

**basic forms** — The four intrinsic three-dimensional forms in art: the cube, cone, cylinder, and sphere; separately or in combination, they can suggest the structure of almost anything, whether natural or man-made

**bas relief** — 1. (French, *low* relief) A form of sculpture in which figures project only slightly from the background. 2. In photography, the technique of printing two identical negatives slightly out of register to create a two-dimensional imitation of this effect

**bassetaille** — (French, *cut low*) In jewelry-making, a process in which gold or silver is engraved with a design and carved in low relief; transparent coloured enamels are applied, drying between coats, and a clear coat is made level with the rim, followed by enamel fixing

**batik** — Fabric-decorating technique originating in Indonesia, in which a design is drawn in wax and the cloth dyed. Removal of the wax leaves an uncoloured area and the use of successive dye baths can create an intricate effect

**Bauhaus** — A German school of architecture, design, and applied arts founded in 1919 by Walter Gropius, specializing in relating art to industrial technology; some of the artists involved included Lyonel Feininger, Wassily Kandinsky, and Paul Klee

**bead** — A small dotted texture in a design

**bead and leaf** — A running moulding design of a bead shape and a leaf pattern

bead and leaf pattern

**bead and reel** — A running moulding pattern of a bead shape alternated with disk shapes

**beam compass** — A drawing compass with a long beam attachment which draws or cuts circles from 4 to 39cm

**bed** — On a printing press, the surface that establishes the maximum usable sheet size

**beeswax** — Wax from honeycombs, used in encaustic painting, in etching grounds, in wax varnish, and as a resist in batik and other procedures

**beige** — A light brown colour, considered a neutral

**Bell's medium** — An obsolete oil painting medium consisting of blown linseed oil thinned with oil of spike lavender

**bench hook** — A device used to hold a wood or linoleum block in place while cutting

benday screen – one of many patterns

**benday** — In printing, a process using screens of different dot patterns to produce shading effects mechanically, named from its inventor, Benjamin Day (1838-1916). *See also* **shading sheets**

**Bengal rose** — Pigment; a sharp pink, gouache, fugitive

17

**beni-ye, beni-zuri-ye** — (Japanese, *pink picture*) A two-colour print in pink and green

**benzine** — A low-grade petroleum distillate more usually found as a dry cleaner. Used to thin rubber cement

**beret** — A round, soft, brimless tam sometimes worn by artists

**Berlin blue** — Pigment; also called Prussian blue; a term used mainly in France

**bevel** — 1. To give a slanted edge to something. 2. The tool which performs this operation. Typically, aperture mounts are bevelled

**bi** — A prefix indicating *two*

**biacca** — Artist-quality white lead pigment

**biceps** — 1. A front upper arm muscle that flexes the arm and forearm and turns the hand. 2. A large muscle of the upper leg

**bichromatic** — A term describing a work of art created with just two colours

**bicutter** — A tool that cuts two lines at the same time; adjustable from 3mm to 2cm

**Biedermeier** — A term coined from the fictional Philistine poet and applied to a style of art and architecture of Germany and Austria during the period 1815 to 1845; a style geared to the middle class, similar to early Victorian art in Britain, and considered stolid, simple, and sentimental

**billboard** — The American term for an advertising hoarding

**bimetal plate** — In engraving or printing, a plate made with two layers of metal, for example copper over aluminium or copper over stainless steel

**binary colours** — Colours made up of two hues, as orange, green, and purple

**binder** — The adhesive used to hold particles of pigment together in paint: in watercolour – gum arabic, a water-soluble glue; in oil – linseed oil; in tempera – egg yolk or whole egg; in pastels – gum arabic; in acrylics – a liquid plastic

**biomorphic** — A term applied to shapes that resemble the curves of plant and animal life; applied especially to the work of Hans Arp

**bird's-eye** — In textile design, a woven cloth pattern suggesting the shape of a bird's eye in the middle of a diamond

**bismuth white** — A less poisonous paint than white lead; it darkens from sulphur fumes; now obsolete

**bistre** — A brownish colour used as a wash and in inks, made from the soot of burned wood; replaced by more permanent pigments

**bite** — In engraving, to etch with acid from a metal plate

**bitumen** — A native asphalt used in the preparation of asphaltum. *See also* **asphaltum**

**black** — 1. The absence of colour. 2. Black pigment:

**acrylic colours:**
carbon black, makes warm greys, permanent
ivory black, makes warm greys, permanent
Mars black, an artificial earth colour, makes warmer greys than ivory, permanent

**alkyd colours:**
ivory black, a bone black, permanent
lamp black, a carbon black, makes warm greys, permanent

**gouache colours:**
ivory black, makes warm greys, permanent
jet black, makes cool greys, permanent
lamp black, greyer than jet, makes cool greys, permanent

**oil colours:**
ivory black, cooler than lamp, a slow dryer but permanent
lamp black, a pure carbon, warmer than ivory, a slow dryer, permanent
Mars black, an artificial earth colour on the brownish side, opaque, permanent

**watercolours:**
ivory black, *see* **gouache**
lamp black, *see* **gouache**

**black and white** — A term used for any rendering completed in black and white and the greys resulting from mixing black and white

**black iron oxide or black oxide of iron** — Pigment; Mars black, opaque and permanent

**black lead** — Graphite, commonly used in pencils

**black mirror** — See **Claude glass**

**black sable** — A lettering or fine varnish brush

**bladder green** — Now called sap green, a transparent earth green

**blanc d'argent** — (French, *silvery white*) Flake white, toxic

**blanc fixe** — (French, *fixed white*) A white base for watercolour and fresco painting; also called *constant white*

**blanket** — The felt or foam rubber used between the paper and the roller on an etching press; a rubber-surfaced fabric used on the cylinder of an offset press

**Blaue Reiter, der** — (German, *the Blue Rider*) An avant-garde group of early twentieth-century painters who had a notable influence on modern art; members were founders Wassily Kandinsky and Franz Marc, and Paul Klee, August Macke, and others

**Blaue Vier** — (German, *the Blue Four*) Four artists, Paul Klee, Wassily Kandinsky, Lyonel Feininger, and Alexei von Jawlensky, who held exhibitions together in Germany, Mexico, and the United States in the 1920s

**bleach-out** — A bromide print that is underdeveloped and used as a basis for a line drawing, then bleached away

**bleed** — 1. Paint or ink that runs into an adjoining area or up through coats of paint; usually undesirable. 2. A fuzziness or spreading of the edges of a painted area. 3. In the graphic arts, to extend to the edge of a printed page, without a margin; accomplished by allowing an extra 3mm bleed edge, to be trimmed

**bleed marks** — Lines at the corners of a piece of artwork to be reproduced, showing the area that will extend over an edge, usually 3mm

**bleed-proof** — Said of dried paint or ink that will not spread when wet with water

**blend** — In artwork, to merge colours applied to a surface, usually with a brush

**blended roller technique** — *See* **rainbow printing**

**blender** — *See* **badger blender** *and* **fan brush**

**bleu celeste** — Pigment; cerulean blue

**blind pressing** — Making an embossed print with an uninked plate; also called *blind printing. See also* **embossed print**

**block book** — A book in which text and illustrations were printed as one unit, all in one impression; frequently used before the invention of movable type

**blocking in** — Laying in the initial statement of a picture by a broad indication of tone, colour, and line

**block letter** — A typeface, commonly called *gothic*

THE GOTHIC FAMILY OF TYPE
the gothic family of type faces

block letter typeface

tusche used to block out sections of a lithography stone

**block out** — In graphics, to stop out an area with shellac, tusche, etc.; to use a block-out stencil

**block print** — A print on paper or textile, each colour requiring a separate block; the hand-carved wood or linoleum block may be stamped by hand or in a block printing press

**block-printing ink** — A thick ink applied to a wood or linoleum block; available in many colours in an oil-base or a water-soluble ink

**bloom** — In oil painting, an undesirable, dull, foggy, whitish effect on the surface of a varnished picture

**blotting paper** — In printing, an absorbent paper used to dry printed material

**blowtorch** — In metal sculpture, a hand-held gas-fuelled burner that produces a flame hot enough to melt or fuse some metals

**blowup** — An enlargement (slang)

**blue ashes** — Pigment; Bremen blue, toxic, obsolete

**blue bice** — Pigment; Bremen blue, toxic, obsolete

**blue black** — Pigment; a variety of carbon black; another name for ivory black

**Blue Four** — *See* **Blaue Vier**

**blue malachite** — Pigment; azurite, a clear blue, obsolete

**blue pencil, pale** — Used to mark comments directly on artwork prepared for printing. The lithographic printing process uses a film which is insensitive to blue and the marks therefore do not appear on the printed result. *See also* **litho, offset**

**blueprint** — A photographic reproduction in which white lines are on a blue background or blue lines on a white background

**Blue Rider** — *See* **Blaue Reiter**

**blue verditer** — Pigment; Bremen blue, toxic, obsolete

**board** — In artwork a drawing or painting surface with a stiff backing. *See* **bristol board; canvas board; illustration board; Masonite**

**boasting** — In stone carving, the rough shaping of the design

**boasting chisel** — In sculpture, flat chisel used to rough shape the stone

**Bockingford paper** — An acid-free mould-made watercolour paper suitable for general use

**Bocour blue** or **green** — Trade name for phthalocyanine blue or green

**body** — In painting, the viscosity or density of pigment or ink

**body colour** — Opaque colour in paint, often achieved by the addition of gouache or opaque white to transparent colour

**body matter** — In typography, the text or body text

**body type** — The typeface that is used for the text in a book, usually up to 12-point. Most common body type sizes are in the 8- to 12-point range. The body type of this book is 10-point

**bohemian** — 1. (slang). Originally an inhabitant of Bohemia (Czech.), now a nonconforming person, indifferent to convention. 2. Art produced in Bohemia in the late fourteenth century under the patronage of Charles IV

**Bohemian earth** — Pigment; green earth, transparent, permanent, name obsolete

**boiled oil** — *See* **linseed oil**

**bokusaiga** — A Japanese ink painting using the traditional black and colour

**bokuseki** — (Japanese, *traces of ink*) Zen calligraphy

**bold** — Strong, obvious, direct; for example, a bold, black line

**boldface type** — A heavy dark typeface that stands out in comparison to standard or light type

Gothic
**Gothic Bold**

**bole** — Gold size; a dull red ground laid to provide a smooth, nonabrasive base for gold leaf

**Bolognese school** — Group of artists in and around Bologna, Italy, in the twelfth to seventeenth centuries

**bolus ground** — A ground or base for canvas, prepared with a dark brown or reddish earth (bole); eventually shows through and affects the painting

**bon à tirer** — (French, *good to pull*) A press proof of an etching, lithograph, or other print that is approved and so labelled by the artist, and serves as the standard for the edition of the print. Usually abbreviated to B.A.T.

**bond paper** — A good-quality paper used for drawing and sketching

**bone black** — Pigment; a brownish black made from charred bones; artists' grade called *ivory black*

**bone emulsion** — A product added to plaster or moist clay to make it self-hardening

**boneless style** — *See* **mo-ku**

**bone structure** — The body frame, the way the bones affect the surface appearance

**book jacket** — A cover or wrapper used to protect as well as to advertise a book; also called a *dust jacket*

**border print** — 1. In illustration, a design on all four sides of a picture. 2. In textile design, a design on only one edge, such as on the bottom of a skirt or the top of a drapery

**bordering wax** — Wax used around the edges of a large plate as a moulded border so that the plate can be etched without immersion; also called *walling wax*

**boss** — Any formal protuberance, usually sculpted and frequently highly decorated

**boucharde** — A mallet used by sculptors, with short, pyramidal points on both hammering ends to bruise and break up stone and soften it, in the early stages of stone carving; also called a *bushhammer*

**Bougival white** — Bismuth white

**Bourges process** — The use of transparent acetate sheets for colour separation in the printing process where each overlay sheet is produced by the artist; a relatively inexpensive means of achieving colour in printed art

**bow pen** — A ruling pen with two blades which can be adjusted to vary the thickness of the line produced

**box frame** — A frame in which the picture is set in a box behind the glass

**bozzetto** — (Italian, *small sketch*) In sculpture, a small, rough model used as a guide; also called a *maquette*

**bracketing** — 1. In lettering, the rounding off of the corners where the serif connects to the stem. 2. In photography, shooting the same picture with the same lighting, using different exposure settings

**Brangwyn, Frank** — 1867-1956, English artist associated with the Arts & Crafts Movement, whose fame was worldwide, including a gold medal at the Chicago International Exhibition of 1891 and a commission, in 1922, to design the Occidental Museum in Tokyo

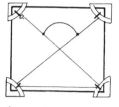

braquette

**Braque, Georges** — 1882-1963, French artist associated early in his career with the Fauves and later a founder, with Pablo Picasso, of cubism, although he was largely non-ideological and tended to keep his work free of outside influences

**braquette** — An inexpensive, frameless frame in which clips are held on the top and bottom of a piece of glass-covered artwork with spring tension and nylon cord; adjustable to different sizes

**brayer** — A hand roller designed for inking printing blocks and plates; also sometimes used by artists in painting large areas

**braze** — 1. In metal sculpture, to solder with hard solders such as an alloy of copper and zinc, zinc and silver, or nickel and silver. 2. To cover a metal with brass

brayer

**Georges Braque**
*Clarinet and Bottle of Rum on a Mantlepiece*

**brazilwood lake** — Pigment; a blood-red lake, now obsolete due to improved, synthetic colours

**breathing** — The expansion and contraction, according to weather conditions, of papers and canvas

**Bremen blue** — Pigment; a semiopaque, poisonous blue available in many shades, now replaced by nonpoisonous ultramarine blue

**Bremen green** — Pigment; a pale green varant of Bremen blue

**brick repeat** — A textile repeat pattern fashioned after a brick wall

**bridge** — *See* **artist's bridge**

**brief** — Instructions to an artist from a client

**bright** — A short, flat brush with a long handle, used mainly for oil, acrylic, and alkyd painting

**bright red** — Pigment; in watercolour, a blend of chlorinated para red and arylamide yellow, transparent and permanent

**brilliant yellow** — Pigment; a bright orangish yellow, permanent; also known as *Naples yellow*

**bristol board** — A durable drawing surface used for all types of general artwork and lettering; can be used on both sides; available in a smooth plate finish or medium vellum

**British Council** — Statutory body concerned with promoting British culture worldwide

**broad manner** — A style of engraving in which the lines are broad and bold; also, a term sometimes used to describe a bold manner of painting

**broadsheet** or **broadside** — A large folded advertisement

**brocade** — In textile design, an interwoven jacquard design of raised flowers or figures with an embossed appearance achieved by contrasting the background of twill or satin with gold or silver threads or by using different surfaces and colours

**brocatelle** — In textile design, a stiff cloth with embossed, twilled figures woven onto a plain ground, producing a high relief effect; similar to damask, it was originally made to imitate Italian leather

**broken colour** — Two or more colours so placed in a painting as to produce the optical effect of another colour, without being mixed on the palette

bright

**bromide print** — In commercial art, a photographic print

**bronze** — An alloy, principally of copper and tin, used for sculpture

**bronze blue** — Pigment; Prussian blue, intense, transparent, name obsolete

**bronze powders** — Powders made in different metallic shades and used decoratively; will tarnish and turn dark

**brown madder** — Pigment; same as alizarin brown, transparent, durable; close to Mars violet on the colour chart

**Brücke, die** — (German, *the Bridge*) Name given to a turn-of-the-century group of German expressionist artists who introduced the influence of Van Gogh, Gauguin, and others into Germany; founding artists were Erich Heckel, Ernst Kirchner, and Karl Schmidt-Rottluff

**Brunswick blue** — Pigment; a variety of Prussian blue, not used in artists' colours

**Brunswick green** — Pigment; a chrome green made from chrome yellow and Brunswick blue, name obsolete

**brush** — The principal means of applying paint to a support. Shapes, sizes and qualities vary and every artist has personal preferences. Natural brushes are made by trimming hairs from the root, relying on natural strength and spring to form and retain the shape. The highest quality watercolour brushes are made from kolinsky sable, but most animal hairs have been used at one time or another with varying success. Hog hairs are used for oil brushes because of their stiffness and resilience. Synthetic materials are being used increasingly and emulate their natural counterparts with considerable success; they also have the advantage of improved wearing properties. Brush sizes vary from 000 (the smallest) to 14 (the largest). Brushes are the artist's most important tool and should be treated with care and respect, cleaned, repointed and dried upright after use

**brush, acrylic** — A nylon-bristle brush compatible with acrylic and polymer paints

**brush, bristle** — Oil painting brushes made from hog bristles, which have a unique taper, or curve. *See* **bright; egbert; filbert; flat; round**

26

**brush cleaner** — A compound used to clean oil, acrylic, varnish, etc. from art brushes; also a receptacle or holder for brush cleaning

**brush, hair** — A brush made of animal hair, such as fitch, badger, ox, and squirrel (called camel hair), with the highest quality called red sable (kolinsky)

**brush quiver** — A container, with a carrying strap, to hold and carry brushes

**brush script** — 1. Calligraphy with a brush. 2. A script typeface

**brushwork** — The distinctive manner in which an artist applies paint with his brush

examples of brush type

**buckle** — Waves, or bulges that appear in paper or canvas, usually from too much moisture and uneven drying

**Buddhist school** — A religious art propagated in Japan by Buddhist priests

**burgundy** — A dark red colour imitating burgundy wine

**Burgundy, school of** — 1390-1420; Flemish court artists under Philip the Bold of Burgundy. The school practised Flemish realism superimposed on the naturalism that was dominant in the Italian schools; from this grew the International Gothic style; among the most noted members were the Van Eyck brothers

**burgundy violet** — Pigment; manganese violet

**burin** — A graver; a tool of different sizes and styles, used to engrave wood or metal plates

**burl** — A knot or growth that may be found in a tree; in a woodblock it is hard to carve, but sometimes can be utilized effectively in a design

**burlap** — A coarsely woven cloth made from jute, hemp, flax, etc., and used for crafts and painting

**burn** — In lithography, the result of too much nitric acid in a gum etch

**burnisher** — A tool used to smooth, flatten, or polish, available in different sizes and materials

a burin or graver

**burnt carmine** — Pigment; a deep dark red, fugitive

**burnt green earth** — Pigment; a dark brown, transparent and permanent

**burnt ochre** — Pigment; a brick-red ochre, permanent

**burnt plate oil** — an extender for etching ink

**burnt sienna** — Pigment; a natural earth colour

(raw sienna) that has been roasted; a warm
brown

**burnt umber** — Pigment; a natural earth colour of
a dark warm brown

**burr** — A rough edge on a cut in metal

**bust** — In sculpture, a portrait that includes the
head, neck, shoulders, and breast

**bust peg** — In sculpture, the wooden support upon
which a bust is modelled

**busy** — Said of areas of a picture that are confusing
or overactive

**butcher's tray** — A white enameled tray used as a
palette for watercolours or acrylics

**butting** — Placing two items close together without
overlapping

**butt joint** — In design, a place where two motifs
meet in a visible or invisible straight line without
overlapping

**Byzantine art** — The term refers to a particular
style rather than the area of the Byzantine Empire
– paintings and mosaics have been found in
Europe, Asia, and parts of Africa. Encompassing
the period AD 330 to the fifteenth century, the art
is religious in nature – early Byzantine art was
called Early Christian art. The style creates
floating figures with large eyes, bright-coloured
mosaics on gold or toned backgrounds; the effect
tends to be flat and decorative, featuring frescoes
and relief carvings

**Byzantium purple** — Pigment; a bluish purple
used in ancient times, now obsolete

# C

**C** — Symbol on tube of paint indicating a fugitive colour

© — a symbol indicating ownership of copyright

**cabinet projection** — A system of projection similar to isometric, where the lines of an object are drawn parallel to three axes, one horizontal, one vertical, and one 45 degrees to the horizontal

**cadmium green** — Pigment; a mixture of cadmium yellow and viridian, permanent

**cadmium orange** — Pigment; bright orange, opaque and permanent

**cadmium red** — Pigment; light – similar to vermilion, bright orangish red, opaque and permanent; medium – a bright medium red opaque and permanent; deep – a dark red, opaque and permanent

**cadmium scarlet** — Pigment; an orangish red, permanent; between cadmium orange and cadmium red light

**cadmium yellow** — Pigment; a bright yellow close to lemon yellow, permanent; light/pale – a bright, light yellow, opaque and permanent; medium – a medium goldish yellow, opaque and permanent; deep – a dark goldish yellow, opaque and permanent

**Caledonian brown** — Pigment; an earth colour similar to burnt sienna but inferior; now obsolete

**Caledonian white** — Pigment; a white lead, now obsolete

**calender printing** — In textile design, same as direct printing

**calendered paper** — A smooth-surfaced paper produced by heavy rolling

**calico** — In textile design, a tiny allover floral print, originally with a bright yellow, dark red, or black background, but now includes all colours

**callipers** — An instrument with two pivoted adjustable arms used to measure thickness or distance between two points

**calligram** — A calligraphic notation, picture, or conveyance

**calligraphy** — 1. The art of fine handwriting. 2. A typeface that resembles such writing. 3. Any calligraphic-type line work used in drawing or painting

**calligraphy brush** — A specially balanced oriental brush made from weasel, raccoon, and horse hairs, used for lettering; only the tip is submerged in ink. *See also* **bamboo brush**

**camaieu, en** — (French, *as a cameo*) – Painted in tones of only one colour, usually for decoration

**camel-hair brush** — Any of a number of soft-hair watercolour brushes made of squirrel, badger, goat, fitch (skunk), etc. (True camel hair is unsuited for brushes)

**cameo** — A small carving in relief, usually on a gemstone

**camera** — The basic instrument of photography

**camera lucida** — (Latin, *light room*) An optical instrument that uses a prism to enlarge or reduce an image, which is projected for tracing; sometimes referred to by artists as a *luci. See also* **epidiascope**

**camera obscura** — (Latin, *dark room*). A device by which an image of a distant object is focused onto a flat surface by means of a lens. In portable versions, sometimes used as a drawing aid. *See also* **camera lucida**

**cancellation proof** — A proof made from a cancelled plate or stone to show that no more prints can be pulled; usually a large X is drawn on the plate before the final proof

**canvas** — A fabric (cotton, linen, jute, etc.), prepared as a surface for painting; also a term for the finished painting

**canvas board** — Canvas laminated onto cardboard

**canvas carrier** — A frame-shaped metal device made to carry two to four wet canvases without touching

**canvas paper** — A paper with a canvas-like surface, used for sketches or practice work

**canvas pins** — Double-point pins used to separate two wet canvases when carrying or storing them

**canvas preparation** — 1. Coating a canvas with gesso or some other primer. 2. On an already primed canvas, painting a tone or underpainting

**canvas scraper** — A tool with a curved blade, used to scrape oils or acrylics from a canvas

**canvas stretcher strips** — *See* **stretchers**

**cap** — A border frame without a liner or mat

**capitals/caps** — Uppercase letters

**cappage brown** — Pigment; similar to umber but inferior, permanent, now obsolete

**caption** — A brief explanation of a picture reproduced in a book or magazine

**caput mortuum** — Pigment; a burned red oxide similar to Indian red only deeper and a little more bluish, permanent, name obsolete

**Caravaggio, Michelangelo Merisi da** — 1571-1610, Italian, considered a tenebrist for his low-key paintings. An accomplished artist who is noted for his precise details and chiaroscuro painting

**Caravaggisti** — The followers of Caravaggio

**carbon black** — Pigment; a pure black, permanent, but not used by artists because it streaks

**carbon paper** — Transfer paper coated with carbon

**carbon pencil** — Drawing pencil made of compressed carbon, often used as a less fragile substitute for charcoal

**Carborundum** — Trade name for an abrasive used in graphics; used as a surface in collagraphs to produce grey masses; available in powder form and as a coated cloth

**cardboard** — A stiff paper board used for mounting pictures, backing, etc.

**cardboard cut** — A design cut into cardboard, used in a printing technique

**cardboard relief** — A collage made up of pieces of cardboard for relief block printing

**caricature** — A distortion of physical characteristics to create a humorous or satirical likeness

**carmine** — Pigment; a fugitive red lake; close to Thalo red rose on the colour chart

**Carolingian art** — Art of a period from the mid-eighth to the early tenth century, beginning with the reign of Charlemagne. Modelled after the style of Rome during the reigns of Constantine and Theodosius, and after Byzantine art of the sixth and seventh centuries; characterized by elaborate illumination of manuscripts and decoration with gold and gems. *See also* **Ada school**

**carpenter's pencil** — A flat, thick pencil supplied in soft grades. Normally used to indicate cut marks on wood, it produces a thick, bold line

**carpus** — In anatomy, a bone of the wrist

**carthame** — Pigment; safflower, a fugitive lake, now obsolete

**carthame pink** — Pigment; a bright pink, moderately permanent, gouache

**cartilage** — In anatomy, a tough, fibrous connective tissue

**cartoon** — 1. A satirical drawing or caricature; a comic strip. 2. A drawing for a mural or large painting used as a full-size guide to the final painting

**cartouche** — 1. An ornamental scroll-like design sometimes used in printing and hand lettering. 2. Studio usage refers to all types of scroll outlines and irregular shapes. 3. A signature in picture form from the Egyptian era

a sixteenth-century cartouche

**cartridge paper** — Generally applied to any smooth, non-glossy paper of reasonable quality. This is not a precise term and grades will vary with supplier

**carve** — To cut into wood, stone, or other hard material; to incise

**caryatid** — In sculpture, a supporting column carved in the form of a woman. *See* **atlantes**

**Casali's green** — Pigment; a variation of viridian green, name obsolete

**casein** — A binder made from casein glue, a milk derivative. Combined with pigments, it resembles opaque watercolour and is used on paper or board, for light impasto, for underpainting, wall decoration, etc., but is too inflexible for canvas. Dries quickly with a waterproof surface and may be varnished

**Cassatt, Mary** — 1844-1926, American-born but spent much of her life in Paris, where she was associated with the Impressionists; a friend of

**Mary Cassatt** *Child in a Straw Hat*

Degas, she is noted for her paintings and prints of mothers and children.

**Cassel earth** — Pigment; an earth colour similar to Vandyke brown, fugitive; close to burnt umber on the colour chart

**Cassel green** — Pigment; manganese green, now obsolete

**Cassel yellow** — Pigment; Turner's lead yellow, now obsolete

**cast** — 1. To form in a mould. 2. A reproduction of classic or other sculpture used as subject in drawing classes

**casting off** — Computing the amount of space a column of type will occupy when set in a desired typeface of a given size and line measure

**cast shadow** — A shadow cast upon a surface, such as a shadow from a tree upon the grass

**catalogue** — A list of works in a gallery or exhibition, giving such information as title, artist, size, medium, ownership and normal location. Historical catalogues can often help with the attribution of an uncertain work

**catching up** — In lithography, the collection of ink or scum on a nonimage area of a plate

**catch light** — The tiny light dot painted into the eye to give it more form and sparkle

**cave painting** — A painting on the walls of caves during the Stone Age, dating from about 40,000 to 3000 BC

cave paintings

33

**cavo-rilievo** — (Italian, *hollow-relief*) In sculpture, relief carving in which the highest part is level with the surface and the rest is below level; also called *intaglio*

**cel**— In animated cartooning, the plastic sheet on which an animation drawing is traced and painted before being photographed: from Celluloid, a trademark for the material of motion picture film

**celadon green** — Pigment; green earth, name obsolete

**celestial blue** — Pigment; a variety of Prussian blue, not permanent

**cellophane** — A thin, transparent acetate film available in crystal clear and colours

**cement** — A general term for *adhesives*; a special mixture of Portland cement is sometimes used as a base for mural paintings. *See* **rubber cement**

**cenacolo** — A painting of the Last Supper

**centre of interest** — The main area of interest in a picture

**centre of vision** — In perspective, the viewer's eye position in relation to the picture plane and the horizon line. *See* **station point**

**centre spread** — The two facing pages in the centre of a newspaper or magazine

**Cercle et Carré** — (French, *Circle and Square*) A group of painters founded in 1929 by Michel Seuphor and Torrés-Garcia. Mondrian was the major figure in the group

**cerise** — (French, *cherry*) A purplish cherry red colour

**Paul Cezanne** *The Gardener*

marc **Chagall** *The Poet Reclining*

**cerography** — Painting in which wax is employed as a binder. Also called encaustic painting

**cerulean blue** — Pigment; bright sky blue, opaque and permanent

**ceruse** — Pigment; white lead, now obsolete

**cervical** — In anatomy, of or pertaining to the neck . or cervix. *See also* **vertebrae**

**Cézanne, Paul** — 1839-1906, Impressionist painter who featured in the Salon des Refusés of 1863 and was included in the first Impressionist exhibition of 1874 as a result of support from Camille Pisarro. For much of the time, however, he worked outside the group at Aix-en-Provence

**Chagall, Marc** — 1887-1981, a Russian who spent much of his career in France, he is classified as an expressionist whose work combines fantasy with Russian folklore. An illustrator, painter, designer, and printmaker, he is well known for his whimsical and decorative paintings

**chalcography** — copper engraving for printing

**chalk** — A powdery substance derived from limestone, compressed with a binder into sticks for easy handling; chalks range from common chalkboard chalks to pastels. *See also* **layout chalk**

**chalk roll** — A tool that is a type of roulette, used in crayon- or chalk-manner engraving. *See also* **roulette**

**chalky** — Said of a paint that has too much white pigment; white and pasty-looking, without enough colour quality

35

**chamois** — 1. A soft, pliable skin used to blend and shade pastels and charcoals, and to wipe plates in graphics. 2. An obsolete name for yellow ochre

**champlevé** — Carving on metal to form a design with raised lines, and wells or cell areas in which enamel is laid. After this the piece is fired, filed, and polished; resembles cloisonné

**character** — 1. In lettering and type, a letter, punctuation mark, or other graphic symbol. 2. Also refers to the personality of the style or face of lettering in relationship to surrounding elements, atmosphere, and mood

**charcoal** — A black porous carbon made from charred wood; vines and twigs make the best charcoal for drawing. *See also* **engraver's charcoal**

charcoal drawing by
Dianne Flynn

**charcoal black** — Pigment made from charcoal, seldom used by artists

**charcoal brown** — Pigment; a dark grayish brown

**charcoal, compressed** — Ground charcoal powder compressed into sticks; harder than vine charcoal and not as easily manipulated; also known as *Siberian charcoal*

**charcoal grey** — Pigment; a dark blackish grey

**charcoal, hard** — *See* **charcoal, compressed**

**charcoal holder** — A handle used to hold charcoal, crayons, or pastels

**charcoal paper** — A paper with a 'tooth' used for charcoal, pastel drawings, and other dry mediums

**charcoal pencil** — A pencil with charcoal as the inner rod or marking material

**charcoal vine** — Thin sticks of charcoal about 15 cm long, available in soft, medium, and hard grades

**charge the brush** — A term generally used in watercolour work, meaning to fill the brush with colour or ink

**chartreuse** — A bright yellow-green mixture; close to cinnabar green on the colour chart

**chase** — 1. To ornament metal by chasing. *See* **chasing**. 2. In letterpress printing, a frame made from metal, used to lock up type and plates so they will retain their position while in the press

**chasing** — A process in metalwork and sculpture in which chasing tools or punches are tapped with a hammer to create an indented design. Also a name for the surface finishing of a metal cast

chasing

**check** — 1. A split or crack in wood. 2. In textile design, a small square repeated in a print

**chequerboard** — In textile design, a repeat pattern using every other square, as on a chequerboard

**cherub** — In design, a winged, nude baby angel

**chestnut brown** — Pigment; umber, a permanent earth colour, name obsolete

**chevron** — A *V* pattern repeated vertically

**chiaroscuro** — (Italian, *light/dark*) Strong emphasis on the change from light to dark in drawing or painting seen at its best in the works of Rembrandt

*chiaroscuro* by Michael Woods

**chih hua** — (Chinese) A painting made by using fingers and fingernails in place of brushes

**chimera** — In design, a fire-breathing monster with the head of a lion, body of a goat, and tail of a serpent

**chinagraph** — A grease-based pencil which will mark glazed surfaces such as china

**Chinese blue** — Pigment; a variety of Prussian blue

**Chinese orange** — Pigment; a burnt orange, permanent, gouache; close to burnt sienna

**Chinese red** — Pigment; a bright orangish red

**Chinese white** — Pigment; a zinc white used in watercolours, gouache, and commerical art; opaque

**Chinese yellow** — Pigment; King's yellow; also a bright yellow ochre

**chinkinbori** — (Japanese) A lacquer technique using gold dust sprinkled on black lacquer

**chinoiserie** — (French, *Chinese things*) European style of decoration that was inspired by Chinese art, beginning in the sixteenth century

**chip carving** — Carving by cutting wedge shapes and triangular shapes from a wood surface

**chiro-xylograph** — A woodblock in which a space is left empty so that text can be put in by hand

**chisel** — A cutting tool with a sharp, bevelled edge used for carving

**chisel brush** — A brush with hairs shaped like a chisel, useful in sign writing

**chisel draft** — In sculpture, marks on the edge of a stone or other solid material that are used as a cutting guide

**chisel point** — 1. A manner of shaping a pencil point as a chisel. 2. A lettering brush

**chop mark** — A signature or identifying mark impressed on paper, often used by commercial printers and workshops. *See also* **watermark**

**chroma** — The intensity, strength, or saturation of colour, distinguishing the chromatic colours from black and white

**chromatic colours** — All colours are chromatic; black, white, and the mixture of black and white to create greys are achromatic, or not possessed of colour

**chrome green** — Pigment; a mixture of Prussian blue and chrome yellow

an artist's chop: the Chinese characters mean water/men

**chrome orange** — Pigment; a soft orange lake, opaque, durable; close to cadmium orange on the colour chart

**chrome red** — Pigment; a bright red, toxic, fugitive, replaced by cadmium red

**chrome yellow** — Pigment; bright yellow, toxic, fugitive, replaced by cadmium yellow

**chromium oxide** — Pigment; a green earth, permanent

**chromium oxide green** — Pigment; a cool earth green, opaque, permanent

**chromolithography** — Colour lithography

**chromo-luminarism** — *See* **neo-impressionism**

**chrysocolla** — Pigment; native green copper silicate, now obsolete

**Chungking bristle** — The finest bristle used for brushes, from the province of Chungking, China

**cinnabar** — Pigment; a native vermilion

**cinnabar green** — Pigment; a combination of chrome yellow, Prussian blue, and raw sienna, durable

**cinquefoil** — (French, *five-leaved*) A motif using five leaves in a pattern

**circle cutter** — An adjustable tool used to cut exact circles

**cire perdue** — (French, *lost wax*) *See* **lost wax process**

cinquefoil design

**citron yellow** — Pigment; any pale greenish-yellow, also zinc yellow

**classical art** — Pertaining to the art of the ancient Greeks and Romans

**classical lettering** — Roman lettering

**Classical style** — Art modelled on the perceived rules of Greek and Roman antiquity. In the eighteenth and early nineteenth centuries this became so highly regarded that little else was thought worthy of consideration. In France, this stultifying effect was only broken by the advent of Impressionism

**Claude glass** — A device which reflects the view of a landscape by means of a darkened convex mirror. Definition is lost, but colour and tone are emphasized. Originally used by Claude Lorrain

**clavicle** — In anatomy, a bone that links the sternum and the scapula; collarbone

**clean colour** — A pure colour, not reduced

**clean lines** — Lines in artwork that are stated simply but superbly

**cleavage** — Flaking off of paint as it cracks and separates from its ground

**cliché verre** — (French, *exposure of glass*) A graphic art in which clear glass is covered with opaque pigment, a design is scratched into the coating with a stylus, and the glass is exposed on photosenstive paper

**clip file** — A collection of pictures arranged for reference according to subject or artist; also known as *swipe file, scrap file, the morgue, research file, and reference file*

**cloisonné** — A form of enamel decoration in which metal lines separate the colours

**cloisonnisme** — A style of painting of the 1880s marked by black lines between areas of colour, developed by Emile Bernard and Paul Gauguin. resembles the metallic separating lines in cloisonné

**close-up** — 1. A very close view of a subject; 2. a section of a subject enlarged

**coal-tar colours** — Synthetic organic colours derived from coal tar

**cobalt blue** — Pigment; a bright clear blue, permanent and nearly transparent

**cobalt drier** — *See* **drier**

**cobalt green** — Pigment; a bright bluish green, opaque, permanent

**cobalt turquoise** — Pigment; a compound of aluminium, cobalt, and chromium oxides, durable; a bluish green

**cobalt ultramarine** — Pigment; a transparent blue, permanent

**cobalt violet** — Pigment; semiopaque, with a reddish or bluish undertone; the artificial product is nontoxic and permanent

**cobalt yellow** — Pigment; a bright transparent yellow, permanent

**cockled** — A term applied to paper that is rippled or slightly wrinkled

**cockle finish** — An irregular surface on paper

**coelin** — Pigment; cerulean blue, permanent, name obsolete

**coffee table book** — An expensive and lavishly illustrated book, usually about art, not generally intended to be read but to be left around (on a coffee table) and to impress by sheer weight

**coil pottery** — A method in which rolled clay (about pencil thick) is coiled into a desired shape, filled in, and smoothed off

**coke black** — Pigment; vine black, an inferior carbon black

**colcothar** — Pigment; a red oxide, now obsolete

**cold** — An expression used to describe artwork that has no feeling or emotion; or a palette or painting where cool colours are dominant

**cold-pressed oil** — Vegetable oil extracted from seeds and nuts by pressing them without heat. *See also* **linseed oil**

**cold-pressed paper** — A handmade watercolour paper with a medium to rough texture, made as chemically pure as possible

**collage** — Objets trouvés or any pieces of material glued onto a flat surface to make an abstract or representative design. Sometimes combined with paint. *See also* **assemblage**

**collage intaglio** — An intaglio printmaking process in which the block is built up as a collage. *See also* **intaglio**

**collage relief print** — In printmaking, a relief print made from a block built up like a collage. *See also* **relief printing**

**collagraph** — A print made by the collage intaglio method

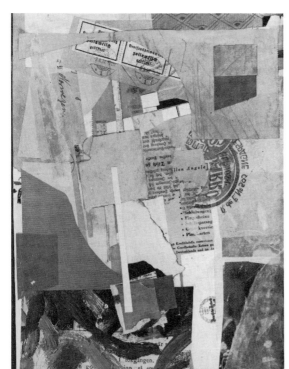

collage by Kurt Schwitters (*Opened by Customs*)

**collagraph plate** — In graphics, a piece of heavy cardboard or wood with a collage glued to the surface, used in printing a collagraph or collage relief print, depending on which is inked, the depressions or the surface *See also* **intaglio; relief printing**

**collarbone** — *See* **clavicle**

**collate** — To collect or assemble in proper order, sheets, signatures, insertions, or similar material for publications, such as magazines and books

**Cologne earth** — Pigment; Cassel earth, umber, name obsolete

**colophon** — (Greek, *finishing touch*) An inscription giving information about a publication or artist, usually placed at the end of a book or on the mat of a picture

**colophony** — A rosin used in the process of relining paintings on canvas

**colour** — Colour is perceived when the components of white light are reflected by an object or refined by filters. As there are only three primary colours (red, yellow and blue), it follows that all other colours are formed by mixtures. To obtain bright, intense colours, therefore, all paint mixtures should be kept as simple as possible to avoid contradictory effects and the introduction of impurities. The means by which the eye and brain perceive colour are extremely complex and beyond the scope of this book. Nevertheless, the artist should be aware that colour can be used to evoke specific responses in the brain and therefore alter the perception of a design. See also **additive colour mixing, subtractive colour mixing**

**colouration** — In textile design, a term for colour variation

**coloured print** — A print that has been handpainted or handcoloured. *See also* **colour print**

**colourfast** — Having colour that does not run or fade

**colour fatigue** — Tiring of certain colour receptors in the eye, causing inaccurate colour perception

**colour-field painting** — An abstract art of the late 1960s using colour applied to the picture surface in a flat or uniform style; seen in the work of Barnett Newman

**colour indication chart** — In animated cartooning, a pencil tracing of a scene with all the colours numbered according to a precise formula

**colour modulation** — A means of creating volume, from its cool dark side to its warm light side in chromatic nuances, by overlapping warm patches of colour over cool patches of colour. Where the colours overlap, solidity is created. This is different from direct dark to light modelling. Cézanne is noted for his colour modulation

**colour painting** — The term loosely applied to a style of painting using flat applications of colour. Creating form is not intended

**colour pencils** — Drawing pencils of different colours; some are made to be blended on the paper with a wet brush

**colour print** — Print on which each colour is printed from a separate block or plate

**colour proof** — Printer's or engraver's proof; shows the colours as closely as possible to their final printed form

**colour scale** — Colours in a series of steps at regular intervals, based on hue, value, or chroma

**colour scheme** — The choice of colours used in a work of art, such as monochromatic, analogous, complementary, or mixed

**colour separation** — 1. A photographic process used in photolithography that separates colours through the use of filters and screens. The standard four-colour process reduces each full-colour picture to four separate plates – magenta, yellow, cyan, and black, but more than four colours can be used; when printed one over the other, a reasonably accurate reproduction of the original is achieved. 2. By hand, colour separation is usually accomplished by using acetate or rubylith overlays keyed to the base art; alternatively, colours can be indicated on tissue overlays from which a camera process creates separate negatives that are used to make the required printing plates

**colour slide** — A photographic transparency; artists often send colour slides, rather than their work, to be viewed for prospective shows or sale

**colour swatch** — 1. In textile design, small squares of painted colour at the side of a design, indicating the colour separations in the design. 2. Examples of the colours to be matched in printing

**colour symbolism** — The use of colour to express an emotional, political, religious, or other meaning

**colour temperature** — *See* **cool colours; warm colours; temperature**

**colour triad** — Three colours spaced an equal distance apart on the colour wheel, such as red, yellow, and blue; or orange, green, and violet. *See also* **colour wheel**

**colour variation** — In textile design, a different-coloured version of the original design

**colour wheel** — A circular representation of colours in which complementaries are opposite each other, with secondaries and tertiaries in between. *See also* **colour chart; colour triad; complementary colour; Ives colour wheel; Munsell theory; Newton's colour wheel; Ostwald system; Prang colour wheel; primary colours, secondary colours; tetrads; tertiary colours**

**combination plate** — In printing artwork, the combination of line and halftone of the same colour on one plate

**comic strip** — A series of drawings in strips or panels, which may or may not be humorous

**commercial art** — Art that is created to serve a specific business purpose, such as selling a product. Advertising illustration, textile designing, packaging, lettering, and fashion illustration are some of the facets of commercial art

**commission** — An authorization to create a work of art for a stated price

**comp** — Slang abbreviation of compositor

**companion pieces** — Textiles, wallpapers, and fabrics made to match or to be companions through related design

**compass** — A drawing instrument used to draw circles or arcs

**compass cutter** — A drawing compass, but with a blade to cut circles

**complementary colour** — Colours directly opposite each other on the colour wheel, such as yellow-purple, red-green, and blue-orange are complementary pairs

**compose** — 1. To put together, assemble, create. 2. To set type. *See also* **design elements**

compass

**composite shape** — A group of two or more objects or shapes (sometimes including shadows) that form an easily recognizable shape or unit

**composition** — 1. Arrangement of forms, lines, values, and other pictorial elements into a picture design. 2. Production or arrangement of type for printing. *See also* **design elements**

**composition brayer** — A soft gelatin roller used in graphics

**compositor** — A person or machine that composes or sets type

**compressed charcoal** — *See* **charcoal, compressed**

**concept, picture** — The visual idea (picture) that takes form through a creative process, sparked by any stimulus, conscious or subconscious

**cone** — A form in which the base is circular and the sides taper upward to a common point (apex)

**cone of vision** — In mechanical perspective, the visual field, in a cone shape of about 45 degrees to 60 degrees, in which a person views the points in a picture

**considered line** — A planned, thought-out line used to show texture, form, etc.

**consistency** — The thickness or softness of a given medium, its apparent viscosity

**Constable, John** — 1776-1837, English painter famous for his East Anglian scenes and a pioneer of the use of broken colour to express the play of light. *The Haywain* was exhibited at the Salon of 1824 and had a major influence on French landscape painting and the development of the Impressionist movement

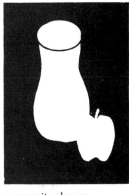

composite shapes

**John Constable**
*Sketch for Hadleigh Castle*

**constant white** — Pigment; blanc fixe, a base for watercolour and fresco painting

**constructivism** — An abstract movement in sculpture, begun in Russia about 1917, that used metal, wood, plaster, tin, and other industrial materials to build three-dimensional sculptures, paintings, and graphics. A form of art designed to bridge the gap between art and everyday life; also called *Tatlinism*, after Vadamir Tatlin (1885-1953), a champion of the art form

**contact points** — Points at which lines or objects meet

**contact screen** — Halftone screen. *See* **half-tone**

**Conté crayon** — Trade name of a unique French drawing crayon that is made in square sticks or in pencil form, is grease-free and available in several colours; the reddish crayon is called a *sanguine*. Conté also manufactures a line of pencils, pastels and chalks

**content** — In art, generally refers to the theme of a work and the aesthetic and emotional sensation it imparts to the viewer. Applies not only to the components of a painting, but also to the way in which the artist has arranged and depicted them

**continuity** — In cartooning, the running story behind a comic strip, animated cartoon, or related themes in illustrations, murals, etc.

**continuous line technique** — A technique based on the 'golden mean'. Using any variation of the golden mean rectangle, an angular line is drawn from a major point to the picture's edge. At this intersection, another angular, horizontal, or vertical line is drawn. Lines are continued in this manner. A picture is then incorporated into the line formation. Often the lines are left visible

**continuous-tone illustration** — In commercial art, any picture or photograph that has not been screened and that contains gradient tones in either black and white or colour

**contour** — The outer limit of a figure, form, or object; an outline

**contour drawing** — A line drawing using one continuing line or as few lines as possible to render a given subject while the artist keeps his eyes on the subject, not on the paper

contour drawing

**contour style** — *See* **kou le**

**contrast** — The difference in high and low values used for emphasis in a picture

46

**convergence** — The tendency of two or more lines or shapes to approach each other or come to a common point

**conversation piece** — 1. A type of group portrait popular in the eighteenth century. 2. Said of an artwork that may or may not be a quality work, but is unusual enough to attract attention and cause conversation among the viewers

**cool colours** — Colours in which blue, green, or violet predominate

**coordinates** — In textile design, two or three patterns that go together, such as a plaid and a floral design in the same colour scheme

**copal painting medium** — A medium made from resin, pure oil, and rectified turpentine, used with oil paints

**copal varnish** — A quality varnish sometimes used as a finish coat on an oil painting after it is thoroughly dry (six to twelve months)

**copper blue** — Pigment; Bremen blue, ultramarine blue, toxic, obsolete

**copper glass** — Pigment; see **Egyptian blue**

**copper green** — Pigment; Bremen green, bluish green, toxic, obsolete

**copper plate** — An engraving plate made from copper

**copper tooling** — Creating a design or picture on copper by means of pressing a tool into the surface either from the front or black; sulphur is then applied to make different values

**copper wheel engraving** — The process of engraving a design on glass with various copper wheels and abrasives. The copper wheels are fitted on a small lathe and the object to be engraved is held against the spinning wheel

**Coptic art** — Early Christian art, mainly in Egypt during the fifth to eighth centuries

**copy** — 1. A duplication or imitation. 2. Any text or illustration to be reproduced. 3. Also refers to the written matter in an advertisement to differentiate from visual matter

**copyboard** — 1. The area of a process camera that holds the material to be photographed. 2. Any board or surface on which art or other material is placed to be photographed

**copy counter** — An instrument that is rolled over copy to be measured and registers length in agates, picas, inches, and/or centimeters

**copying process** — The use of a photographic emulsion that is sensitive to light, or a form of radiation to produce an image

**copy negative** — In comercial work, a negative made of the original artwork

**copyright** — Exclusive legal right of an author or artist to make or control copies of his work. Remains with the originator for a specific term of years unless otherwise assigned. This right is automatic and does not have to be registered (although it may have to be proved), as is sometimes believed. This is a very precise legal term and the above should not be taken as an exhaustive definition

**coquille board** — A textured illustration board available in several different stipple finishes, used to make halftone effects through line reproduction

**cork black** — Pigment; vine black or Spanish black; name obsolete

**cornsilk** — Pigment; a pale yellow mixture

**cornucopia** — (Latin, *horn of plenty*) In design, a cone-shaped horn overflowing with fruit, vegetables, and flowers; a symbol of prosperity or plenty

**correction tape** — A white, lightweight, opaque tape used mainly in commercial art for masking and making corrections

**correction white** — An opaque white paint used in commercial art to make corrections or to block out an area of artwork

**corrosion** — A gradual wearing away by a chemical process, especially of metals; oxidation of iron-producing rust

**corundum** — An extremely hard mineral abrasive used to smooth or grind

**Cotman, John Sell** — 1782-1842, a major figure of the Norwich School and an introverted character, subject to bouts of depression. Cotman worked almost exclusively in watercolour and possessed an excellent sense of design and colour. Professionally ambitious, he became Professor of Drawing at King's College, London, but continually over-reached himself and died in penury

**Cotman watercolours** — Trade name of a range of students' quality watercolours

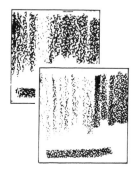

coquille board

**John Sell Cotman**
*Norwich Market Place*

**cotton canvas** — Heavy-duty cotton, usually already primed, used as a painting surface

**counterchange** — In textile design, a figure-ground reversal; the background colour or value is the reverse of that of the main subject; may be referred to as *interchange*

**counter-etch** — To resensitize a lithographic or other printing plate so that it will accept crayon or tusche

**counterproof** — 1. After a plate of woodblock has been printed, and while the proof is still wet, a clean sheet of paper is placed on the wet proof and run through the press, making an offset or reverse image called a counterproof. 2. When a pastel or chalk drawing is put through a press face-to-face on a damp paper, a reverse impression is pulled from which a new study is developed

**Courbet, Gustave** — 1819-1877, classically educated painter whose interest in socialism brought him into contact with writers such as Daudet and Zola. Rejection from the Exposition Universelle of 1855 caused him to hold a one-man exhibition in defiance, and he flourished during the 1860s, having a strong influence on Monet and Renoir

**coverage** — In textile design, the amount of design within a given space

**cover paper** — A heavy-duty coloured paper used for covers of brochures, catalogues, cards, etc. *See also* **cover stock**

**cover sheet** — *See* **flap**

counterchange

**cover stock** — A type of smooth or textured paper produced in single or double weight, in white and colours, and used for covers, advertising, greeting cards, etc.

**Cow gum** — Trade name of an inert latex-based adhesive suitable for mounting artwork

**C.P.** — *See* **cold-pressed paper**

**crackle** — A network of fine cracks on a painting caused by the paint becoming brittle and cracking; often due to unequal drying times of paint layers; sometimes called *alligatoring* because of the pattern formed

**cradle** — The wood stripping on the back of a painting panel that helps to stiffen it. *See also* **rocker**

**craftsmanship** — The skill with which one uses tools and materials

**cranium** — The skull

**craquelure** (French, *crackle*). *See* **crackle**

**crawling** — Term given to a tendency of paint, inks, or dyes to spread outward on application in a crawling fashion

**crayons** — Drawing sticks of coloured wax. Also sometimes used to refer to pastels and coloured pencils

**Cray-Pas** — Trade name for oil stick colours that combine qualities of crayons and pastels, do not need to be fixed, and can be used with turpentine to create a special effect

**creative** — Having the ability to use imagination, to express ideas, and to present them in an individual and effective manner, especially through the arts

**creep** — 1. The tendency of ink or paint to move by itself on the surface of a paper or support. 2. Moving forward of the blanket during the printing process

**creeping bite** — Etching performed in stages by gradually submerging the plate into the acid

**Cremnitz white** — *See* **white**

**crêpe paper** — A paper with wrinkled texture, available in many colours, used for decorations and crafts

**crest** — In design, a crown or coat of arms. *See also* **heraldic**

**crevé** — In etching, the collapse of a whole area of a plate where lines are close together and the plate is left in the acid too long

50

**John Crome (Old)**
*Yarmouth Harbour –*
*Evening*

**criblée** — Covered with dots punched on an engraving plate to create an image; also a technique of surface decoration with dots; also called *dotted manner; manière criblée; schrottblatt*

**crimson** — A deep red hue; close to cadmium red deep on the colour chart

**crimson lake** — Pigment; a transparent lake colour similar to alizarin crimson, permanent

**critic, art**— One who expresses his personal judgment of works of art; usually also a writer on art

**critique** — A constructive discourse covering a work or works of art, pointing out areas that are well done as well as things that might be improved

**Crome, John (Old)** — 1768-1821, oil painter strongly influenced by the Dutch school who is generally regarded as the founder of the Norwich School. An extrovert character, his style is brash but competent

**Crome, John Berney** — 1794-1842, eldest son of John Crome, by whom he was much influenced. He built up a strong reputation during his lifetime and is best known for his moonlight scenes

**crop marks** — Marks or indications on artwork or photographs to be reproduced that give instructions where to crop or cut

**croppers** — Two L shaped pieces of mat board held around a picture to judge how a composition can most effectively be cropped

**cropping** — Cutting a picture down or trimming it from its original dimensions to a specific size

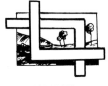

croppers

51

crosshatching by
Michael Woods

**croquis** — (French, *sketch*) Sketch and notes that will be used for a full art rendering at a later date; often used in fashion drawing

**crosshatch** — A means of creating a tonal effect by repeated and parallel horizontal, vertical, or diagonal lines

**crossmarks** — *See* **registration marks**

**cross section** — A rendering that shows an inside section of an object by cutting through it, usually at right angles

**cross-sectional paper** — A finely milled graph paper on which the square-inch lines are accented

**crow quill pen** — A small dip pen with a fine steel nib, used for sketching or drawing, where thin lines are needed

**crux ansata** — *See* **ankh**

**Cryla** — Trade name of a range of acrylic colours

**cube** — A solid form consisting of six equal square sides

**cubism** — An abstract art movement of the early twentieth century, initiated by Pablo Picasso and Georges Braque. In painting, a means of representing volume in a two-dimensional plane without resorting to the illusion of depth as usually developed within the picture space. In sculpture, in Africa, Oceania, and Alaska, cubistic form was used at much earlier dates

**Cupid** — In design, a chubby, nude infant; derived from the gold of love in Roman mythology

**Cupid's bow** — The middle hollow above the upper lip

**cursive** — Flowing, as in lettering or type that imitates handwriting; also used to describe flowing design

**curve** — *See* **French curve**

**curve ruler** — A piece of rubber or plastic that can be bent into various curves as an aid in scribing lines

**curvilinear** — Having curved lines

**cushion** — *See* **engraver's pad**

**cushion blanket** — In intaglio printing, the middle blanket on the press that pushes the paper into the hollows of the plate

**cut** — Originally meaning *woodcut*, used loosely to describe any type of plate for printing and the print thus made

**cutaway** — A drawing or other artwork where the outside of an object is cut away to reveal the interior. *See also* **cross section**

**cut-out** — In printing, a half-tone illustration where the background has been removed or another illustration inserted. *See also* **silhouetting**

**cutter** — A flat bristle brush with its edge cut on an angle, used by sign painters. *See also* **mat cutter; paper cutter**

**cutter, paper** — *See* **paper cutter**

**cutting** — In textile design, a small sample of fabric showing a design and its colours

**cyanine blue** — Pigment; a mixture of Prussian blue and cobalt blue, permanent

**Cycladic art** — Art of the islands of the Aegean Sea called the Cyclades, about 2600-1100 BC; consisted mainly of pottery and sculpture

**cylinder printing** — *See* **direct printing**

**Cyprus green** — Pigment; almost a blue turquoise, moderately permanent, gouache

**Cyprus umber** — Pigment; Turkey umber, raw umber, name obsolete

cursive

curve ruler

# D

**dabber** — In graphic arts, a pad of leather or cloth used to apply ink to a plate or type

**Dada** — (French, *hobby horse*, a word picked at random from a dictionary) An anti-establishment art movement during World War I expressing outrage at the conditions of the world and cynicism and rebellion toward traditional art forms. Major artists were Hans Arp, Man Ray, Max Ernst, and Marcel Duchamp (who produced a porcelain urinal and sent it to a New York art show); considered a forerunner of surrealism

**dagger** — A dagger-shaped brush used by sign painters for striping

**Daler Board** — A prepared painting board available in a variety of surfaces for oil and watercolour use

**Dali, Salvador** — 1904- , major Surrealist whose realistically rendered paintings contain disturbing images. Collaborated with the film-maker Luis Buñuel to make *Un Chien Andalou*

**Dalon** — Trade name of a range of synthetic watercolour brushes

**damask** — In textile design, a firm cloth with an elaborate raised pattern of fruit and flowers, made by directions of thread against a plain background

**dammar varnish** — A final varnish for oil and tempera paintings, used when the picture is completely dry (about six to twelve months for oils); colourless; available in spray or liquid form

**damp press** — In graphics, a means of dampening paper, using a box lined with oilcloth, rubber, or zinc

54

**dance of death** — In the Middle Ages, a recurring *subject* of pictures, depicting skeletal figures accompanying human figures to their deaths

**danse macabre** — (French, *dance of death*) *See* **dance of death**

**D'Arches** — *See* **Arches**

**Davy's grey** — Pigment; a warm grey used in watercolour, permanent

**dead area** — 1. An area not desired in a picture and dropped out by use of retouch white. 2. In a painting, an area that has little appeal and weakens the composition

**deadline** — The final time or date when artwork is due

**dead metal** — 1. Excess metal in areas not to be printed from a relief printing plate. 2. Discarded type that will be melted down for reuse

**death mask** — A mould of the face taken immediately after death to preserve the features

**debossment** — The act of pushing into or cutting below the image surface. The exact opposite of **embossing**

**decal** — A design or picture that is transferred from paper to another surface

**decalcomania** — 1. The process of transferring specially prepared printing from its paper to another surface. 2. A technique of blot drawing used by the surrealists for inspiration in painting

**deckle edge** — The decorative ragged edge on quality watercolour paper and on many paper stocks used for printing (one edge deckled on each sheet)

**décollage** — A reverse collage made by tearing away parts of paper layers and revealing colours or images that are part of the final artwork

**decor** — The decorative style employed in an interior; may sometimes pertain to an area or period of time, such as Spanish, Louis XIV, Pennsylvania Dutch, etc.

**decorative** — Ornamental, fashionable or beautiful objects used in interiors; embellishing a surface, as furniture or pottery

**decorative overload** — Too much surface decoration in an artwork

**découpage** — (French, *cut out*) A decorative technique in which cut-out pictures or designs are pasted onto a firm surface and then varnished

**Edgar Degas**
*Woman at her Toilet*

**deep etch** — The preparation of a printing plate for a long print run

**Degas, Hilarie Germain Edgar** — 1834-1917, Impressionist painter most noted for his pastels and paintings of racecourse scenes, the theatre and ballet. He was taught drawing by Ingres at the Ecole des Beaux Arts in the 1850s. Failing sight caused him to turn to sculpture in later years

**del.** — (Latin, abbreviation for *delineavit, he drew it*) On an engraving, the artist who drew the original for the print

**deltoid muscle** — A thick muscle covering the shoulder joint, triangular in shape; raises and rotates the arm

**demi-teinte** — (French, *half-tone*) or mezzotint

**density** — Thickness, used in relation to paint thickness or amount of opacity

**derby red** — Pigment; a bright chrome red, fugitive, toxic, obsolete

**descender** — The part of a lowercase letter that descends below the line, as in p, q, g

**descriptive art** — Art that is realistic or representative of actual things

**desensitize** — In lithography, to render areas insensitive to grease on a stone or plate with acidified gum etch

**design** — 1. To plan the grouping or arrangement of the elements in a composition. 2. In flat design, the motif or pattern. *See also* **design elements**

**Design Centre** — *See* **Design Council**

**Design Council** — Statutory body established in 1944 to promote excellence in industrial design. A permanent exhibition is held at the Design Centre in The Haymarket, London

**design elements** — Line, shape, size, value, colour, direction, and texture

**designer** — One who creates or designs art or applied art

**designer's colours** — gouache; high-quality opaque watercolour

**De Stijl** — A Dutch art movement, 1917-1928, also known as neo-plasticism, employing rectangles and primary colours; the major artist was Piet Mondrian. A magazine of the same name was published by the group, featuring articles on pure abstraction

**devil's mask** — (Chinese) Two animals, birds, or other motifs made into a design forming a third and larger animal design

**De Wint, Peter** — 1784-1849, English watercolourist noted for his drawings and paintings in and around his native Lincoln

**diagonal** — Oblique line or pattern in a composition

**diameter** — A straight line passing through the centre of a circle or sphere; the length of such a line

**diamond black** — Pigment; carbon black, name obsolete

**diamond point** — A diamond-tipped needle used to incise a plate directly. *See* **drypoint**

**diamond repeat** — In textile design, a repeat pattern in the shape of diamonds or lozenges

**diaper** — 1. In textile design, small squares or diamond shapes connecting to form a net-work, as a block or diamond repeat pattern. 2. An identifiable fold pattern in drapery

**diffused light** — Light that is distributed or spread, rather than focused

**diffusion** — In painting, a spreading, blending, or blurring

**dimensions** — In art, the measures of spatial extent – height, width, and length

diamond repeat

**Peter De Wint**
*Bridge over a Branch of the Witham, Lancs.*

57

**diminution** — In visual perspective, the effect of things appearing smaller as they recede

**Dingler's green** — Pigment; a variety of chromium oxide green, a dark green close to Phthalo green on the colour chart; name obsolete

**dioxazine purple** — A synthetic true purple, durable, acrylic

**dipper** — Small container attached to a palette to hold the painting medium

**diptych** — A pair of carved or painted panels, hinged together like a book

**direction** — In art, the pattern of movement the eyes follow through a picture; the 'eye path' that is controlled by careful manipulation of the elements of design

fourteenth-century ivory diptych

**directoire style** — Late eighteenth-century French style in decorative arts that was a simplified combination of Louis XVI neoclassicism and the Empire style

**direct printing** — Calender, roller, or cylinder printing where the paper is in direct contact with the printing plate. In textile design, it is the same method as newspaper printing, but each colour has a separate roller, some machines taking up to sixteen colours

**direct transfer** — In lithography, transfer of an image directly to the stone from an inked object

**discord** — Lack of harmony in a composition

**display** — A branch of commercial art given to the design of exhibits

**display face** — *See* **display type**

**display letters** — Large letters in various fonts made in plastic, cardboard, wood, aluminium, etc., used for indoor and outdoor advertising and exhibits

**display type** — A large typeface for headlines, to attract attention

**disposable palette** — A pad of oil-proof paper in the general shape of a palette; after use, the tope sheet can be torn off and thrown away

**dissymmetric** — Not symmetrical. *See* **symmetrical**

**divided interest** — The effect of two or more points of equal interest in a composition

**dividers** — Drafting instrument used for dividing lines and transferring measurements

**divine proportion** — *See* **golden mean/golden section**

**divisionism** — A term for pointillism or optical mixing. *See also* **pointillism**

**doctor** — 1. In lithography, a greasy fluid used to strengthen the work. 2. A painting knife or scraper used to remove paint from a surface. 3. In general artwork, to repair or correct any mistake

**documentary** — In textile design, an original fabric and design, as very old cloth from China from which a present design is copied

**dominant** — In art, having paramount importance in a picture or design

**dominant colour** — The main colour; the predominating colour in a composition

**dominant tint** — *See* **mother colour**

**donkey** — Artist's seat with combined easel

**doodle** — To draw or scribble with little or no conscious thought about the result

**Dorland's wax medium** — Trade name of a concentrated wax used for encaustic painting and for preserving sculpture, carvings, and paintings

**dorsal** — *See* **vertebrae**

**dotism** — Slang for pointillism

**dotted manner** — *See* **criblé**

**double elephant** — *See* **watercolour paper sizes**

**double image** — In drawing or painting, a subject that can be two different things, such as a tree that is a hand or a cloud that is an eye

**double load** — To fill a brush with one value or colour and then tip the brush with a second value or colour

**double run** — Running a plate through the press twice to create a heavier impression

**double-sided tape** — Adhesive tape which is tacky on both sides

**double spread** — Illustration or copy occupying two facing pages of a publication

**double truck** — A newspaper printing term meaning two facing pages dealing with the same story or material; a double spread. *See also* **truck**

**dovetail joint** — 1. An interlocking joint. 2. In textile design, a point where a portion of a repeat fits into a part of the next design without touching it

**double primed** (D.P.) — Said of canvas having two coats of priming, such as gesso

**drafting film** — A polyester film used for drafting in ink

**drafting machine** — Mechanical parallel-motion device attached to a drawing board enabling lines and angles to be quickly and accurately repeated

**drafting tape** — A self-adhesive paper tape used to secure a drawing to the drawing board, mat, etc.; similar to, but not as sticky as *masking tape*, is easily removed without damage to drawing

**drag** — To pull a paint brush across an area of a painting so it drags and catches, leaving an uneven texture. *See also* **dry brush**

**dragon's blood** — 1. A red resin used as an etching resist in photoengraving. 2. A blood-red transparent resin once used in Europe, now obsolete

**draughtsman** — One with excellent drawing ability; one who renders architectural, mechanical, or engineering drawings

**drawing** — 1. An art technique using pencil, pen, brush, charcoal, crayon, pastel, or stylus. 2. An entity in itself, or may be used as a preliminary for a rendering in another medium

**drawing board** — A rectangular panel, usually wood, used as a base for drawing

**drawing bridge** — A wooden support for the artist's hand and to keep it off the surface of the picture; often used while working over a wet paint area, or on a litho stone

**drawing table** — A table used for artwork, adjustable in height and slant

**draw through** — Drawing the back, unseen side of a subject

**draw tool** — In graphic arts, a tool with a hooked blade used to 'hand cut' a plate

**dressing** — 1. In tole painting, the medium that is commonly called *goop*. 2. The ornamental top strokes applied to folk art

draw tool

**dried lacquer work** — *See* **kanshitsu**

**drier** — A prepared liquid (a siccative) added to paint to speed the drying process; cobalt drier is used in artists' materials, Japan drier in sign painting and industrial paints

**drizzle** — In painting, to drip paint or let it run into a pattern

**drop black** — Pigment; a carbon black made from burnt vegetables and animal matter

**drop-out** — 1. A section of a half-tone where the original has not been adequately reproduced. 2. To leave an area of white around a half-tone illustration. *See also* **silhouette**

**dropout marker** — Light blue pen or pencil that will not reproduce when photographed with normal reproduction film; used for instructions on copy and mechanicals

**dry-brush** — With ink, watercolours, or other mediums, a method of painting with very little colour or moisture on the brush, creating a 'skipped' or 'missed' effect

**dry-brush blend** — A flat dry-brush stroke that blends two values or colours

**dry-cleaning pad** — A small pad containing a powder that absorbs dirt, used to clean drawings

**dry-in** — Name given to oil paint that gets dull as part of the picture dries-in and loses its shine; retouch varnish is used to restore the lustre to the level of the newly added paint

**drying oil** — In graphics, an oil such as linseed or tung oil, which changes to a solid as a result of the action of oxygen

**dry lithography** — A lithographic printing method using a chemical coating that repels ink

**dry mounting** — A method of attaching a print, drawing, or photograph to a cardboard backing by placing a sheet of dry mounting tissue betwen the artwork and the cardboard and then applying heat for adhesion

**dry-mounting press** — A machine that adheres drawings, photos, and other papers to cardboard, using heat and pressure

**dry-mounting tissue** — Tissue with a thermosetting heat seal adhesive used between a paper and a cardboard surface for dry mounting

**dry offset** — A process in which ink is transferred from a relief to a printing blanket, and from there to the paper

**dry pigments** — Pigments in a dry powder form, ready for grinding

**drypoint** — A graphic art in which a needle scratches directly onto the plate and the burr is allowed to remain, producing a soft effect in printing but limiting the number of prints obtainable

dry brush

**dry-relief offset** — A type of offset printing in which photomechanically made plates print without dampeners or water; also called *high etch*

**dry-transfer lettering** — *See* **pressure-sensitive lettering**

**Duchamp, Marcel** — 1887-1968, a French painter and sculptor. He shocked the art world at the 1913 Armory Show when he exhibited his *Nude Decending a Staircase*, a cubistic, futuristic work. He was part of the Dada movement and often used found objects to stand as works of art.

**duck canvas** — A durable cotton canvas ranging in weight from 5 to 24 ounces per square yard, used mainly as a painting support and available in different weaves

**duotone** — The process of using two halftone cuts of the same black and white illustration; the screened plates are angled slightly so the printed dots do not overlap; one plate is usually printed in black, the other in a second colour, such as red or blue

**duplex paper** — A paper made with a different finish or colour on each side

**duplicating process** — A process for making a number of copies from an original, with images being formed by transference from plates, type, or stencils onto white or coloured paper

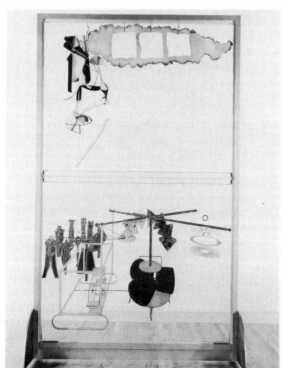

**Marcel Duchamp**
*The Bridge Stripped Bare by Her Bachelors*

**durable** — A term used for class *A* pigments

**Dürer, Albrecht** — 1471-1528, German Renaissance artist principally known for a series of highly detailed engravings and drawings, many of religious subjects and mostly executed on copper. He was also the author of several aesthetic and technical treatises.

**dust bag** — Ground-up rosin in a cloth bag, used in making aquatints

**dust box** — A box in which rosin is applied to a plate for an aquatint

**dusting brush** — A brush used to clean artwork

**dust jacket** — *See* **book jacket**

**Dutch mordant** — A mordant used for the etching of fine lines. *See also* **mordant**

**Dutch pink** — Pigment; in addition to a tint of red, a yellow lake, fugitive; also called English pink, brown pink, and stil-de-grain

**Dutch white** — Pigment; a white lead, toxic, darkens with age

**dyes** — Pigments that dissolve completely, are transparent, and have no bulk

**dyes, batik** — Highly concentrated dyes used to colour cloth. *See also* **batik**

**dyestuff, natural** — Natural colouring matter taken from plants and animals

**dye transfer** — A photographic process used to produce high-quality prints or transparencies. The process can be manipulated and is most used in graphic applications where a high degree of retouching is required

**dynamic symmetry** — A theory of design linked to the formula of the golden section; at one time many artists followed it as an aid to achieving the perfect composition, but the system is now rarely used. *See also* **golden mean/golden section**

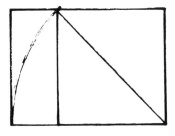

dynamic symmetry, or root-2 projection, is based on extending a square according to the arc of the square's diagonal

# E

**E.A.** — (French, *epreuve d' artiste*) Artist's proof

**Early Christian art** — *See* **Byzantine art; Coptic art**

**earth colours** — Pigments, such as yellow ochre, burnt sienna, the umbers, made from minerals such as iron, manganese, copper, etc.; yellow ochre, for instance, is refined clay coloured by iron oxide and chrome yellow. Such colours have been used since prehistoric times

**easel** — A free-standing structure used to hold a canvas while painting

    **French easel** — A folding, adjustable easel originally made in France, having an attached box for supplies and a place to hold a canvas or paper

    **portable studio easel** — A sturdy and adjustable easel, but lighter than a studio easel; folds for convenience in storage

    **sketching easel** — A lightweight, adjustable wood or aluminium easel; folds for convenience in carrying or storage

    **studio easel** — A sturdy easel in design and structure; adjustable and often has casters for easy movability

    **table easel** An easel that is set up on a table; folds for convenience

    **watercolour easel** — An adjustable, folding, portable easel that may be used outdoors, mainly for watercolour painting

**ébauche** — A monochrome lay-in over a drawing, later to be painted in full colour; an underpainting

**ebony** — Pigment; a brownish black colour

**ebony pencil** — Sketching and layout pencil, very dark black, and having a rod of a larger diameter than a standard pencil

studio easel

folding easel

64

**echo** — In composition, repeat of an element such as a shape, texture, or colour

**echoppe** — (French, *graver*) An etching and engraving needle ground to an oblique face

**Ecole des Beaux Arts** — The French academy established in 1648, producing in 1680 a set of rules governing all aspects of painting. Like all regulatory systems, it eventually failed, but the Ecole was re-established in 1816 as the Académie des Beaux Arts. However, this rigid approach probably encouraged the artistic rebellion which eventually produced Impressionism

**ectype** — A copy or replica of an original artwork

**écru** — A golden tan, considered a neutral colour

**edges, hard** — Sharp lines and forms that do not blend into adjacent areas

**edges, soft** — Limits having no definite line but allowing a value or colour to blend and blur into the adjacent areas

**edition** — The number of prints, such as lithographs or etchings, pulled from the original stone or plate, each print identified by the artist according to the total number and the sequence in which they were pulled. The fifth print in an edition of twenty would be stated in the margin in pencil as 5/20; an edition can be of any number, but seldom more than 100

**egbert** — A long-haired, round-tipped brush with a long handle

**eggshell** — An off-white or neutral colour

**eggshell finish** — Finish on a paper that resembles the surface texture of an eggshell

**egg tempera** — *See* **tempera**

**Egyptian art** — A stylized, flat, decorative art developed and practised in ancient Egypt

**Egyptian blue** — Pigment; an artificial blue used in Egypt about 3000 BC, now replaced by a mixture of cobalt blue, cerulean blue, and viridian, or of cerulean blue, a small amount of white, and phthalocyanine green; also called Alexandrian blue, coeruleum, copper glass, Italian blue, Pompeian blue, Pozzuoli blue, and Vestorian blue

**Egyptian cross** — *See* **ankh**

**Egyptian green** — Pigment; a greenish Egyptian blue, obsolete

**eikon** — *See* **icon**

**electric eraser** — A revolving, rubber-tipped eraser driven by a small electric motor

**electron painting** — A graphic art developed by Caroline Durieux in which radioactive isotopes are used for the image-making process

**electroplating** — An electrochemical process by which a thin layer of metal is deposited on another metal's surface

**electrotype (*electro*)** — A facsimile printing plate made from an original plate by means of electroplating

**electrum** — A natural gold and silver alloy, used for casting and in sculpture; also, an alloy of nickel, copper, and zinc, sometimes called *German silver*

**elements** — *See* **design elements**

**elephant** — *See* **watercolour paper sizes**

**ellipse** — A curved, elongated, oval shape

**ellipsograph** — A tool that draws mathematically true ellipses, using a pencil, pen, scriber, or cutting knife

**elliptic graver** — A special graver for wood engraving, having curved sides that can produce thick and thin lines; sometimes called a *spit-sticker*

**em** — A unit of type measurement; the width of the type is equal to the point size; for instance, a 6-point em is 6 points wide

**embellish** — To ornament or add decoration

**emblem** — A design that is a symbol or insignia, such as a heraldic crest used on seals, stationery, clothing, etc.

emblem – the British coat or arms

**emboss** — To create a relief or raised design

**embossed print** — A relief print made by pressing into the paper with an intaglio plate; also called a *gypsographic print* and *inkless intaglio. See also* **white-on-white; blind pressing**

**embroidered design** — A design made with needlework; may be handmade or machinemade

**embu** — A dull area in an otherwise glossy picture, usually caused by the paint sinking into the canvas

**emerald chromium oxide** — Pigment; viridian green, name obsolete

**emerald green** — Pigment; a brilliant green, toxic and fugitive; obsolete

**emeraude green** — Pigment; a confusing name

for viridian green. Although *emeraude* means
emerald, it is not emerald green; transparent

**emery** — A polishing and grinding agent for metals
made from corundum

**empaquetage** — *See* **wrapping**

**emulsion** — A suspension of small drops or
globules of one liquid in a second liquid with
which they do not mix; a condition found in egg
tempera

**en** — A type measurement term meaning one half
of an em. *See* **em**

**enamel** — A vitreous glaze applied to metal or
ceramics, then fired in a kiln. *See also*
**champlevé; cloisonné**

**enamel paint** — Paint that dries hard and shiny,
suggesting the quality of baked enamel

**enamel paper** — Paper with a fine clay finish

**enamel white** — Pigment; *blanc fixe*, a base for
watercolours and frescoes

**encaustic painting** — A method of painting with
hot wax mixed with pigment, difficult to control
but extremely durable; some examples exist that
were done in the first century BC; also called
*cerography*

**English finish** — A paper finish that is between
machine finish and supercalendered finish

**English pink** — Pigment; *see* **Dutch pink**

**English red** — Pigment; a light red iron oxide,
close to Venetian red on the colour chart,
permanent

**English varnish** — *See* **megilp**

**English vermilion** — Pigment; a bright red close
to cadmium red light on the colour chart

**English watercolour technique** — A technique
using transparent washes, alone or as a means of
building up colour through glazing

**engrave** — To incise, carve, or cut into a hard
surface

**engraver's charcoal** — Charcoal in block form,
used to polish plates in graphics

**engraver's pad** — A leather-covered pad filled
with sand, used to support a plate during the
engraving process; also called a *cushion*

**engrossing** — Decorating with calligraphy and
border designs on certificates, citations, etc.

**en kin** — (Japanese, *what is far and what is near*)
Perspective

partially completed
engraving

**epidiascope** — A projector designed to throw an image of a flat, opaque original

**Epstein, Jacob** — 1880-1959, English sculptor known for his large, controversial figures on public buildings. Those he produced for the British Medical Association building in the Strand, London (1907-8) were literally emasculated and began the opposition and attacks that followed his career

**eraser** — A device for cleaning off finger marks or pencil marks, or correcting a drawing; there are many kinds, such as pink pearl, kneaded, artgum, and felt erasers. *See also* **air eraser; electric eraser**

**erasing shield** — A metal or plastic shield with various-shaped slots, used along with electric erasers and manual stick erasers to avoid errors in erasing

**espagnolette** — A bust of a smiling young woman, originally in bronze

**esquisse** — (French, *outline*) A preliminary sketch and notes, for a painting or sculpture with more than a croquis

**etching** — An intaglio process of creating a design on the surface of a metal or other plate with a needle, and using a mordant to bite out the design; the resulting print is called *an etching*

**etching ground** — A thin, usually darkened acid-resisting coat applied to a plate, on which the design is incised

**etching ink**— A special thick ink made for etching, available in different colours

**etching needle** — A tempered piece of steel, sometimes in a wooden handle, used to incise a design on a plate for etching

**etching paper** — Paper specifically made for etching, lithographs, and block printing, available in hot- (smooth-) pressed or semismooth finish

**etching press** — A printing press designed especially for printing intaglio plates

**Etruscan art** — Art from early Etruria, a part of Italy; the culture dates from the seventh century BC to about the first century BC

**euchrome** — Pigment; burnt umber; name obsolete

**exc.** — (Latin, abbreviation for *excudit, he executed it*) Used on a print as credit for the one who printed it, as differentiated from the one who engraved it

**expressionism** — A twentieth-century art movement that turned away from the representation of nature and to the expression of emotional intensity; forerunners were Vincent Van Gogh and the Fauves; other such artists were Georges Rouault, James Ensor, Marc Chagall, and Emil Nolde

**extender** — A substance added to an inert pigment in order to increase its bulk or reduce its colour strength

**extensors** — Muscles in the lower arm that move the fingers

**eyedropper** — An implement useful for transferring or measuring water or other liquids, one drop at a time

**eye level** — The horizon line, in mechanical perspective, where two parallel lines meet at the vanishing point

**eye path** — The movement pattern the eyes follow when studying a picture

**eye trap** — An element that attracts attention to a particular area of a picture, sometimes a void

# F

**façade** — The main face or front of a building, usually given special treatment, as the façade of a cathedral

**face** — A front surface; the front part of a human head. *See also* **typeface**

**fan brush** — A bristle, sable, or synthetic brush made in the shape of a fan with a long handle; used to blend colours or to create texture in a painting, especially in trees and shrubs; more sparsely bristled than a badger blender

**fantastic realism** — Very realistic rendering in fantasy art

**fantasy** — A product of the imagination; an artwork produced from the imagination

**fantasy art** — Highly stylized form of illustration, usually by airbrush and related to science fiction. Exponents include Roger Dean and Boris Vallejo

**fast frame** — *See* **braquette**

**fat over lean** — In oil painting, the practice of painting 'lean' or with less oil at first, with top layers painted 'fat' or with more oil, to allow changes in the lower layers (expansion, contraction) without cracking the surface

**Fauves, les** — (French, *the wild beasts*) The first major aesthetic movement of the twentieth century, it was led by Henri Matisse in France in 1905-6. The outstanding characteristic of the Fauves was their use of pure, bright, explosive colour (often squeezed straight from the tube for directness and emotional effect) rather than tone; other important artists in the movement were André Derain, Maurice Vlaminck, Georges Rouault, Raoul Dufy, and Georges Braque

**fawn brown** — Pigment; a combination of dark ochre with either raw or burnt umber, also called *velvet brown*; names obsolete

**F.B.A.** — *See* **Federation of British Artists**

**feather** — To blend an edge so that it fades off or softens; to overlap values and colours in the manner of the overlapping feathers on a bird

**feathering** — In etching, to stir or move around the bubbles of the acid with a feather, brush, or pipe cleaner

**Federation of British Artists** — Umbrella body for many art societies, providing administration, accommodation and exhibition facilities

**felt finish** — Term describing paper that imitates felt

**felt side** — Said of the smoother side of paper, the top side in papermaking

**felt-tip markers** — Pens or cartridges with soft, felt-like, fine to broad tips, used for sketching, drawing, and layouts; permanent or watercolour, in a wide range of colours

**femur** — The thighbone, located between the pelvis and knee

**fence** — In sculpture, the piece of metal or clay used as a separation in a piece mould of plaster

**ferric chloride** — In etching, a liquid used on both copper and zinc printing plates as a mordant

**ferrule** — The metal part of a brush that holds the hairs or bristles

**Ferrarese school** — Mid-fifteenth-century Italian and Flemish artists around Ferrara, Italy, who painted in the Gothic and Renaissance styles; leading artists were Piero della Francesca, Pisanello, Jacopo Bellini, and later Dosso Dossi

**Festival of Britain** — Major exhibition of art and technology held in 1951 on the South Bank of the Thames in conjunction with many minor events up and down the country, intended to inspire national confidence. Strongly influential in the formation of a post-war style in British art

**festoon** — A decorative motif made up of flowers or fruit and leaves held together or interlaced with ribbons

**fibreglass eraser** — A fibreglass brush in a holder, used to remove ink and other marks difficult to eradicate from paper

**fibula** — The smaller bone in the lower leg occupying the outside and posterior part of the leg

**field** — The overall illumination in a picture; for example, if the majority of elements appear bright, the field is bright; if greyed, the field is greyed

**field of vision** — Everything that is visible without moving the eyes. *See also* **cone of vision**

**figurative** — 1. Representational. 2. A painting depicting a human figure(s), more real than abstract

**figure-ground reversal** — In design, the background and the main subject reverse colours and/or values; same as counterchange

**filbert** — A flat artist's brush with an oval-shaped point

**filigree** — Delicate, ornamental openwork of fine wire; lacelike ornamentation mainly used in jewellery

**fill** — 1. In textile design, the crosswise (horizontal) yarns, woof, or weft. 2. The small designs that are added to fill in around a major motif

**filler** — An inert pigment added to a paint or pigment to extend it or cheapen it. *See also* **extender**

filigree

**film stripper** — In platemaking for photolithography, the person who handles the films and negatives for plating; fits, positions, and assembles the negative film elements

**fine art** — Art primarily produced for the artist's satisfaction rather than for direct commercial purposes; does not necessarily denote quality

**Fine Art Trade Guild** — A trade association regulating quality and practice in the fine art publishing industry

**fine manner** — A means of engraving with a fine crosshatching that can approach a wash effect

**finish** — Treatment of the surface of a painting or photograph, such as glossy or matt, or of paper, such as smooth, kid, etc.

**finished artwork** — Artwork ready to go to the printer or exhibition

**finished, highly** — Having a very glossy finish; said also of a work of art with exact and complete details

**fire** — 1. In artwork, a characteristic of colours that are vivid or exciting, or of a piece of artwork that is exciting. 2. To bake in a kiln

**firmer** — In wood carving, a chisel that is flat-bladed and double-bevelled

**fish-scale motif** — A pattern resembling fish scales

**fitch** — A long, flat sign-painting or lettering brush with a chiselled edge; fitch, or polecat, hair is also used in some 'camel hair' brushes

chiselled edge fitch brush

**fixative** — A permanent waterproof spray used to protect artwork such as pencil drawing, charcoal, pastels, etc. from smearing

**fixed palette** — A limited number of colours to be used for a particular painting

**flake white** — Pigment; *see* **white**

**flaking** — Separating of small particles of paint from a painting

**flame black** — Pigment; a brownish carbon black, inferior to lampblack

**flame red** — Pigment; an orange red similar to cadmium red light; gouache; permanent

**flap** — A cover for artwork; often made of transparent paper or acetate; also called a *cover sheet*

**flat** — 1. Term describing the finish of a picture as lustreless. 2. Term for an application of paint that has no variations in value or colour and no brush marks showing. 3. A brush with oblong hairs and a long handle, available in bristle, sable, and synthetic. 4. Painted stage scenery

**flat wash** — An even colour or value of wash over an area in a picture

**flavine lake** — Pigment; yellow quercitron lake, fugitive

**Flemish white** — Pigment; a lead white, toxic

**flesh tint** — Pigment; a prepared Caucasian flesh colour, permanent; since flesh tones vary considerably, most professionals prefer to mix their own flesh colours

**flesh tone** — Any colour imitating flesh, be it white, black, brown, red, or yellow; usually a mixture of two or three colours

**flexible ruler** — *See* **curve ruler**

**flimsy** — The transparent overlay paper used on a piece of artwork for protection and notations

**flint paper** — A highly coated paper with a glossy finish, used for packaging and displays, available in many colours and white

**flip board** — Usually a gesso-coated cardboard or hardboard used in graphics to turn over or flip a print

**flock** — A soft-textured, pulverized product of wool, cotton, rayon, etc. that is glued or sprayed

73

onto cloth or paper, creating a velvety effect, either solid or in a pattern

**flong** — A term referring to strong tissue paper pasted to thick blotting paper, used in making stereotype printing plates

**floodlight** — A portable light used for lighting effects when painting portraits or still life, and for photography

**flop** — To reverse or turn over a design or photograph from left to right or vice versa

**Florentine brown** — Pigment; a brownish Vandyke red; toxic; darkens

**Florentine lake** — Pigment; crimson lake, obsolete

**flourishes** — Fancy or decorative embellishments on calligraphy or lettering

**flour paste** — Flour and water mixed together to form a paste

**flow** — 1. The ability of a printing ink to spread. 2. The movement of the eyes through a picture, influenced by colour and composition

**fluorescent pigments** — Brilliant, synthetic, luminous paints that glow or have a fluorescent effect in daylight and in the dark under black light; familiar as Day-Glo colours, a trade name

**flush** — Up tight to a line or edge, next to or touching without overlapping

**flush left** or **flush right** — Lined up at the left or the right of a column without indention

**flux** — In metal sculpture, a substance applied to metal to make the solder flow and stick

**foamcore board** — Board with a plastic foam centre faced with white paper on both sides; lightweight and sturdy, used, among other things, for mounting or backing pictures

**focal point** — The centre of interest in a picture

**foil** — 1. Any visual means in a picture employed indirectly to enhance or support another area, often accomplished through contrast of colour, value, texture, etc. 2. Thin leaf of metal used in jewellery making, sign painting, etc. 3. A small arc or lobe used in threes and fours, as in Gothic tracery. *See also* **trefoil; quatrefoil**

**foliated** — Decorated with leaves or with foils

**folk art** — Art and handicrafts produced by untrained people, usually of a traditional decorative style, such as tole painting, hand carved toys, handcrafted ironwork, embroidery, calligraphy, scrimshaw, etc.

**font** — A complete set of pieces of type of one size and face including upper and lower case letters, symbols, numbers and punctuation marks

**Fontainebleau school** — A group of Italian and French painters working at Fontainebleau, France, in the mid-sixteenth century. *See* **mannerism**

**foreground** — The area in a picture that seems to be closest to the observer

**foreshorten** — To shorten forms in a drawing as they recede from the foreground in order to maintain the proportions that appear natural to the viewer

**forgery** — The deliberate creation of an imitation of another work or artist's style with the intention to deceive. The best forgers are often considerable artists in their own right and some, such as the late Tom Keating, have achieved a degree of respectability

**form** — The three-dimensional shape and structure of an object

**formal balance** — The creation of areas of equal importance either side of the perceived centre of interest of a picture

**formalism** — The tendency toward symmetrical balance; a devolution from naturalism toward the stylized

**format** — Layout or makeup of a book, paper, magazine, etc.; its appearance in size, shape, type, and design

**foul bite** — In etching, the accidental biting of an area, causing unplanned inking

**foundation white** — Pigment; a variety of flake white used for priming or foundation coats

**found object** — *See* **objet trouvé**

**fountain** — In printing, a reservoir on a press for the ink supply

**fountain sumi ink brush** — A fountain brush (sable) with a barrel for the ink; takes refills

**fractured planes** — In pictorial composition, planes that have been 'chopped up' and realigned; also referred to as *split planes*

**frame** — A border of moulding surrounding a picture to enhance it and to facilitate hanging it

**Frankfort black** — Pigment; a carbon product, name obsolete

**free** — Applied to art, a loose and not exact treatment in drawing or painting; a broad manner, not clipped or tight

**free-form** — Irregular in shape; usually used to describe forms that depart from the rectangular and flow in linear freedom

**freehand drawing** — Drawing without the use of mechanical aids

**freelance artist** — One who does artwork for several different employers, not on salary or on a specific day-to-day basis

**French blue** — Pigment; French ultramarine blue, permanent

**French bristle** — A silky, thin bristle, usually white, used for brushes

**French chalk** — *See* **talc**

**French curve** — A thin template, usually made of clear plastic, used to draw curves; available in many sizes and shapes

**French easel** — *See* **easel**

**French ultramarine** — An artificial pigment replacing the prohibitively expensive lapis lazuli ash in genuine ultramarine

**French Veronese green** — Pigment; viridian, name obsolete

**French watercolour** — A coined name for watercolours that are runny or dribbly in handling

**French white** — Pigment; a flake white, zinc white, or silver white; toxic, permanent

**fresco** — A type of mural painting using limeproof pigments painted on a fresh lime plaster, becoming a permanent part of the wall; many masterpieces were done in fresco; no longer commonly used

**fret** — *See* **Greek key pattern**

**frieze** — A horizontal band high on an external wall, often decorated with relief sculpture, or a band below the ceiling on an internal wall

**frisket** — A transparent paper or other material with adhesive backing, used as a stencil, or to protect areas of artwork from a wash or airbrush treatment

**frog perspective** — *See* **sotto in sù**

**frontality** — Presentation of the straight-on view of an object or scene, as in Egyptian and other early painting

**frontispiece** — An illustration that appears at the front of a book, near the title page

76

**frothing etch** — In lithography, a strong etch that appears to 'boil' on the stone

**frottage** — (French, *rubbing*) The technique of taking an impression of wood, stone, or any other texture, by placing paper over the object and rubbing with a pencil, crayon, chalk, or charcoal over the surface. Max Ernst used this type of work in some of his collages. Similar to the rubbings from tombstones, sculpture, etc.

**frottis** — Term for a glaze or thin layer of paint

**fuchsia** — A reddish purple mixture

**fude** — An oriental brush 20-23cm long with a bamboo handle, made of various combinations of squirrel, horsehair, weasel, rabbit, wolf, and raccoon; soft, round and makes a hairline point

**fugitive pigment** — Said of colour that is not stable but changes chemically under different circumstances, usually fading

**full-colour rendition** — Using a wide range or full spectrum of colours

**full drop** — In design, a repeat motif directly below the first motif

**full length** — In painting or drawing, from the top of the head to the feet (of a figure)

**futurism** — An artistic movement founded in Italy in 1909 as a glorification of machinery, speed, and violence; followed the colour approach of neo-impressionists. Important artists were Boccioni, Balla, Carrá, and Severini

**fylfot** — A design made up of the Greek letter gamma, called a gammadion, one of which is the swastika. *See* **gamma** and **gammadion**

frottage taken from a tombstone

# G

**gag line** — A colloquial term for a caption

**Gahn's blue** — Pigment; cobalt ultramarine, permanent, name obsolete

**Gainsborough, Sir Thomas** — 1727-1788, English painter in the Classical mould who began as a landscape artist but in later life became a very fashionable portrait painter. Born at Sudbury in Suffolk, his early contact with the countryside enabled him to keep a sense of naturalness in his commissioned work

**gallery** — A room or rooms where artworks are exhibited

**gallery picture** — A painting in which the figures are larger than life and therefore requires to be hung in a large room to be viewed properly

**gallery tone** — The golden brown tone acquired by many Old Masters' paintings due to age, poor varnish, dirt, and the use of bituminous pigments

**galley** — 1. A section of movable type or assembled hot-metal slugs made up ready to be placed in the press. 2. A proof made from a galley

**Galliolino** — Pigment; a Naples lead yellow, obsolete

**gallstone** — Pigment; a variety of Dutch pink, obsolete

**Thomas Gainsborough**
*Wooded Landscape with Buildings on a Hillside*

**gamboge** — A natural gum pigment used in watercolour; a transparent yellow close to cadmium yellow medium on the colour chart, permanence questionable

**gamboge, New** — A trade name for a watercolour close to cadmium yellow, transparent and permanent

**gamma** — A Greek letter resembling an upside-down *L*, sometimes used in design

**gammadion** — A design made up of four gammas, an example of which is the swastika or fylfot

**'gang of Batignolles'** — Nickname for a group led by Claude Monet who met at the Café Guerbois in Batignolles, a district in Paris; the group included artists, writers, musicians, and critics

**gang up** — To put a number of items together for the printing or platemaking processes

**garance** — Pigment; madder lake, obsolete

**gargoyle** — A carved, grotesque human or animal figure projecting from the roof of a building. Most popular in the Middle Ages, it was originally used as a rain conductor, the water spouting from the mouth

**gas black** — Pigment; carbon black, name obsolete

**gauffrage** — An embossing process, using a tool called a gauffer, for decorating various surfaces

**Gauguin, Paul** — 1848-1903, born in Paris, a French post-Impressionist, he is best known for his use of broad planes and symbolic colour depicting the life of the South Seas

**gel** — 1. A transparent oil colour medium, packaged in tube form, used to alter the viscosity and elastic quality of paint for ease of handling, drying time, and certain effects. 2. A thick, colourless acrylic medium that adds gloss to acrylic paints. 3. A non-rigid coloured acetate filter

**gelatin** — A protein product, colourless, transparent, used as an adhesive or for sizing

**gelatin roller** — In graphics, a firm but flexible roller used for inking and used by some artists in painting; also called a *brayer*

**Paul Gaugin**
*Harvest: Le Pouldu*

**gellert green** — Pigment; a variety of cobalt green (bluish green)

**genre painting** — A type of painting that portrays a phase of everyday life, such as the interior of a room, a child at play, or a person cooking; most of Jan Vermeer's work is genre painting

**geometric abstraction** — The use of geometric shapes – lines, squares, triangles, rectangles, circles – to design a composition; Piet Mondrian is a leader of this style

**Georgian colours** — Trade name of a range of students' quality oil and watercolours

**geranium** — Pigment; a dark cherry red close to cadmium vermilion on the colour chart, moderately permanent, gouache

**geranium lake pale** — Pigment; a bright pink lake close to cadmium vermilion, fugitive, gouache

**German black** — Pigment; drop black, a carbon product, name obsolete

**gesso** — A white primer made of gypsum or chalk used as a base for painting canvas, wood, hardboard etc.; can be textured or sanded smooth

**gesso engraving** — Process in which gesso is built up to a 1.5mm thickness in multiple layers and an engraving is made on this hardened surface; a sealer is used to provide a good printing surface

**gestural drawing** — A way of drawing action or movement, generally of a figure or object in motion; drawn rather quickly to express the feeling of movement, not as a detailed work of art

**ghost** — 1. In lithography, the remnant of a previous drawing reappearing on a wet stone. 2. The remnant of a previous painting appearing through a painting done over it. *See also* **pentimento**

**giallorino, giallolino** — Pigment; a lead yellow, obsolete

**gilded** — Covered with gold leaf or gold paint, as on a picture frame

**Gillott pen** — A range of steel dip-pens in a variety of sizes, used for pen and ink drawing

gingerbread

**Thomas Girtin**
*The White House, Chelsea*

**gingerbread** — A lot of unnecessary decoration or ornamental details, especially in architecture (it is this sense of the word that appears in the phrase 'putting the gilt on the gingerbread')

**Girtin, Thomas** — 1775-1802, English watercolourist and rival of Turner, noted for his landscapes of Yorkshire

**glair** — A glaze or size made from the white of an egg, used in gilding and in egg tempera

**glassine** — A thin, transparent cover paper used over artwork or as sleeves for photo negatives

**glass stain** — A transparent paint in a full range of colours, used on glass, ceramics, or metal, to imitate stained glass

**glaze** — 1. A transparent layer of paint mixed with a medium, applied over a dry area, allowing the underpainting to show through. 2. In ceramics, a fired-on finish for pottery. 3. To impart a high gloss finish to a photograph

**glisten** — A stage in the drying of a watercolour when the paper reflects light with a slight shine or lustre, best seen at about a 45-degree angle to the paper

**glory** — *See* **aureole**

**gloss medium** — An acrylic medium that is used to increase the gloss in pigments, and can be used as a final varnish on acrylics

**glossy** — A photograph printed on shiny paper

**gluteus** — Any of three large muscles of the buttocks: *gluteus maximus* – the muscle forming the prominence of the buttocks; *gluteus medius* – the muscle that adducts and rotates the thigh; *gluteus minimus* – the muscle that adducts and extends the thigh

**glycerine** — A heavy, colourless, and odorless oil used in making watercolour paints, or added to watercolour paints and gouache to delay drying time

**Gmelin's blue** — Pigment; artificial ultramarine, name obsolete

**golden mean/golden section** — An idealized proportion based on the division of a line so that the ratio of the shorter section to the longer is equal to that of the longer section to the whole; based on a mathematical theory of Euclid

**gold ink** — an ink made of gold-coloured metallic particles in suspension; used with pen or air

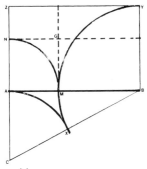

golden mean – one way to locate the ideal placement of a picture's centre of interest. Start with base-line AB of any length. Drop a perpendicular line from A to point C so that AC is one half AB. From C scribe an arc the measure of AC to point X on triangle ABC. From B swing an arc the measure of BX. The perpendicular from B to intersection of arc at Y is the height of desired rectangle. Complete rectangle ABYZ. Point M on line AB establishes the golden ratio. An arc from A, the length of AM, will place N. M and N are the co-ordinates for the golden section at G.

brush; requires frequent agitation to keep particles from settling

**gold leaf** — Extremely thin beaten gold for gilding; standard is 23½ carats, but available in a number of weights and quantities

**gold ochre** — Pigment; transparent, permanent

**goldpoint** — A technique in which gold wire is used to draw on specially prepared paper. *See also* **silverpoint**

**gold size** — *See* **bole**

**goop** — In tole painting, the medium used to thin the paint

**Gothic** — Pertaining to European art and architecture, between the twelfth and fifteenth centuries. The building style emphasized pointed arches, cross-ribbed vaults, and flying buttresses; the scope was monumental in scale, with much ornamentation. Gothic painting emphasized human qualities striving for classical ideals

**Gothic type** — Also known as *spire gothic, sans serif*, and *block letter*; gothic type today is a plain sans serif face

**gouache** — French for opaque watercolour, permanent. Designer's colours and casein are gouache, also the mixture of opaque white with transparent watercolours can be used. Sometimes referred to as tempera

**gouge** — A kind of chisel used on wood, linoleum, etc.

**gradation** — In composition, a gradual transition from one form or element to another, usually with slight changes in value

**graded wash** — A wash with variation in colour or value from dark to light or light to dark

**gradine** — In sculpture, a toothed chisel used to remove large pieces from marble or stone

**graffiti** — (Italian, *graffiare, to scratch*) Originally a drawing on an ancient wall, in modern times has come to mean crude drawing or writing disfiguring walls, doors, or any available public space. In certain quarters it has become an art form in itself

**graffito** — *See* **sgraffito**

**grain** — Refers to the texture of paper, as fine or rough

**graining** — In lithography, a slight roughening of the stone to give it a tooth to catch the grease crayon

**grandee paper** — A 36-kilo cover stock in a medium texture, 51 × 66cm, available in a variety of colours and white

**grand manner** — A term applied to the lofty style and noble themes advocated in the Academies; Michelangelo, Poussin, and Reynolds, among others, are said to be painters in the grand manner

**granosis** — In sculpture, toning or dulling the glare of stone by using an application of colour mixed with wax

**granular board** — A sand- or marble-textured board prepared by the artist and used for pastels, etc.

**grape black** — Pigment; vine black, a carbon product

**graphic arts** — This term differentiates between fine art and art produced for commercial purposes. Originates from the need to redraw illustrations for engraving prior to the use of half-tones. Also applies to any form of art producing original prints, such as aquatint, drypoint, etching, lithography, silkscreen, woodcut, etc.

**graphics** — In a broad sense any representation by printing, drawing, and painting

**graphic symbols** — 'Press style' symbols, such as dots, lines, stars, borders, etc., used to decorate type for advertising and other printed material

graphic symbols

**graphite pencils** — Drawing pencils in which the centre rod is graphite; H to 9H are graduated degrees of hard (light); HB and F are between hard and soft; and 2B to 6B are graduated degrees of softness (dark)

**graphite transfer paper** — A thin paper coated with graphite, used for transferring a drawing

**graph paper** — Paper with a printed grid, available in various sizes and grids

**graver** — *See* **burin**

**gravity folds** — Folds in cloth that follow the least resistance or 'fall' of the cloth

**gravure, photogravure** — A commercial intaglio printing process using plates or cylinders, known for its quality in halftone and colour reproduction

**grease pencil** — *See* **lithographic crayon**

**Grecian purple** — Pigment; Tyrian purple, an inferior purple used by the Greeks and Romans; obsolete

**Greco, El Theotocopulos Domenikos** — 1541-1614, born in Crete, settled in Spain where he was known as *the Greek*. His style is often mystical and full of exaggerated proportions. His work had a great influence on all who followed

**Greek cross** — A cross with four equal arms, vertical and horizontal, as in the plus sign

**Greek fold** — Folded cloth in an angular shape with rounded ends

**Greek key pattern** — A running design popular in Greek and Roman decoration, also called *Greek fret* and *Roman key*

Greek key pattern

**green bice** — Pigment; green earth, name obsolete

**green earth** — Pigment; transparent earth green, permanent, made in yellowish (Cyrian), bluish (Verona), and dull blue (Tyrolean)

**green ultramarine** — Pigment; a semitransparent, permanent greenish blue, not widely used

**green verditer** — Pigment; Bremen green, toxic, obsolete

**grenadine** — A bright to medium cherry colour, permanent, close to cadmium vermilion, gouache

**grey** — Commonly the mixture of white and black; can also be produced by mixing any complementary colours

**grid** — A graph pattern of proportional divisions with many uses, including enlarging or reducing a composition

**griffin** — In design, a mythical beast, half eagle and half lion

**grinding stone** — In lithography, a pumice stone used with a mixture of sealing wax and alum solution to smooth the stone

**grisaille** — (French, *grey*) 1. A Renaissance technique of underpainting with greys; transparent or semitransparent colours were then glazed on. 2. Contemporary usage has come to mean a monochrome painting rendered in greys, often in imitation of bas-relief

grotesque decoration

**grotesque** — Decorative art that combines fanciful human and animal forms

**ground** — 1. A base coating of paint or gesso applied to a panel, canvas, paper, or board on which a picture is painted or scratched. 2. In textile design, the first screen or the base colour of a design, often white. 3. An acid-resistant coating for plates used in etching

**ground colour** — Base or background colour

**grounding** — In sculpture, the polishing of marble with a fine abrasive

**ground line** — In linear perspective, the line on which the object (often a building) rests, parallel with the horizon line

**ground plane** — In linear perspective, the horizontal plane on which the viewer stands, theoretically extending to the horizon

**G.S.M.** — Grams per square metre. A measure of the weight (and therefore thickness) of paper

**Guignet's green** — Pigment; viridian, name obsolete

**guillotine** — A machine which cuts (paper, board and sometimes frame moulding) by means of a heavy knife

**gum arabic** — A natural gum material from the acacia tree used in solution with watercolours and other art products to increase gloss and transparency, now nearly unobtainable; synthetic or cellulose substitutes, referred to as 'gum', are usually used

**gum eraser** — A firm but soft crumbly eraser used to clean artwork

**gumming up** — In lithography, brushing a solution of gum (arabic) and water over the stone to seal off and desensitize a nonpainting area

**gum water** — A gum solution used with watercolours to increase gloss and transparency and improve flow and wetting; a binder of watercolours

**gutter** — The inner margin (white paper) of a printed page and the empty space between two facing pages

**gwa** — (Japanese) A drawing or a picture

**gwafu** — (Japanese) A book of sketches

**gwajó** — (Japanese) An album of folding prints

**gypsographic print** — *See* **embossed print**

# H

**Haarlem blue** — Pigment; Antwerp blue, a reduced Prussian blue, name obsolete

**Haarlem checks** — Named from Haarlem, The Netherlands; a textile design, originally red and white, or blue and white checks; now other colours are also used

**Hague school** — Dutch realist artists who painted at The Hague during the last half of the nineteenth century

**hairline register** — A very close register; in printing, a register within plus or minus one-half row of dots

**hairline spacing** — Very fine, tight spacing of type or elements in a layout

**hake** — An oriental flat brush made of sheep or goat hair, used for washes (pronounced *hokey*)

**half-drop** — In textile design, a repeat motif that is dropped halfway down from the first motif

**half-tone** — 1. Any value between the lightest and darkest tone or shade of a colour. 2. A printed image where the full tonal range is produced by dots of colour of varying size and proximity

**halo, halation** — 1. A glowing or halo effect usually about the head of religious figures. 2. In graphic arts, the same type of effect around headlines, products, etc.

**hamstring muscles** — Three muscles on the back of the thigh that flex the leg, adduct and extend the thigh

**hand-blocked** — Printed by hand with the use of a block plate

**hand burnishing** — In printmaking, a method of rubbing a plate, often achieved with a wooden spoon

**hand colouring** — *See* **pochoir**

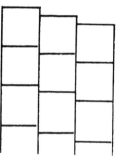

half-drop

enlarged half-tone screen of photo

**hand-primed** — As opposed to mechanically primed canvas, the primer is brushed or rolled on by hand rather than by machine

**hand screen printing** — *See* **silkscreen**

**hand-tacking iron** — An electrically heated iron used to tack or fix, in the dry-mounting process

**Hansa yellow** — Pigment; a pale yellow, both transparent and semi-transparent, permanent; close to cadmium yellow pale

**hard realism** — A realism with an exact and flat painting style; Grant Wood (1892-1942) painted in this manner

**haricot** — In design, a kidney bean shape

**harmony** — The pleasing combination of elements; order, agreement, balance

**hatch, hatching** — Lines superimposed upon lines to create texture and value. *See* **crosshatch**

**Hatchett's brown** — Pigment; a brownish Vandyke red, name obsolete

**Hawaiian prints** — In textile design, brightly coloured, large floral or abstract prints

**haze** — An atmospheric condition that clouds an area

**H D** — Handmade

**head animator** — The person responsible for an animated cartooning operation

**heartwood** — In woodcarving, the harder and darker part of the tree near the centre

**heat transfer printing** — In textile design, the procedure of transferring a design to fabric, using heat and pressure

**heavy** — Said about any element in a composition if it is strong and compelling

**heel (of a brush)** — The portion of hair on a brush where the brush and ferrule meet

**hell box** — A printer's receptacle for discarded metal type to be melted down in a furnace

**heraldic** — pertaining to a design or emblem symbolizing or identifying a family or a profession, especially a coat of arms

**herm** — A rectangular block or slab of stone having a head carved at the top, used as a dedication to a god, or as a grave marker

**hickey** — In graphics, an undesirable mark or imperfection in printing, caused by dirt in the ink or on the press

heraldic

87

**hide glue** — An adhesive made from the hides of animals – rabbit, calf, and others

**hiding power** — The degree of opacity of a coat of paint; how it covers an area, whether lightly or completely

**hieroglyphics** — Pertaining to picture characters (signs or symbols) in Egyptian and other early writings; any emblematic markings

**high etch** — *See* **dry-relief offset**

**high-key painting** — The use of upper values on the value scale in a composition, creating a light, sometimes pale picture

**highlight** — A spot of the highest or lightest light or value on a subject or in a painting

**highliner** — A square-tipped, long or extra long lettering brush, the best being red sable

**highlining** — In lettering, an edge on letters like a highlight

**high surface** — A smooth surface on paper

**HMP** — Handmade paper; the pattern is more random, therefore will not tear as easily as mould-made paper

**Hockney, David** — 1937-  , like many trained draughtsmen who turn to fine art, Hockney rejects the obviously graphic, yet the quality of drawing is always central to his pictures. He is a keen experimenter and brings a depth of understanding to what are often superficially banal subjects

**Hogarth's line** — *See* **line of beauty**

**David Hockney**
*The First Marriage*

**hog hair** — *See* **bristle**

**Hokusai (Katsushika Hokusai)** — 1760-1849, a Japanese master printmaker famous for the *Great Wave* and *View of Mr. Fuji*, among others. His sketchbooks are an invaluable source of Japanese life and custom.

**holding line** — A line on a mechanical, usually in black, to be printed unless otherwise indicated; not a key line

**holly green** — Pigment; green earth, name obsolete

**holograph** — A special photographic plate from which, by means of laser light, a three-dimensional image can be projected

**Homer, Winslow** — 1836-1910, an American illustrator, graphic artist, and painter. He recorded the Civil War but is best known for his rural, small-town genre paintings, and later for pictures of men and the sea

**honeycomb** — In design, a small raised geometric network resembling the honeycomb of bees; also called *waffle*

**Hooker's green** — Pigment; a mixture of gamboge and Prussian blue in two shades, one with a yellowish undertone and one more bluish, neither permanent; the mixture of phthalocyanine blue and cobalt yellow is permanent and transparent

**Horace Vernet green** — Pigment; a type of Bremen green, toxic, now obsolete

**horizon line** — In perspective, a straight horizontal line at the line of sight. *See* **line of sight**

**horizontal** — Parallel to the horizon; horizontal composition is one in which the dimensions are more wide than high

**horsehair brush** — An oriental painting brush with stiff hairs, originally made from horsehair

**hot-metal setting** — *See* **linotype**

**hot pink** — A bright pink colour

**hot pressed paper** — (H.P.) – Smooth, dense paper used for drawing and opaque watercolour painting

**hot wax painting** — *See* **encaustic painting**

**H.P.** — *See* **hot pressed paper**

**Hudson River painters** — A nineteenth-century group of American romantic landscape artists who painted mainly in the Hudson River valley and the Catskill Mountains, though some roamed as far west as the Sierras. Famous painters of the early group included Cole, Doughty, Durand, among others; the second group were called the Luminists and included such artists as Church and Bierstadt

**hue** — The basic attribute of a colour, such as red, blue, green

**humanism** — A Renaissance doctrine centered on the potential of mankind, with some rejection of supernaturalism; in art, brought a tendency toward secular themes

**humerus** — The arm bone reaching from the shoulder to the elbow

**hyalography** — Engraving on glass with diamond or emery cutting tools, or with an etching solution

**hydrochloric acid** — In etching, a colourless acid best used on zinc plates

**hygroscopic** — Capable of absorbing moisture from the air; said of paper that changes character and size with humidity

# I

**I.C.A.** — *See* **Institute of Contemporary Arts**

**icon, ikon, eikon** — A religious image, particularly of the Eastern orthodox churches; a sacred likeness or representation, often painted on wood

**ideogram** — A sign or symbol representing an object or idea

**illumination** — The art of decorating manuscripts with fanciful letters, pictures, and designs; the earliest known example was found in the *Book of the Dead* in Egypt

**illusionism** — *See* **trompe l'oeil**

**illustration** — A picture that tells a story or is used to support and accompany a written text

**illustration board** — A good-quality paper mounted to a stiff backing board; available in two thicknesses and two textures, hot pressed and cold pressed; used in a variety of types of artwork

illumination – initial letter from a tenth-century manuscript

**image** — 1. A representation of a person or thing, translated in an artwork. 2. Abstractly, a form or semblance of creative thought, which may also be translated in an artwork

**imbrication** — A pattern in which the motifs overlap like the shingles on a roof

**imp.** — (Latin, abbreviation for *impressit, he printed it*) Same as exc. *See* **exc.**

**impasto** — A thick application of paint on a painting. Usually oil or acrylic, but possible with any thick, opaque medium

**imperial** — *See* **watercolour paper sizes**

**imperial green** — Pigment; a form of emerald green, toxic, name obsolete

**imposition** — In printing, the positioning of pages on the press so they will be in proper sequence when printed and folded

**impression** — An imprint made by means of pressure

**Impressionism** — French landscape movement arising out of dissatisfaction with the classical basis of art laid down by the Académie des Beaux Arts. The original members of the Impressionist group regularly had their work refused by the Salon and, in 1863, held their own exhibition, the Salon des Refusés, which was neither a critical nor public success. Impressionism was one of the first art movements to attract general hostility, although today it is one of the most influential and admired. Its style relies not on realism, careful modelling or great technical mastery, which had characterized previous advances in artistic style, but rather on an interpretation of the play and value of light. Many artists of the group would paint the same scene under a variety of different conditions, achieving quite contradictory effects. The movement is not exclusively French and J.M.W. Turner and the American Mary Cassatt are often included with it. Strictly, though, they are not part of the Impressionist group, whose members included Cézanne, Degas, Gaugin, Manet, Monet, Pisarro, Renoir and Sisley

**improvise** — To create spontaneously without a definite plan

**inc.** — (Latin, *incidit, he cut it*) Found on a print as credit for the engraver or etcher when different from the artist

**India ink** — A dark black liquid ink, available in what is called waterproof or nonwaterproof formulae

**Indian blue** — Pigment; a deep transparent blue, fugitive, an obsolete name for indigo

**Indian red** — Pigment; a reddish earth colour with bluish undertone; opaque and permanent

**Indian yellow** — Pigment; a synthetic yellow similar to a warm cadmium yellow medium, transparent and permanent

**India oil stone** — A stone used to sharpen knives, burins, and scrapers

**indigo** — Pigment; no longer available from the natural plant; in oil, a mixture of ivory black, Prussian blue, and ultramarine; in watercolour, a mixture of alizarin crimson, lamp black, and phthalocyanine blue; durable

**indo orange red** — Pigment; similar to scarlet vermilion, durable, acrylic

92

**informal balance** — Equilibrium between compositional elements without total symmetry. *See also* **formal balance**

**Ingres paper** — A textured drawing paper particularly suited for use with pastels

**ink** — Pigment in liquid or paste form. *See* **India ink; sumi ink; printer's ink; etching ink**

**ink stone** — *See* **sumi ink**

**inkers** — Artists who do portions of ink drawings for animated cartoons or comic strips

**inking roller** — *See* **brayer**

**inking slab** — Any heavy flat surfaced material on which ink can be placed (butcher's tray, glass, marble, hardboard), to roll ink onto a brayer

**inkless intaglio** — *See* **embossed print**

**inlay** — To decorate by making slots in a surface and 'laying in' small pieces of precious metals, ivory, or other material. *See* **intarsia**

**insert frame** — *See* **liner**

**in situ** — (Latin, *in position*) On the spot; said of a painting when painted on location

**instant lettering** — *See* **press type; pressure-sensitive letters**

**instant mount sheets** — Double-faced adhesive sheets used where heat, glue, or wax may damage artwork

**Institute of Contemporary Arts** — Body specializing in promoting and exhibiting contemporary work in all fields of art

**intaglio** — 1. In sculpture, hollow or concave relief. *See* **cavo rilievo**. 2. In printmaking, design or lettering cut below the surface of a plate, with ink left only in the depressions, as in etching, drypoint, aquatint, photogravure, and line engraving

**intaglio relief plate** — A plate that has been inked on the surface rather than in the lines

**intarsia** — Inlay work, usually wood inlaid with contrasting wood, but may be ivory, mother of pearl, or other material. *See also* **marquetry**

**intense blue** — Pigment; phthalocyanine blue, similar to Prussian

**intensify** — To make bright or strong; to strengthen in some way

**intensity, colour** — The brightness or saturation of a colour

**interchange** — *See* **counterchange**

**interference colours** — Pastels made with two different colours in one stick

**interlacing** — In textile design, a pattern made up of lines or bands that are interwoven, or painted so they look interwoven

**intermediate colours** — *See* **tertiary colours**

**interpret** — In art, to represent or illustrate in light of the artist's belief; not necessarily a literal copy of real things

**intervals** — In art, the spaces between elements of a composition that set up a rhythm

**in the round** — *See* **sculpture in the round**

**intimism** — A style of painting, concerned with intimate domestic settings; major artists were Pierre Bonnard and Edouard Vuillard

**intuitive painting** — Painting from a subjective, or personal, frame of refrence

**inv.** — (Latin, abbreviation for *invenit, he invented it*) Credit given on a print to the one who designed it

**investment casting** — *See* **lost wax**

**iridescence** — Delicate tints of rainbow colours caused by diffraction of light

**iris green** — Pigment; sap green, name obsolete

**iron blue** — Pigment; Prussian blue, an intense transparent colour, name obsolete

**iron brown** — Pigment; Prussian brown, iron hydroxide, name obsolete

**iron gall ink** — An ink made from tannin or gallotannic acid, which comes from oak galls; used in the Middle Ages

**irregular curve** — *See* **French curve**

**isometric projection** — A form of axonometric projection used in mechanical drawing which has equality of foreshortening of the three planes of an object, with the height, width, and depth drawn on the same scale. Horizontal lines are usually all drawn at 30 degrees to base, and verticals perpendicular to base; distortion is evident. First used by East Indian and Persian artists

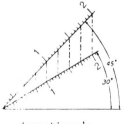

isometric scale

**Italian blue** — Pigment. *See* **Egyptian blue**

**Italian earth** — Pigment; an old name for sienna

**italic** — 1. Calligraphic hand characterized by lateral compression, branching and flourishes. Developed as a reaction to more formal and complex scripts. 2. Name of an alphabet of type that is slanted or leans upward to the right; most type fonts have an italic, as well as a Roman alphabet

**Ives colour wheel** — The red, yellow, blue colour wheel introduced by Herbert Ives, an American (1882-1953); red was called achlor, yellow was zanth, and blue turquoise was cyan

**ivory** — Pigment; an off-white colour, usually with a yellow undertone; a medium for carving, from animal tusks. *See* **scrimshaw**

**ivory black** — *See* **black**

# J

**jacaranta brown** — Pigment; umber, name obsolete

**Jacquard** — In textile design, a raised, figured pattern woven into cloth like tapestry, damask, brocatelle, etc.; invented by J.M. Jacquard, an eighteenth- and early nineteenth-century French weaver

**Japan colours** — A sign painter's quick drying paint, available in many colours in tubes or cans

**Japan drier** — *See* **drier**

**japanning** — An imitation of oriental lacquer. *See* **lacquer, oriental**

**japan paper** — Paper made with an irregular mottled surface, used for greeting cards

**Japonisme** — The influence of Japanese art and decoration, especially in France, 1854-1910; a number of French artists were influenced by the simplicity of Oriental design, among whom were Monet, Whistler, Tissot, Degas, Bracquemond, and Jacquemart

**jaune brillant** — Pigment; a reddish variety of Naples yellow made from cadmium yellow, flake white, and vermilion; toxic but durable

**jaune d'antimoine** — Pigment; Naples yellow

**jeweller's rouge** — A compound used to buff and polish metals

**jigger** — *See* **levigator**

**Jugendstil** — The German term for art nouveau after the Munich publication *Jugend*, meaning youth. *See* **art nouveau**

**jungle print** — In textile design, a pattern of animals and foliage that are found in the jungle

**justify** — In typesetting, to space out letters and words so that each line is exactly the same measure and both margins form perpendicular lines

96

**jute** — a coarse natural fibre used for making burlap and a cheap canvas that does not last well

**juxtaposition** — In painting, the close placement of adjoining colours or forms; side by side

# K

**kakemono** — (Japanese, *hanging scroll*) A vertical scroll displayed periodically, often following seasonal changes or as a dedication to a friend's visit, a birth, or the like. *See also* **makimono**

**Kandinsky, Wassily** — 1866-1944, Russian, associated with the Blue Rider group and the Bauhaus. His work is nonobjective, based on a spatial feeling rather than the depiction of objects realistically. Many theoretical writings on art are credited to his name.

**Kano school** — (Japanese), founded in the sixteenth century by Kanō Masanobu; known for its boldness, the life of the brush stroke, and the play of values in the ink paintings. *See also* **sumi-e**

**kanshitsu** — (Japanese) Sculptural forms produced by the use of lacquer-saturated cloths placed on an armature

**kara-zuri** — (Japanese) Blind embossing. *See also* **embossed print**

**Wassily Kandinsky**
*The Battle*

**Kassler yellow** — Pigment; Turner's lead yellow, now obsolete

**Kauffer, Edward McKnight** — 1890-1954, American-born poster and graphic artist who came to prominence under Frank Pick at London Transport, designing more than a hundred posters promoting bus and underground services and special events

**kelly green** — Pigment; a bright green

**kerf** — In woodcarving, the path cut by a saw blade

**kermes** — Pigment; crimson lake, obsolete

**kern** — In typesetting, to adjust the letter spacing of type such as TA, VC, AY, to improve appearance and legibility

**kernel black** — Pigment; vine black, a carbon product made by burning kernels

**kerosene** — American term for paraffin

**key** — 1. The dominant tone or value of a picture – high (light), medium or low (dark). 2. A wooden or plastic form used in the holes of stretcher strips to tighten the canvas

**key block, key plate, keystone** — In multicolour printing, the block, plate, or stone that has the complete drawing on it, the other colour blocks, plates, or stones being made from this key

**key lines** — In commercial art, the outline, usually in red, indicating the placement, size, and shape of elements such as photographs and drawings on the mechanical; not printed, but a guide for the platemaker

**khaki** — A light brown/tan mixture, considered a neutral

**kid finished** — Describes a medium-textured drawing paper, also called *vellum*

**kinetic art** — Popular in the 1950-1960s and continuing into the present, includes any artwork that moves or has moving parts, such as mobiles and motorized sculpture

**king's blue** — Pigment; cobalt blue, name obsolete

**king's yellow** — Pigment; a bright yellow, opaque, toxic, and fugitive, name obsolete

**kiss impression** — In printing, a very light impression, just enough to show the image

**kitchen prints** — In textile design, motifs pertaining to fruit, vegetables, pots and pans, baskets, etc.

TA VC

normal spacing

TA VC

kerned

**Klee, Paul** — 1879-1940, Swiss artist whose earliest association was with the Blue Rider group. He later taught painting at the Bauhaus and featured in the 1925 Surrealist exhibition in Paris

**Klimt, Gustav** — 1862-1918, Austrian painter who was one of the founders of the Vienna Secession movement. His style is personal, based largely on Art Nouveau

**kneaded eraser** — A pliable, nonabrasive eraser that can be shaped to a point; used for cleaning artwork, picking out highlights, and softening pencil lines

**knife** — *See* **mat knife, painting knife, palette knife,** and **X-Acto knife**

**Knight, Dame Laura** — 1877-1970, English artist best known for her paintings of circus life and scenes from the ballet. She pictured many other subjects, however, and was also a major war artist, producing many portraits at the Nuremberg trials

**kolinsky** — *See* **sable**

**Korin school** — Japanese school of painting emphasizing decoration; the artist Korin was a superb painter in lacquer

**kou le** — (Chinese, *contour style*) A style of painting in which light outlines are drawn to establish a basic structure, darker lines are used to reinforce them, and finally colour is added if desired. *Pai-miao* is the name given to the drawing or painting; *shuan kon* is a form of kou le with a double outline

**Kremnitz/Krems white** — *See* **white**

**Paul Klee** *They're biting*

# L

**laboured** — Overworked; said of artwork that has lost a feeling of spontaneity

**lacework** — 1. A flat, filigree design, chainlike or similar to strapwork. *See also* **strapwork**. *2.* Calligraphy-type strokes in a painting

**lacquer, modern** — Coating made of cellulose materials, made for ease in spraying to create a fast-drying, shiny, tough, hard film, used mostly in industrial work

**lacquer inks** — Used for commercial silk-screen work, available in many colours, can be thinned to transparency with a special base. One type of lacquer ink can be used on aluminium foil; toxic and flammable

**lacquer, oriental** — Name given to a coating used in Asia to create artwork, usually platters, bowls, boxes, etc., coated with multiple applications and built up to a hard, tough, permanent surface, sometimes thick enough to be carved; the artwork is also called *lacquer*

**laid paper** — Paper with a pattern of equally spaced parallel lines made by a screen on which the paper is formed, giving a ribbed effect to the surface

**lake colours** — Pigment make by fixing a dye on an inert base in a manner similar to dyeing cloth. Transparent and usually impermanent

**laminated** — 1. Formed into a bond in layers, as in plywood; also applies to papers, paperboard, etc. 2. Said of a transparent film permanently applied to artwork, book jackets, etc. to preserve and protect the surface

**lampblack** — Pigment; pure carbon black, permanent

**landscape** — A view of scenery – fields, trees, rocks, sky, etc. – as the subject of a picture or design

**landscape shape** — A term occasionally used in reference to a horizontally shaped piece of paper, canvas or other support

**lapis lazuli** — Pigment; a true ultramarine blue made from the semiprecious stone; practically obsolete

**latissimus dorsi** — A large back muscle that originates in the lower thoracic and lumbar region and extends up the side under each arm, adducting, extending, and rotating the arm

**lattice** — An open framework of crossed strips, or a design resembling such a framework

**lay figure** — A wooden manikin with movable parts; can assume almost any desired position, to substitute for a life model

lay figure

**lay in** — To apply a rough application of paint, pastel, or other medium to a section of a picture at a preliminary stage

**layout** — A rough or general planning of a page, advertisement, brochure, etc., showing positioning of type and illustrations

**layout chalk** — Chalk used for layouts, made in different colours and in different values of greys

**layout paper** — A bond or offset text, vellum-finished, able to accept paint, chalk, pencil, etc. and usually translucent

**layout pencils** — Soft, smooth, usually black pencils, used for layouts and sketching (ebony, negro, and flat carpenter's pencils)

**lazuline blue** — Pigment; native ultramarine, practically obsolete

**lead/leading** — Originally a strip of lead separating lines of type, still used to designate the space between lines. For example: ten on twelve (10/12) means a ten-point typeface cast on a twelve-point body, allowing two extra points between lines, referred to as 'leaded two points'

**lead adhesive** — A presure-sensitive adhesive brushed on lead tape so that it can be applied to glass, metal, etc.

**lead casting** — A form of sculpture using lead

**lead holder** — A mechanical, handle-type tool that holds lead (graphite) for drawing

**lead tape** — A pliable, soft, lead stripping used to create a stained-glass window effect

**lead white** — *See* **white**

**leaf** — Metal that has been rolled or beaten to a very thin sheet, used in gilding; available in gold, silver, palladium, and aluminium

**leaf green** — Pigment; chrome green, fugitive, name obsolete

**leaflet** — A printed circular, handbill or flier, usually consisting of a single sheet of paper

**lean** — Said of oil colours that are thin or low in oil content, giving a matt finish. A lean quality can be achieved by squeezing the oil paint onto a blotter to absorb some of the medium

**leather brayer** — In lithography, a roller covered with soft leather

**L'Ecole de Paris** — (French, the *School of Paris*) A term that implies 'contemporary art'. It started about 1900 when Paris was the world art centre

**leek green** — Pigment; chrome green, fugitive, name obsolete

**Leipzig yellow** — Pigment; chrome yellow, fugitive, name obsolete

**Leithner blue** — Pigment; a form of cobalt blue, name obsolete

**lemon yellow** — Pigment; barium yellow; a pale, cool yellow; permanent

**Leonardo da Vinci** — 1452-1519, Italian, a Florentine painter, sculptor, architect, and designer. Among his best-known paintings are *The Last Supper* and the *Mona Lisa*. His notebooks and sketches show the scope of his remarkably agile mind.

**Letraline tape** — Trade name of an opaque tape (glossy or matt) used in commercial art; available in 10 widths and in different colours

**Letraset** — Trade name of a pressure-sensitive lettering system, sometimes used generically

**letterhead** — The heading on business stationery, giving the name, address, etc. and often carrying a unique logo design

**lettering** — Letters drawn by hand as opposed to type or other mechanical forms

**lettering brush** — Brushes used by a hand letterer, such as a quill, chisel brush, liner, striper, single-stroke brush, or cutter

**lettering pen** — A pen used for hand lettering

**lettering quill** — A quill brush for lettering, available in a long, flat, squarecut brush that produces sharp, clean work, and a pointed quill,

lettering quill

103

used for outlining, shading, and highlining. *See also* **quill**

**letterpress** — Commercial relief printing used mostly for newspapers, books, and magazines

**letter spacing** — Adjusting the spaces between letters so they appear proper and consistent, legibility and ease of reading being the prime considerations

**levigator** — In lithography, a circular tool used to grind the stone; also referred to as a *jigger*

**Leyden blue** — Pigment; a form of cobalt blue, name obsolete

**liberty print** — An early American design, usually limited to one or two colour variations on a white or natural background

**life (of a brush)** — 1. The spring or bounce of a brush, making it easy or hard to use. 2. The length of time that a brush will last – a month, five years, a lifetime

**life drawing** — Drawing of the human figure; usually refers to drawing from a nude model

**life mask** — An impression of the face of a living person, usually made of plaster

**life size** — Of the same size as the person or animal used as a model

**lift** — In watercolour, a term for taking out unwanted pigment, using dry brush, a sponge, tissue, paper towel, finger, or cloth

**lift-ground etching** — Using aquatint as a base, positive images of lines or brush strokes are etched into the plate, which is then inked with a lift-ground solution (e.g. 50 per cent saturated sugar dissolved in 50 per cent India ink); also called *sugar bite*

**lifting** — In gouache and some other mediums, the mixing of an undercoat with a second coat; prevented by using a fixative on the first coat

**ligature** — In typography, two or more letters joined together in one body, such as *fl, fi,* etc.

**light and shadow** — The change from pronounced light to pronounced dark. *See* **chiaroscuro**

**light box** — A translucent glass-topped box with a light under it, used for tracing

**light face** — The lightest and thinnest form of a typeface

**lightfast** — Resistant to fading on long exposure to sunlight

Helvetica
Helvetica
**Helvetica**

10 point type in light face, regular and semi-bold

**light green oxide** — Pigment; a light yellowish green, extremely permanent, acrylic

**light, medium, dark** — Terms used to denote values and to 'key' a picture. *See* **key**

**light red** — Pigment; an earth red, between burnt sienna and Venetian, permanent

**light-sensitive plate** — Plate that is treated with a light-sensitive coating, used in photogravure and photolithography printing procedures

**light source** — The location that the light appears to be coming from in a picture, as indicated by cast shadows, highlights, etc.

**lime blue** — Pigment; Bremen blue, toxic, obsolete

**lime white** — Pigment; whiting, used as a filler in inexpensive paints

**limited edition** — In graphic arts, a limited number of prints, determined by the artist, that are pulled from a plate and numbered, after which the plate is destroyed

**limited palette** — A selected number of colours on the palette, which by mixing can often suggest a full range; for example, alizarin crimson, cadmium yellow, and cobalt blue

**limner** — An artist who paints miniatures

**linage** — The size of an advertisement; the depth in agate lines, 14 lines to 2.5cm; example: a 5cm ad is 28 lines deep

**line** — 1. A continuous mark as made by a pencil, pen, or brush in an artwork, as distinguished from shade, colour, mass. 2. A set of marks, shapes, colours, or other elements that lead the viewer's eye through a work of art. 3. The 'line' in textile design is the presently salable designs pertaining to a given subject, as the designs for bed linens and related products

**line and wash** — A line drawing combined with a wash of ink or watercolour

**linear** — Of or pertaining to lines; said of an artwork that is dominated by lines

**linear perspective** — Mechanical, geometric perspective, a means of giving the illusion of distance in three-dimensional space on a two-dimensional surface by the location of lines

**line art** — In commercial art, black and white drawings, type, etc., achieving greys or variations in values by line hatching and not requiring halftones; may be called *linecopy*

**line block** — *See* **linecut**

**line board** — Smooth finished white board used in the production of mechanicals to mount copy and half-tones

**line conversion** — The process of photographing continuous tone photos with line film in which the values are all reduced to either black or white

**linecopy** — *See* **line art**

**linecut** — A printing plate photoengraved from a line drawing, executed in only black and white or one colour and white; flat screens are used to produce a grey tone with black and white solids (no variable screen); other names are *line engraving, line block, line etching,* and *line plate*

**line drawing** *See* **line art**

**line engraving** — *See* **linecut**

**line etching** — *See* **linecut**

line drawing

**line film** — Film used to create extreme contrasts of white and black by dropping out greys; used in graphic and commercial arts

**line leading** — *See* **lead/leading**

**line matter** — *See* **line art**

**line measure** — In typography, the maximum length of any line in a block of text

**line movement** — The arrangement of elements in a picture so that the viewer's eye is directed from one area or object to another

**linen canvas** — Linen cloth used as a support for painting; may be primed or unprimed, in different textures and qualities

**linenfold** — A decorative Gothic fold in cloth, straight in line with soft and hard ends

**linen tester** — A small, powerful magnifying glass originally designed to count threads in linen; now also used to examine the dot structure in plates, printed materials, and negatives

linen tester

**line of beauty** — Called Hogarth's line after the English painter William Hogarth (1697-1764), it takes the form of a graceful *S* curve in a composition

**line of sight** — In linear perspective, the line extending from the viewer's eyes to the picture plane, in the exact centre of the cone of vision; also called the *line of vision*

**line of vision** — *See* **line of sight**

**line plate** — *See* **linecut**

**liner** — 1. A brush used by sign painters to create straight lines and sharp edges; available in different shapes and in pointed quill and square liner quill sizes. *See also* **dagger**. 2. A strip of wood, linen, hemp, velvet, etc., that lines the inside of a frame immediately next to the picture

**line spacing** — Adjusting the space between lines in copy for better layout or fit

**line, weighted** — A line that is heavy in either value or thickness

**linocut** — *See* **linoleum cut**

**linoleum** — A durable floor covering material used for linoleum cuts

**linoleum block** — A piece of wood with linoleum mounted to the surface, cut and inked to make a block print called a *linoleum cut* or *linocut*

**linoleum cut/linocut** — A relief print similar to a woodcut. *See* **linoleum block**

**linotype** — A machine that sets type by keyboard, to be cast by the line in hot metal. The procedure, which dates from the 1870s, is being replaced by various computer typesetting systems

**linoxyn** — The dried linseed oil skin of an oil painting

**linseed oil** — An oil made from flax seed, used as a medium with oil paints and as a drying oil in pigments

    **boiled linseed oil** — Processed with heat or driers; not used by artists

    **cold pressed oil** — No heat involved; oil from the crushed seed is left to stand until the impurities have settled out, and is then filtered

    **raw linseed oil** — Seeds are heated before being pressed; used only in lower-quality paints

    **refined linseed oil** — Steam pressed, refined, and bleached; less expensive than cold pressed oil; most often used in grinding paints

    **stand oil** — The molecular structure has been changed by polymerization; a heavy oil, dries slowly but creates a tough, flexible film

    **sun-thickened oil** — Of honey-like consistency, is thicker and quicker drying than cold pressed oil or refined oil; has been partly oxidized, thickened, and bleached by exposure to the sun

**liquid eraser** — used on drafting film to completely erase an area

**liquid mask** — A liquid frisket used to block out

areas on paintings in watercolour, gouache, commercial art, etc.; can be removed by rubbing with the fingers

**liquid opaque** — A light-proof liquid used to retouch line negatives used in the production of photolitho plates. *See also* **lithography, offset**

**liquid resin ground** — In aquatint, a saturated solution of resin mixed in denatured alcohol

**liquin** — Trade name of a medium used to thin oils and alkyd; speeds drying time

**Liquitex** — Trade name of a range of acrylic colours

**lithographic crayon or pencil** — A black grease crayon or pencil with which the drawing is made for the lithographic process; also used to write on glass, china, stone, or where a dense black line is desired; may be used on rough-textured paper to create halftone effects with line

**lithographic ink** — A printing ink available in colours, used in reproducing lithographs; not to be confused with the tusche in lithography used for drawing and painting on the stone

**lithographic points** — Needles or points used for scratching in the crayon areas on a lithograph stone to create white-line effects

**lithographic printing** — *See* **lithography, offset**

**lithograph stone** — A flat slab of limestone, prepared with a grain to be used for lithography

**lithography** — A process that involves drawing with a grease crayon on limestone or a metal or plastic plate, which is wet with water and then inked with a roller; the oily printing ink adheres to the oily drawing and resists the blank areas, making it possible to pull prints with a litho press. Since its invention in 1798 it has been a popular process with such artists as Daumier, Degas, Toulouse-Lautrec, Picasso, and Miró

**lithography, offset** — A term applied to printing by offset press in which the image is transferred to the plate by a photographic process; not to be confused with the lithographic process

**lithography press** — The printing press used to pull prints in lithography

**lithography, transfer** — A process in lithography that allows an image to be transferred from paper to the stone

**lithol red** — A bright cherry red used in inks and commercial products, not permanent

**livering** — The turning of oil paint to a rubbery mass in the tube, caused by impurities in the pigment

**loaded** — Fully charged; said of a brush filled with paint

**local colour** — The actual colour of a subject

**logo/logotype** — An identifying symbol, signature, or trade name for commercial use

**London Transport** — The governing body of London's buses and underground railways became an unlikely patron of the arts in the 1920s and 30s under the influence of its Vice-Chairman, Frank Pick (1878-1941). In a manner similar to the Arts & Crafts Movement, Pick believed in the importance of outward appearance in overall fitness for purpose. Applying this to everything from architecture to publicity posters, he saw this as a means not only of selling tickets, but also of bringing good art to the man (literally) in the street. Although institutional patronage is often conservative and regressive, Pick championed modern design and played an important part in the development of a characteristic British style in art and architecture in the middle of the twentieth century that came to fulfilment in the Festival of Britain exhibition and the period that followed it. It was really only superseded by 1960s pop art and culture and the rising influence of America. Pick commissioned many of the leading artists of his day, as well as encouraging new talent. Frequent exhibitions of posters are held at the London Transport Museum in London's Covent Garden and include artists such as Frank Brangwyn, E. McKnight Kauffer, Tom Eckersley, Laura Knight, Edouard Paolozzi and many others. The architect most responsible for LT's building design was Charles Holden. London Transport's patronage continues today, particularly in underground station design and the introduction of mosaics as part of individual station identity

**long shot** — A view of a subject or scene from a distance

**loose painting** — Painting characterized by free, broad handling of areas and brushwork, lost-and-found contours, broken or loose lines, or patches of colour

**lost and found** — A painting quality in which lines and/or contours dissolve, fade, or blend into others and then reappear at intervals

**lost-wax process** — A procedure for casting metal sculpture and jewellery, used from the fifth century AD to the present time; also called cire perdue and investment casting

**lotus** — A flower design originating from the lotus flower, a kind of tropical water lily; a Buddhist symbol

**lowercase letters** — The uncapitalized letters of a font

**low key painting** — Using the darker section of the value scale, likely to be subtle, subdued, or moody

**Lowry, Laurence Stephen** — 1887-1976, English painter whose work is mainly associated with the industrial landscapes of Manchester and Salford, in which stick-like figures became his trademark. He also painted smaller compositions which exhibit humour (*Man Lying On A Wall*) as well as demonstrating a more disturbing side to his nature (*Head of a Boy in A Yellow Jacket*)

**luci/lucida** — *See* **camera lucida**

**Lukasbrüder** — Order of St. Luke. *See* **Nazarenes**

**lumbar** — In anatomy, the region between the thoracic vertebrae and the sacrum. *See also* **vertebrae**

**luminous** — Appearing to give off a glow from under the surface, as from under a glaze on a painted work; also describes a paint that glows in the dark

**lunette** — A half-moon shaped panel decorated with artwork

**lustre** — A deep glow, often metallic or iridescent

**Lutschism** — *See* **Rayonnism**

**lyrical** — A poetical term used to describe art that is graceful and flowing

**lyrical abstraction** — In the early 1970s, an outgrowth of abstract expressionism, featuring large picture sizes and muted colour harmonies; the term is sometimes applied to the work of Mark Rothko (1903-1970) who is also classified as an abstract expressionist

# M

**macaroni** — An uncomplimentary colloquial term for a stringy design or pattern

**macchia** — (Italian, *spot* or *stain*) A style of painting or sketching in spots or patches of colour in an impressionistic manner

**Macchiaioli** — A group of nineteenth-century Florentine landscape artists who painted with patches of colour and called their work *macchie*

**mace-head** — A tool used in mezzotint to produce graininess or burr where desired; also called a *mattoir*

**machine composition** — Setting of type by machine, usually hot metal type

**machine finish** — A finish on paper made by calendering or polishing by mechanical means

**machine screen printing** — *See* **screen printing**

**macle** — A hollow lozenge or diamond shape

**maculature** — In intaglio printmaking, pulling a second print without re-inking, to remove surface ink or colour

**madder** — Organic pigment produced from the root of the madder plant (Rubia Tinctorum)

**madder brown** — Pigment; alizarin brown, transparent, permanent

**madder lake** — Pigment; a transparent colour similar to alizarin crimson, moderately durable

**Madonna** — Usually refers to a representation of the Virgin Mary

**magenta** — Pigment; a purple with a red undertone, moderately permanent

**Magic Markers** — Trade name for a type of felt-tip markers. *See* **felt-tip markers**

**magic realism** — A type of painting of the twentieth century where almost photographic realism is achieved. Sometimes the realism is combined with the fantastic through strangely related subject material and mysterious light-source treatment, creating metaphysical effects reminiscent of de Chirico and others

**mahlstick (or maulstick)** — A stick about 76cm long, of wood or telescoping aluminium, used as a rest to balance the hand and arm when drawing or painting. *See also* **artist's bridge**

**maize** — Pigment; a corn yellow

**makeover** — In graphic printing, any plate which is reworked or remade

**make ready** — 1. In printmaking, to level relief printing plates on the bed of the press, so a good impression is possible. 2. In commercial printing, all work done on printing presses prior to starting the print run, including setting the plates, adjusting the ink fountains, grippers, etc.

**makimono** — A Japanese horizontal scroll painting that is unrolled with the left hand and rolled up with the right hand; after the viewing, the scroll is rewound so it can again be viewed from right to left. *See also* **kakemono**

**Malevich, Kasimir** — 1878-1935, Russian; his early work was fauve, then cubistic and finally he founded Suprematism, a nonobjective geometric movement.

**mallet** — A woden hammer used in sculpture, leatherwork, and woodcarving

**Maltese cross** — An eight-point cross, named for its use as an emblem by the medieval Knights of Malta

**mandala** — A Hindu or Buddhist symbol of the universe; any circular design can be considered a mandala

Maltese cross

**Kasimir Malevich**
*Dynamic*
*Suprematism*

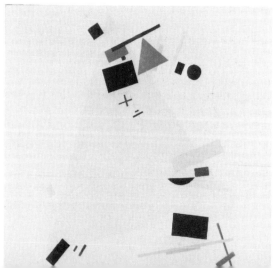

**Edouard Manet**
*Woman with a Cat*

**Manet, Edouard** — 1832-1883, French painter
much influenced by Spanish masters including
Velasquez, Murillo and Goya. Featured
prominently in the Salon des Refusés of 1863
and was a strong influence on the emerging
Impressionist movement, although he never
exhibited with the group
**manganese black** — Pigment; a black oxide,
obsolete
**manganese blue** — Pigment; a bright greenish
blue, transparent and permanent
**manganese brown** — Pigment; a brown oxide,
obsolete
**manganese green** — Pigment; a greenish
manganese blue, obsolete
**manganese violet** — Pigment; a deep bluish
purple, permanent
**manière criblée** — *See* **criblée**
**manifesto** — A public declaration of the theories of
an art movement
**manikin, mannikin, mannequin** — *See* **lay
figure**
**mannerism** — A style of painting in Italy and
France about 1525-1600, marked by emotional
distortion, harsh colouring, and individualism,
said to be a reaction to the art of the High
Renaissance; major artists were El Greco and
Tintoretto
**maquette** — In sculpture, a small, rough model,
used as a guide for the larger piece; also called a
*bozzetto*

**marble dust** — A crushed marble used as a texture in printmaking and pastels or mixed into plaster for frescos

**marble paper** — A paper that imitates a marble pattern

**marbling** — 1. In painting, a mingling of colours that form an irregular pattern as found in marble. 2. A process for making a convoluting marble-like pattern for decorating books, etc., by floating colours in a gum solution, swirling them, and transferring the pattern to paper by contact

**marigold yellow** — Pigment; an orange close to cadmium yellow deep in gouache; permanent

**Maroger medium** — A gel-like medium or megilp. *See* **megilp**

**maroon** — Pigment; a dark red colour mixture

**marouflage** — The process of attaching a painted canvas to a wall with acrylic binders

**marquetry** — A decorative art in which small pieces of wood, ivory, metal, or other material are inlaid in furniture, usually forming floral or geometric patterns

**Mars colours** — Earth colours made from artificial oxides of iron

**Maruyama school** — An eighteenth-century Japanese school using a realistic approach to painting; started by the scholar Maruyama Okyo

**mask** — 1. White paint or paper used to cover or hide an area. 2. A film or resist used to cover and hold an area in silk screen and airbrush. 3. A mould of a human or animal face, used as a wall hanging. 4. A cover worn over the face, often weird and bizarre

**masking film** — A thin, plastic film coated with a thin, coloured plastic emulsion, used for overlays for colour separation and in silk-screen positives

**masking tape** — A paper-adhesive, pressure-sensitive tape that sticks tighter than drafting tape, but can be removed without damaging artwork

**Masonite** — American tradename for hardboard

**mass** — 1. In artwork, a sizable area of a composition, as opposed to a line. 2. The bulk of an object

**massicot** — Pigment; yellow lead, toxic and fugitive, obsolete

**mass tone** — The surface colour of a pigment

**master** — A knowledgeable artist, usually with extensive experience

**masterpiece** — A work of art of an excellence that has stood the test of time; originally an example of work presented to a guild to qualify for the rank of master

**mastic** — A resin used with turpentine to make varnish; has a tendency to turn yellow with age

**mastic varnish** — used as a final gloss varnish on oil paintings

**mat** — See **mount** (definition 2)

**mat board** — See **mount board**

**mat cutter** — See **mount cutter**

**Matisse, Henri Emile Benoît** — 1869-1954, French painter influenced by the later part of the Impressionist movement and a leader of the Fauves group

**mat** — A dull, lustreless finish; sometimes spelled *matt* or *matte*

**mat medium** — An acrylic medium used with acrylic paints to reduce the gloss; can be used as a final mat finish

**mat varnish** — A non-glossy, flat varnish

**matting wheel** — A variant of the roulette, used in *crayon manner* or *chalk manner. See also* **roulette**

**mattoir** — See **mace-head**

**mature style** — An artist's individual style, method of paint application, composition, etc., usually developed after years of painting

**mauve** — Pigment; any of several shades of purple

**McGuilp** — See **megilp**

**meander pattern** — The Greek key pattern

**Henri Matisse**
*Standing Nude*

115

**measure** — The length of line in characters specified when copy is being typeset

**mechanical** — A working board made to guide the printer when making reproductions; consists of all the camera-ready components – type, illustration, etc. – in correct size and pasted up

**mechanical perspective** — Linear perspective with the use of tools

**medallion** — A circular or round design; a large medal

**media** — *See* **medium**

**medium** (plural, **mediums** or **media**) — 1. The liquid used to thin paint. 2. Material used to create art, such as pencil, pen, watercolour, oil colour, gouache, pastel, alkyd, acrylic paint, wood, stone, and various found materials. 3. (usually media) Channels for advertising, such as newspapers, magazines, and television

**medium key** — Using the middle value range as a picture's dominant tonality

**megilp** — A gel-like, quick-drying painting medium used in the nineteenth century that gave an enamel-like finish but had a tendency to darken and crack with age; also called *McGuilp* and *English varnish*

**memento mori** — (Latin, *remember death*) A skull as part of a painting or other artwork; may also be a clock or other symbol of the passing of life. Such a still life is also called *vanitas*

**memory picture** — *See* **mind's eye**

**mermaid** — A legendary creature with a woman's body and the tail of a fish, appearing as a design motif

**Merz** — A form of dada, started by Kurt Schwitters, an abstract artist. The name Merz originated from a collage he made which had MERZ in red capital letters (torn from a bank advertisement) in the composition

**metacarpus** — The five bones in the hand between the wrist and the fingers

**metal-foil paper** — Paper-backed foil available in colours of gold, silver, red, green, and blue

**metal modelling compound** — Metal in paste form, used on sculpture; applied to the surface, dried and buffed; available in aluminium and bronze

**metal point** — A procedure in which a pointed

metal rod is used as a drawing instrument on an abrasive, coated surface; the metal stylus may be of silver, lead, copper, or gold. Much used by artists before the development of the graphite pencil in the sixteenth century

**metamerism** — An undesirable condition in which two areas of matching opaque colour that have a reflective surface, as in an oil painting, appear to match in colour under one kind of illumination and not under another form of light; usually caused by not using exactly the same pigments to paint both areas

**metaphysical painting** — Painting with a dreamlike quality combined with realism, created by de Chirico and others, where unusual perspective and colour create a mysterious or unreal effect. *See* **magic realism**

**metatarsus** — The five bones between the tarsus and the toes

**métier** — The field or specialty in which an artist performs best, as painting or sculpture, or the subject field, as landscape, portraiture, or other

**mezzo fresco** — A painting done on partially dry plaster; a line surrounds the forms because the paint sinks partially into the semidry plaster

**mezzotint** — (Italian, *halftone*) A relief print made on a metal plate; a rocker is used to roughen the whole surface, then the white areas (not to be printed) are burnished and smoothed below the surface; halftones are created by removing only part of the burr

**Michelangelo Buonarroti** — 1475-1564, Italian, a painter, sculptor, poet, and architect. Famous for his sculpture *The Pieta*, among others, and his vast undertaking of frescos on the ceiling of the Vatican's Sistine Chapel

**middle ground** — The middle area in a picture between the foreground and the background

**middle key** — Using the middle values on the value scale as the dominant tonality in a picture

**migration** — The bleeding or spreading of colour outside the allotted area

**millefiori** — Jewellery design made from pieces of coloured glass inlaid with gold

**mill blank** — A white coated mounting board for photos and artwork

**Milori blue** — Pigment; a high-quality Prussian blue

**mimosa yellow** — Pigment; a yellow earth brighter than Naples yellow, permanent, gouache

**minaret** — A tall tower near a mosque from which the faithful are called to prayer; often used as a motif in Islamic design

**mind's eye** — The faculty of the mind to imagine or remember visual things

**mineral black** — Pigment; vine black; also a name for black iron oxide

**mineral blue** — Pigment; manganese blue, brilliant, transparent, and permanent

**mineral brown** — Pigment; burnt umber, permanent

**mineral green** — Pigment; Bremen green, toxic, obsolete

**mineral spirits** — A substitute for turpentine, used as a brush cleaner and a paint thinner, also called *petroleum spirits* and *white spirits*

**mineral violet** — Pigment; manganese violet, also ultramarine violet, obsolete

**mineral white** — Pigment; a native calcium sulphate, not recommended for oil paints

**mineral yellow** — Pigment; Turner's lead yellow, obsolete

**minette** — Pigment, ochre; name obsolete

**mingling** — The mixing of several colours right on the painting rather than on a palette; most often done in watercolours or gouache

**miniature** — Often simply refers to a very small picture, but technically it is one which is painted on ivory or vellum. The style developed from the decorated capitals in medieval illuminated manuscripts. The name derives from the Latin word 'minimum' for *red lead*, which was used to make the contemporary red ink and has no connection with 'minimus', meaning *small*

**minimal art** (ABC art) — A 1960s American movement related to the nonart theories of Duchamp, in which the artist's means are reduced to an apparent minimum. Closely related are the bare surface paintings of Frank Stella, and the publicized wrapping of buildings and mountains by Christo

**minium** — A red lead popular in the Middle Ages

**Minoan art** — Art and culture of Crete about 3400 BC-1100 BC

**mirror image** — A design or picture in reverse as seen in a mirror

**mistletoe green** — Pigment; a light olive green, permanent, gouache

**Mitchell pen** — A range of steel dip-pens in a variety of styles and sizes, used for calligraphy

**MiTeintes pastel paper** — Trade name for a paper especially made for pastels, crayon, casein, and gouache, available in many colours

**mitre box** — A tool used with a saw to cut 45-degree angles for picture-frame corners

**Mittis green** — Pigment; a form of Vienna green, toxic, obsolete

**Mittler's green** — Pigment; a form of viridian, name obsolete

**mixed media** — Two or more media used in one picture, such as transparent watercolour and gouache, or pencil and ink wash

**mixing cup** — *See* **dipper**

**mixing tray** — Tray used as a palette and for mixing colours; available in numerous shapes

**M O** — Mould made, said of paper products

**mobile** — A sculpture with a delicately balanced arrangement of movable parts, suspended on thin wire and generally moved by air currents. The Chinese made wind chimes, which are mobiles, hundreds of years before Alexander Calder built his famous sculptures

**mock-up** — A three-dimensional model, full size, of a future structure

**model** — 1. A person posing for an art class. 2. A scaled-down representation. 3. In fashion, a mannequin

**modelling** — 1. In sculpture, the act of shaping and manipulating the clay or other material into desired forms. 2. In drawing or painting, the suggestion of three-dimensional forms through use of planes, values, and colour

**modelling board** — In sculpture, a board on which the artist works with clay or other material

**modelling clay, self-setting** — A moist, ready-to-use clay that sets hard but does not have to be baked

**modelling paste** — A thick acrylic paste, used in reliefs or for any area that needs to be built up; easily modelled while wet, can be carved and sanded when dry

**modelling stand** — A turntable, usually about 90cm high, on which a sculpture is formed

**modelling tools** — Various-shaped tools made from boxwood and wire, used in sculpture and ceramics

**modello** — (Italian, *model*) A sketch (often in paint) or a more finished model to show a patron the idea for an artwork

**model's stand** — A low table-like construction, sometimes on wheels, normally about 1.8m square, used by a life model for sitting, standing, or reclining

**modern art** — Generally indicative of the art of the twentieth century that is nonobjective or abstract in nature

**modern folk art** — In America, art that includes posters, baseball cards, car stickers, etc.

**Moderne Kunstkring** — (Dutch, *modern art circle*) A group of painters who first exhibited together on Oct. 11, 1910; included were Cézanne, Mondrian, Toorop, Sluyters, Braque, Picasso, Derain, Dufy, Vlaminck, and Redon

**modified realism** — Stylized representation of real and recognizable things

**Modigliani, Amedeo** — 1884-1920, Italian painter and sculptor who worked in France. His stylized figures with smooth, long oval forms are expressive and moody. His sculpture was influenced by African art and by Constantin Brancusi

**modular colours** — A line of acrylic colours already mixed to different values, put out in America under the trade name of Liquitex

**moiré** — A shifting, wavy pattern caused by

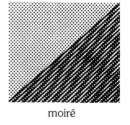

moiré

**Amedeo Modigliani**
*The Little Peasant*

superimposing a halftone screen over another one, an undesirable condition. In textile design, another name for *watered silk*

**moist paper** — In watercolour, the condition when the shine has disappeared from the surface of wet paper

**mokkotsu** — A traditional Japanese ink painting with colour

**mo-ku** — (Chinese, *boneless style*) No lines are used; the picture is painted freely, with each brush stroke creating a form

**Mondrian, Piet** — 1872-1944, born in the Netherlands and known as a Neoplasticist. He is famous for his purely abstract compositions using the three primaries plus white, black, and grey. All lines are parallel to the sides and no obliques are used

**Monestial colours** — Trade name of a variety of pigments which substitute for expensive or impermanent colours in the artists' range

**Monet, Claude Oscar** — 1840-1926, French, one of the leaders of French impressionism. A *plein air* painter who is noted for his series of paintings of the same subject, done at differing times of day. (See illustration over.)

**monochrome/monochromatic** — Rendered in variations of one colour

**monogram** — A design composed of one or more letters, for identification and decoration

**monolith** — A single standing stone or other material, carved or cast in one piece, sometimes used as a monument

**monotype** — 1. Process in which a one-of-a-kind original print is made by painting on a glass or smooth surface, then pulling a single print from the plate before the paint is dry. 2. (cap) Trademark of a kind of hot lead typesetting

**Piet Mondrian**
*Composition with Grey, Red, Yellow and Blue*

121

**Claude Monet**
*Poplars on the Epte*

machine similar to Linotype. Now largely
replaced by photosetting

**monotonous art** — indicates an overall similarity
in shapes, values, textures, colours, or lines

**montage** — A picture made by mounting other
pictures, photos, etc. onto a flat surface; not
three-dimensional as in *assemblage* or *collage*

**Montpellier green** — Pigment; verdigris, fugitive,
obsolete

**Montpellier yellow** — Pigment; Turner's lead
yellow, now obsolete

**mood** — An emotional impression or feeling that
may be created through visual means

**Moore, Henry** — 1898-1986, English sculptor
whose work was strongly influenced by natural
geological formations. He is particularly known
for a series of momumental figures whose appeal
is as textural as representational

**mop** — An oval-shaped watercolour brush used to
lay washes

**mordant** — 1. An acid solution used in etching.
2. An adhesive film used in applying gold leaf.
3. Any of a number of substances used in
photography and fabric manufacture for dye-
toning

**morphoplasticism** — A word used to describe
realistic, natural art which has form, colour, etc.,
as opposed to *neoplasticism*

122

**Morris, William** — 1834-1896, English artist and designer, founder and leading member of the Arts & Crafts Movement

**mortar and pestle** — *See* **pestle and mortar**

**mosaic** — 1. An ancient process of decorative art using small coloured pieces of tile, glass, or pebbles pressed into plaster or other ground. Contemporary mosaics are made from tile, metal, beads, stone, etc. 2. In photography, a term for photos pieced together from a number of separate exposures, often used in aerial surveying

**mosaic gold** — A metallic gold-coloured powder used as a substitute for real gold leaf or powder, obsolete

mosiac by Arthur Goodwin

**mosaic tesserae** — *See* **tesserae**

**moss green** — Pigment; chrome green, fugitive, name obsolete

**mother colour** — A touch of one colour added to every colour used in a picture; a dominant tint that results

**mother-of-pearl** — A hard, internal, iridescent layer in some shells, used in design and ornamentation

**motif** — A repeated design or pattern; the main idea or theme in a design

**motion in art** — 1. Movement suggested by the placement of compositional elements. 2. Figures depicted as bending, walking, etc.

**mottle** — To make a variegated or spotty effect

**mould** — A hollow form used to cast or shape something, as a mould for a mask or a piece of pottery

**moulding** — Narrow strips of wood or metal used to make frames; available in simple or highly decorated styles

**mould-made** — Describes paper where sheets are made individually by hand. *See also* **paper**

**mould-made paper** — Paper made by machine rather than by hand

**mount** — To place on top of, as to mount a photograph on a cardboard. 2. Board with cut out aperture, placed over a picture prior to framing. Also referred to as a mat

**mountain blue** — Pigment; dark azurite blue, obsolete

**mountain green** — Pigment; a form of Bremen blue, toxic, obsolete

**mountant** — A glue, paste, cement, or other adhesive for mounting

**mount cutter** — Mechanical or hand-held device used to cut aperture mounts. Most can give a square or bevelled edge

**mounting adhesive, dry** — A sheet of adhesive that transfers to the back of the work to be mounted

**mounting board** — A heavy cardboard, usually white, used to mount photos and artwork

**mounting tissue** — *See* **dry mounting tissue**

**mouse** — *See* **pick-up**

**movable type** — Type of which each letter is separate so it can be moved and placed where desired; referred to as 'hand set'

**Mozarabic** — A style produced by Spanish Christians using Moslem art and decoration during the Moorish domination of Spain

**muddy** — Said of colours in a painting that have lost their sparkle; usually caused by overworking or mixing too many colours together

**mud-glyph** — A coined word used to describe symbols, designs, and pictures inscribed in mud on cave walls

**mulberry paper** — A thin Japanese rice paper

**muller** — A tool used for grinding pigments

**multicolour** — Having many colours; polychromatic

**multicolour print** — A print made with a number of colours

**multiliner tool** — A scratchboard tool that makes several parallel lines with one stroke

**multiple graver** — A graver with two or more evenly spaced points, used to cut several lines with one stroke

**mummy** — Pigment; a brown ash colour once made from Egyptian mummies; obsolete. The colour apparently came from asphaltum, used in the embalming process

**Munch, Edvard** — 1863-1944, Norweigian, a painter, printmaker, and one of the leaders of expressionism. His mature work was simplified, stark, and often focusing on morbidity

**Munich lake** — Pigment; carmine, a fugitive lake, obsolete

**Munich school** — A group of nineteenth-century American painters who were influenced by their teachers at the Munich Academy; paintings tended to be dark in value and based on the works of Rembrandt, Hals, and Velasquez. Prominent artists were Alexander, Bacher, Chase, Currier, Dielman, Duveneck, Fitz, Marr, Muhrman, Neal, Rosenthal, and Shirlaw

**Munsell theory** — A colour system introduced in 1915 by Albert Munsell in which colour has three components to which the human eye responds: hue, value, and chroma. The method of colour identification uses five hues: red, yellow, green, blue, and purple; based on visual mixture of colour rather than pigments

**mural** — A wall of ceiling painting painted directly on the surface or permanently fixed in place, large in scale to match its setting

**muscle** — A tissue made up of fibres, capable of contracting and relaxing to effect bodily movement

**museum** — A building in which artistic or scientific works are preserved, housed, and displayed

**museum mounting** — *See* **archival mounting**

**museum mounting board** — A high-quality acid-free mounting board used for archival mounting

**Mycenaean art** — Art and culture from Mycenae, a city on the Greek mainland *c.* 1600 BC-1100 BC; characterized by rich artefacts, often of gold. *See also* **Aegean painting**

**Mylar** — Trade name for gum-backed coated paper used in graphics. A transparent, tough, dimensionally stable acetate used for overlays; also used in the offset printing process for stripping

**myosotis blue** — Pigment; a dark blue close to Prussian blue, fugitive, gouache

**myrtle green** — Pigment; chrome green, name obsolete

**Edvard Munch**
*The Sick Child*

125

# N

**Nabis, Les** — (Hebrew, *the prophets*) In the 1890s, a group of French artists, including Bonnard, Vuillard, Denis, Roussel, and others, who were influenced by Gauguin and by naive painting, mysticism, and rebellion against artistic conventions

**nacarat carmine** — Pigment; carmine, fugitive lake, obsolete

**Nagasaki school** — Japanese eighteenth-century school of painting in a realistic style derived from traditional Chinese painting

**naïve painting** — Originally used to describe the work of untrained artists who nevertheless have some innate ability. Some artists have, however, taken up the style and it has become a more recognizable school. Among the best-known genuine naïves are Grandma Moses and Douanier Rousseau. Modern naïves include Beryl Cook and Martin Leman. *See also* **primitive painting**

**Nangwa school** — Japanese late seventeenth- to nineteenth-centuries school of painting noted for graceful brush strokes and the use of changing values throughout the painting

**Pierre Bonnard**
*Bathing Woman seen from the Back*

**naphtha** — A petroleum distillate used as a solvent for wax; has little effect on oil and is sometimes used as a picture cleaner; toxic

**naphthol crimson** — Pigment; an acrylic colour similar to alizarin crimson, permanent

**Naples yellow** — Pigment; a permanent pale yellow, a lead product; toxic

**narrative art** — Art that tells or suggests a story

**National Academy of Design** — A society of conservative American painters, sculptors, and engravers headquartered in New York City since 1826; associate members are entitled to use A.N.A. after their name, and when elected to full membership, N.A. is used

**National Gallery** — The major British national art collection, housed on the north side of Trafalgar Square in London. Began as a national collection only in 1824 and was originally housed in Pall Mall. *See also* **Tate Gallery**

**National Portrait Gallery** — London gallery close to the National Gallery, housing portraits in paint and sculpture of distinguished men and women in the history of the country

**native green** — Pigment; native chromium oxide, obsolete

**natural dyestuffs** — Colours extracted from natural sources such as plants and animals, as opposed to synthetic material

**naturalism** — Realism in painting, not influenced by distortion, mysticism, etc., and not by romanticism

**natural pigments** — Pigments from animal, mineral, or vegetables sources

**natural texture** — Texture from natural sources such as stones, bark, etc.

**nature morte** — (French, *still life*) *See* **still life**

**Nazarenes** — Mocking name given to the Lukasbrüder, Order of St. Luke, a group of artists and writers founded in Vienna in 1809, and dedicated to encouraging art as a religious devotion. Members included Friedrich Overbeck, Peter von Cornelius, Karl Begas, Julius Schnorr, and Franz Pforr

**near complement** — The colour on either side of the direct complement; for example, a near complement of yellow is blue violet or red violet

**near symmetry** — A nearly equal visual balance of elements in a composition

**needle** — A pointed tool used in etching and other graphic arts

**negative** — A photographic image in which the darks of the original subject appear light and the lights dark; a tonal reverse of the original

**negative space** — The space in an artwork not occupied by subject matter but utilized by the artist as part of the design

**negative tint** — White dots or pattern against a dark background

**neoclassical** — Pertaining to a style, mainly in eighteenth-century Europe, influenced by classical Greece and Rome

**Neo Dada** — *See* **pop art**

**neo-expressionist painting** — Abstract painting stemming from the emotions or accidental happenings, as distinguished from planned, geometric forms

**neo-impressionism** — An art movement started in France about 1880; also called chromo-luminarism, pointillism, and divisionism. Consists of applying tiny dots of pure colour in such a manner that intermediate colours are created in the eye of the observer. Prominent artists were Seurat and Signac, although the principle had been practised by earlier artists including Watteau, DeCaerech, Turner, and others

**neoplasticism** — *See* **De Stijl**

**neoromanticism** — A movement of escapism in painting in the late 1920s; the mood was dreamlike or mournful, similar to but more lyrical than surrealism; prominent artists were Berman and Bérard

**net lines** — In textile design, the 'visible or not visible' lines of the network

**Neue Gestaltung** — *See* **de Stijl**

**Neue Sachlichkeit** — *See* **new objectivity**

**neuter figure** — A manikin or comic figure that can be either male or female

**neutrals** — Pigments; beige, tan, putty, cream, khaki, etc.

**neutralization** — In lithography, the process that removes the water retentive film from the stone so the surface again becomes receptive to grease

**neutralized colour** — Colour that has been toned or greyed

**neutral tint** — Pigment; a watercolour made from

alizarin crimson, lamp black, and phthalocyanine blue; durable

**new blue** — Pigment; a form of either cobalt blue or ultramarine blue

**New English Art Club** — Founded in 1886 by John Singer Sargent at a time when the standing of the Royal Academy was very low among creative artists. The Club represented what was then seen as a progressive movement, although in reality was little more than a love of naturalism in preference to romantic idealism. Sargent spent part of his life in France and was strongly influenced by the Impressionist movement. *See also* **Pre-Raphaelite Brotherhood**

**Newlyn colony** — Group of artists specializing in *plein-air* painting, who settled at Newlyn, Cornwall, in the late nineteenth century. The most important of these were Frank Bramley and Stanhope Forbes

**new objectivity** or **Neue Sachlichkeit** — Painting that was a reaction to expressionism that developed in Germany in the 1920s; it was representational and exact in detail to the point of unreality; prominent artists were George Grosz and Otto Dix

**new realism** — *See* **pop art**

**newsboard** — *See* **strawboard**

**newsprint** — A cheap paper used for sketching, not durable, turns yellow with age, and tears easily

**Newton's colour wheel** — The first colour circle, developed by Sir Isaac Newton about 1666, using seven colours to correspond with the seven notes of the diatonic scale and the seven known planets. Based on refracted light, they were red, orange, yellow, green, blue, indigo, and violet

**New York school** — A group of painters working in and around New York City after World War II; most are associated with abstract expressionism; among them were DeKooning, Gottlieb, and Pollock

**nickel titanate yellow** — Pigment; a pale lemon yellow, durable

**nihilism** — A philosophy denying the existence of any basis for truth. In art a revolt against established values and smugness. *See* **Dada**

**nimbus** — *See* **aureole**

**nitric** — A mineral acid used as an oxidizing agent in etching

**noboyka** — Sixteenth- to eighteenth-century Russian designs crafted from wood blocks and printed on fabric, using florals and geometrics as repeat patterns

**nocturne** — A painting of a night scene

**noncontinuous-tone art** — Artwork that has been screened, usually for reproduction

**nondirectional** — In textile design, a pattern in which direction is not conspicuous

**nonfigurative** — Without figures; sometimes not representational

**nonglare glass or plastic** — A mat finish, framing glass or plastic used to avoid glare

**nonobjective art** — Art arrived at without the influence of real or natural forms

**nonrepresentational art** — Art that does not represent real or natural things in any manner

**nontoxic** — Not poisonous

**noodling** — An artist's term for rendering intricate details; usually derogatory, implying overdone, over involved

**Norwich School** — One of the few art movements to have developed in England and unusual in its frequent use of watercolours. It grew out of the Norwich Society founded in 1803 'to make an enquiry into the rise, progress and present state of painting, architecture and sculpture with a view to point out the best methods of study to attain greater prefection in these arts'. The movement was traditionally founded by John Crome (old), who was generally influenced by Dutch landscape painting. Crome was joined by John Sell Cotman, who was his opposite in almost every respect. Crome's approach to nature was blunt and spontaneous, with unrefined technique. Cotman, by contrast, was subtle in his use of colour and composition. Other artists associated with the school include John Thistle, Robert Ladbroke, Henry Ninham, Joseph Stannard and Henry Bright

**nouveau realisme** — (French, *new realism*) Equivalent of American pop art

**nude** — 1. A live model without clothing. 2. A picture, sculpture or photograph of a person without clothing

**nylon brushes** — Brushes made from nylon, a man-made fibre; used mostly for acrylic painting

# O

**oak gall ink** — *See* **ox gall ink**

**oak tag** — A tough stock paper used for stencils and mounting

**objective art** — The rendering of a subject as it appears; representational art

**objet d'art** — (French, *art object*) A work of art

**objet trouvé** — (French, *found object*) An object such as a piece of driftwood, a dried weed, a piece of machinery, that is seen as beautiful by an artist and exhibited as a piece of art or used in collage and assemblage

**oblique** — Diagonal; in type, a face that slants to the left

**oblique perspective** — *See* **two-point perspective**

**oblique projection** — Projection in which the object has two of its axes parallel to the picture plane. *See also* **axonometric projection**

**ochre** — Pigment; generally applies to the earth colour yellow ochre

**ochre de ru** — Pigment; English red, an obsolete name

**oeuvre** — (French, *works*) The life's work of an artist

**offset litho** — *See* **litho, offset**

**offset reproduction** — A printing process in which the text and artwork are photographed and the negatives are used to make printing plates; on press, the ink is transferred (offset) from the printing plate to a rubber blanket, which in turn prints the paper

**off-white** — Pigment; a colour that is not pure white; may lean in any colour direction such as yellowish white, greenish white

**ogee** — Moulding or design consisting of a continuous double curve, concave below and convex above

**ogive** — A Gothic arch or point in decorative design

**oil black** — Pigment; carbon lampblack, name obsolete

**oil green** — Pigment; a form of chrome green or Bremen green, obsolete

**oiling out** — A process of rubbing an oil medium into dry areas in an oil painting, then painting into the oil-wet surface with fresh colour

ogee

**oil of spike lavender** — As essential oil often preferred by artists who object to the odour of turpentine

**oil pastels** — Pigments in stick form with an oil-based binder. Usually of better quality than wax crayons, but similar in use. Can be applied with a heated knife to form an impasto

**oils** — Usual term for oil-based artist's paints

**oilstone** — A grinding stone used to sharpen knives and tools

**oil wash** — An application of oil paint greatly diluted, usually with turpentine, and applied to the canvas or other support as an undercoating or as a glaze, sometimes used over an acrylic painting to add depth and character

**Okyo school** — *See* **Maruyama school**

**old English** — A style of lettering and type

**Old Masters** — Any of the accomplished European artists who lived from about 1500 to the early 1700s, whose work has stood the test of time; usually refers to painters

**'old style' hand lettering** — A style based on a structural and proportioning system using a broad pen at a natural writing slant

**old style typeface** — A roman type face such as Caslon O.S.

Caslon

**oleograph** — A chromolithograph printed with oil-based inks on a textured board or canvas to suggest the appearance of an oil painting

**oleopasto** — A medium used with oils so they can be applied thickly without cracking

**olive branch** — In design, a branch from an olive tree, a symbol of peace

132

**olive green** — Pigment; yellow-green earth, permanent

**one-man show** — A showing for the public of one artist's work, usually provided by a gallery or musuem

**one-point perspective** — Perspective in a drawing or painting, usually of a structure, having a single vanishing point

**one-stroke brush** — A square-tipped, flat brush used mostly for sign painting, lettering, and watercolour detail work; similar to a *flat* in shape

**opalescence** — A cloudy iridescence. *See* **iridescence**

**opal medium** — A beeswax solution dissolved in turpentine, used as a mat medium for oils

**opaque** — Opposite of transparent; not allowing light to pass through

**opaque projector** — *See* **epidiascope**

**opaque white** — Pigment; a zinc white paint used with watercolours and gouache, or used to block out unwanted areas in a painting

**op art** — A term coined in the 1960s to denote a style of nonobjective art in which geometric designs and certain colour combinations create an illusion of movement through visual vibrations

**opening** — The time set aside for invited guests to view an art show or exhibition prior to the public showing

**open up** — In lettering, to adjust the space between letters, words, or lines of words

**open weave** — In textile design, a loosely woven design

**opposites** — In colour, the same as complements (opposites on the colour wheel)

**optical** — Relating to vision; the means of seeing

**optical balance** — Elements that appear to balance in a composition. May be formal or informal balance

**orange peel texture** — A surface that has a pocked effect similar to that of an orange peel, occurring during the drying of some shellacs and varnishes

**orange vermilion** — Pigment; a form of pure vermilion

**orbicular muscles** — Muscles that open and close the mouth (oris) and the eyes (oculi)

**Order of St. Luke** — *See* **Nazarenes**

**organdy** — A lint-free cloth used to wipe plates in graphic arts

**organic line** — An unconsciously handled line in a drawing that flows in such a way as to take on a meaning of its own

**organic pigments** — Pigments that are compounds of carbon with sulphur, hydrogen, oxygen, etc.

**oriental design** — Chinese/Japanese/East Indian or other Eastern design

**oriental perspective** — An intellectual assumption that the top of the picture is the farthest away from the observer and the bottom of the picture is the nearest

**orient yellow** — Pigment; a deep cadmium yellow

**original** — 1. An authentic work of art conceived and produced solely by the artist. 2. In graphics, a print from a stone, plate, or block is considered an original since the print is the only manifestation of such work. 3. A printing plate used as a master plate

**original print** — A print pulled under the artist's control in graphic arts, such as etching, lithography, etc.; not a mechanical or photographic reproduction

**ornamental** — Decorative; having the purpose of embellishing an object or surface

**orphism** or **orphic cubism** — A type of early twentieth-century cubism using overlapping planes of brilliant colour; also called *simultaneism, synchronism,* and *colour orchestration*

**orpiment** — Pigment; a native king's yellow, toxic, obsolete

**orthographic projection** — A means of projection in which every side of an object is drawn on one flat plane

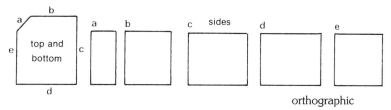

orthographic

**O.S.** — Referring to typefaces, meaning *old style*

**Osnaburg** — A lightweight cotton canvas, generally not as durable as duck, used as a painting support

**ostrum** — Pigment; Tyrian purple, an obsolete purple used by the Greeks and Romans

**Ostwald system** — The colour system of Wilhelm Ostwald, a psychologist who, in 1916, based a colour wheel on a visual mixture of colours, using red, yellow, sea green, and ultramarine blue

**Ottonian Art** — Art in Germany around 950-1060, named after the Ottonian emperors. A combination of the Carolingian, Early Christian, and Byzantine styles, notable in sculpture and manuscript illumination

**outline** — A drawing in which the outer limits are defined by lines, with no modelling of lights and darks

**oval wash brush** — A brush made of various hairs (pony, goat, squirrel, etc.), used to lay washes; sometimes called a *sky brush*

**overlapping joint** — In textile design, a portion of one unit overlapping a portion of the next unit

**overlays** — 1. Transparent papers, clear or in colour, used one over the other for changes, corrections, instructions, and for colour separations in multicolour reproductions. 2. In textile design, a transparent sheet placed over a design which is then painted or copied in another colour, directly on the transparent sheet

**overpainting** — Colour applied on top of an underpainting or undercoat

**overprinting** — Printing colours or lines over a previously printed area

**ox gall liquid or paste** — A wetting agent added to watercolours to allow painting on a glossy surface

**ox hair brush** — Brush made from hair of an ox ear; an imitation, without the spring of sable, and much less expensive

**oyster shell white** — Pigment; an off-white mixture

**ozalid** — Rough proof taken directly from artwork or typesetting before printing plates are made. Bluish in colour

# P

**pai-miao** — *See* **kou le**

**painted woven** — In textile design, a painted design imitating a woven cloth

**painterly** — Appearing free in style or technique, with more use of mass than of line; having the effect of spontaneous, expert paint application

**painting knife** — A flexible steel knife used to apply colours to a painting; different sizes and shapes are available

**paisley** — In design, a stylized leaf or teardrop pattern, originated in India but later named after a city in Scotland

**pale** — Light in value or colour

**palette** — 1. A flat support (wood, glass, plastic, metal) upon which colours are held and mixed, available in various sizes and shapes depending upon the medium used. 2. The colours that an artist chooses to work with, whether limited in number or consisting of many paints

**palette cup** — *See* **dipper**

**palette knife** — A type of knife used to mix colour on the palette, to clean the palette, to apply ground to a canvas, and sometimes as a painting tool

**palette-knife painting** — A painting rendered with the use of a palette knife, but more often with painting knives

**palette, limited** — A restricted number of colours used to execute a painting

**palmette pattern** — A design made up of small palm shapes. *See also* **anthemion**

**pan colours** — Watercolours supplied in hard blocks as opposed to tubes

**panel** — 1. In painting, a section of wood, plywood, or other hardboard, used in place of stretched

canvas. 2. In cartooning, a sequence of several
cartoons, also called a *strip*; or a single frame
where the gag is complete with one drawing

**Pannetier's green** — Pigment; viridian green;
name obsolete

**panorama** — A broad, extended scene suggesting
an unlimited view of a landscape or seascape

**pantograph** — An instrument used to enlarge or
reduce a drawing; the tracing arm activates a
pencil point that reproduces the traced image at a
desired size

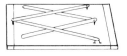

pantograph

**paper** — The basic support for watercolours,
drawing and printmaking. Paper consists of
pulped cellulose fibres dried on a mesh screen to
form a solid mat. The process can be continuous,
or each sheet can be made individually, in which
case the paper is referred to as mould-made.
Quality varies with the ingredients and fibres
used; these can be wood chips, rag, plants or
recycled paper. The best paper is made from
pure linen rag and the cheapest from wood pulp,
which ages rapidly. Pulp with a high acid content
will yellow and harden with age and exposure to
light. It is therefore important that any paper
product, especially mounts, which are to be in
contact with artwork should have as low an acid
content as possible. The best are described as of
museum or archival quality. Papers for writing
and drawing are generally smooth-surfaced, but
for painting a wide variety of surfaces is available.
ROUGH is untreated, or sometimes covered with a
felt while still damp to increase texture; HP (Hot
Pressed) is compressed or calendered with
heated rollers to give an absolutely smooth
surface and NOT (Not Hot Pressed) is cold-rolled
to leave some texture, the amount dependent on
pressure. Actual textures vary by manufacturer
and these terms have no standard definition.
Paper sizes are now largely metric, based on an
841 x 1189 mm sheet referred to as A0; each size
down is produced by folding on the long edge.
Thickness is normally referred to by the weight of
the paper. Commercial papers are now sold in
grams per square metre (G.S.M.), which is a
measurement independent of sheet size. *See also*
**watercolour paper sizes, watercolour paper
weights**

**paperboard** — A cardboard or composition board

**paper foil** — A thin sheet of metal laminated to a piece of paper, available in gold, silver, bronze, red, green, and blue

**paper mark** — The name of a company pressed into a paper produce

**paper palette** — *See* **disposable palette**

**paper plate lithography** — A procedure using a special paper plate (in place of a stone or zinc plate) that can be carried and used for outdoor sketching, then printed on a variety of presses

**paper wipe** — Wiping of inked plates with thin tissue paper

**papier collé** — (French, *stuck paper*) A form of collage using papers to build up three-dimensional forms

**papier mâché** — (French, *chewed paper*) Ground paper materials mixed with glue or paste, which can be moulded when wet

**paraffin wax** — A white wax of lamino-crystalline structure, used in batik

**parallel perspective** — *See* **one-point perspective**

**parallel rule** — A mechanical drawing tool consisting of two rulers (straight edges) that are attached with movable arms so the rules always swing parallel to each other

**para red** — Pigment; a bright cherry red toner (paranitraniline)

**parchment** — A processed animal skin used for scrolls, illuminated writing, and painting, through the sixteenth century; occasionally used in modern times, but replaced by papers that resemble parchment. *See also* **vellum**

**Paris black** — Pigment; an inferior grade of ivory black, name obsolete

**Paris blue** — Pigment; Prussian blue, name obsolete

**Paris green** — Pigment; emerald green; the pigment powder is also an insecticide; poisonous

**Paris, school of** — 1. Thirteenth-century manuscript illuminators of the time of St. Louis. 2. A term broadly used for any artists who were involved with modern painting in the 1920s and 1930s, mostly in Paris; included are such groups as: les Fauves, les Nabis, cubists, etc.

**Paris yellow** — Pigment; chrome yellow

parallel rule

**parma violet** — Pigment; a violet somewhat more blue than manganese violet on the colour chart, fugitive, gouache

**parquetry** — Wood mosaic floor pattern; a design motif simulating a mosaic floor pattern

**parting tool** — A gouge used in woodcut or wood carving

**passage** — Term sometimes applied to a section, segment, or area of a painting

**paste blue** — Pigment; Prussian blue, name obsolete

**pasteboard** — Paperboard made of layers of paper pasted together

**pastel** — An inexact term suggesting a soft, pale, nonstrident hue. *See also* **pastels**

**pastel chalk** — *See* **pastels**

**pastel paper** — A textured paper with a 'tooth', used for pastels, crayon, and other media; a paper made especially for pastels, with a special surface

**pastel pencil** — A pencil-shaped drawing tool of which the inner material is a pastel pigment; made in assorted colours

**pastels** — Pigments pressed into stick form; permanent; available in many colours that are not limited to the common meaning of *pastel*; of soft or hard quality. Like chalk, the sticks are broken into convenient sizes when used; can be overlaid with more colour to obtain various effects; can be rubbed smooth or not. Art in pastels is classified as painting

**pasteup form** — In publishing, a bristol or other board printed with an appropriate grid of light blue (a colour that does not reproduce when photographed with standard films), used to save time in pasting up standard page sizes of magazines, books, etc. to keep copy aligned

**pasteups** — pictures, type, etc. that are mounted onto a mechanical to form a page for a magazine, book, brochure, etc. to be printed

**patchwork** — In textile design, various patterns that imitate patchwork quilting

**patent yellow** — Pigment; Turner's lead yellow, now obsolete

**patina** — 1. A thin deposit of poisonous pigment, often greenish or brownish, caused by corrosion or age, that appears on copper or bronze artworks. 2. Also the name given to a mellowing with age, and may be imitated in painting by glazing. Also called *aerugo, aes ustum, verdigris*

**patriotic colours** — Colours pertaining to a country's flag, as red, white, and blue for the Union Jack

**patron** — A person who supports or buys the work of an artist

**pattern** — 1. In textile design, a single motif or several repeated motifs. 2. A plan or diagram that is repeated, as in stencilling. 3. More abstractly, the colours, values, lines, or textures, regular or irregular, that form a configuration in a composition

**Payne's grey** — Pigment; a prepared blue grey, permanent

**peacock blue** — Pigment; bright to medium blue close to thalo blue on the colour chart, fugitive, gouache

**pectoral muscles** — Muscles that cover the chest
   **major** — flexes, adducts, and rotates the arms
   **minor** — raises the ribs and draws down the scapula

**pedestal** — A support or base for sculptural work

**peinture à l'essence** — (French) A painting procedure in which oil paint is squeezed onto absorbent paper to remove the oil, then turpentine is used as a thinner; often applied in dry brush on pastel paper

**peinture claire** — (French) A procedure in which a bright, flat colour is placed next to a dark, flat colour to create form, in place of a gradual change from light to dark

**pelvis** — The skeletal structure that rests on the legs and supports the spinal column

**pen and wash** — A wash drawing including line work

pen and wash by
Dianne Flynn

**pencil** — 1. A writing or drawing implement consisting of a thin rod of graphite or similar material encased in wood or held in a plastic or metal mechanical holder; commonly called a lead pencil. 2. Type of fine brush

**penholder** — The part of the pen that holds the pen point

**Pennsylvania Dutch patterns** — Distinctive folk designs of the Pennsylvania Dutch, related to designs used in Europe during the eighteenth century; used on furniture and as household decorations. The colourful hex signs seen on barns are usually wheel-shaped

**pen point** — The part of a pen that fits into the holder; the writing or drawing part; the nib

**pentimenti** — Lines drawn in searching for the correct movement or placement. A line is put down and if it is felt to be incorrect the artist adds another line he feels is more correct without removing the first line

**pentimento** — (Italian, *repentance*) The reappearance of a previous drawing or painting on the surface of an oil painting, caused by the tendency of the linseed oil used in the paint to become transparent with age; also called *ghost*

**pepper-pot tints** — In acquatint, a small jar covered with a fine screen (often an old nylon stocking) is used to sprinkle aquatint or bitumen on the plate

**perception** — The act of perceiving, understanding, and discerning

*pentimenti* by John Croney

**perforating wheel** — *See* **pouncing**

**periwinkle blue** — Pigment; a colour close to cobalt blue on the colour chart, permanent, gouache

**Permalba** — Pigment; a trade name for a white oil colour

**permanence** — A standard reference to the susceptibility to fading of artists' colours –
 AA– Extremely permanent
 A – Durable, generally sold as permanent
 B – Moderately permanent
 C – Fugitive

Manufacturers' catalogues will also usually contain notes on colours which are affected by particular substances or conditions. Students' and cheaper ranges usually only contain colours of permanence AA or A

**permanent blue** — Pigment; a colour close to ultramarine blue, permanent

**permanent carmine** — Pigment; a synthetic red, permanent

**permanent colours** — Colours that will not fade or deteriorate

**permanent green** — Pigment; a bright opaque green, permanent, made in a light and a dark shade

**permanent magenta** — Pigment; a reddish purple, permanent

**permanent rose** — Pigment; pink or rose colour close to thalo red rose on the colour chart, transparent and permanent

**permanent violet** — Pigment; manganese violet, permanent

**permanent white** — Pigment; synonymous with titanium white

**permanent yellow** — Pigment; lemon yellow, permanent

**Persian miniatures** — Small, brightly decorated Persian art depicting hunting scenes, gardens, heroes and kings, animal illustrations, etc., often including calligraphy in the design

**Persian orange** — Pigment; a reddish orange, opaque orange lake, fugitive

**Persian red** — Pigment; English red, also a form of chrome red, name obsolete

**perspective** — A linear method of representing a three-dimensional subject

**perspective chart** — A prescaled grid chart used for accurate perspective drawing of architecture, interiors, package design, etc.

**pestle and mortar** — Stoneware bowl and club-like instrument used to crush and grind dry materials

**petit point** — A small dot used in pointillist painting, from *petit point* embroidery, made of very small stitches

**petroglyph** — A line drawing or symbol incised on a cave wall or slab of stone as in prehistoric rock carvings

**petroleum spirits** — *See* **mineral spirits**

**phalanges** — The short bones of the fingers and toes

**photoengraving** — A process for photographically recreating line or continuous-tone art on a

petroglyph in New Mexico

chemically sensitive metal printing plate. A reproduction made by this method

**photographic printing** — In textile and other design processes, the method of transferring designs to the desired surface with photoengraved rollers; fine details and colour effects are possible

**photography** — The use of light-sensitive materials to record an image of any object. Conventionally two-dimensional, a variety of systems allows an illusory three-dimensional image to be created

**photogravure** — *See* **gravure**

**photolitho** — Abbreviation of **photolithography**

**photolithography** — *See* **lithography, offset**

**photo-offset printing** — *See* **offset reproduction**

**photo oil colour** — Permanent, transparent oil colour used specifically for colouring photographs

**photo oil colour pencils** — Oil colour pencils used to draw in highlights, shadows, and details in photographs

**photorealism** — The effect of a picture painted to resemble a photograph or having the realism of a photograph

**photosetting** — A typesetting process in which characters are recorded as a negative image on a disc which spins at high speed, and flash-exposed onto light-sensitive paper, the whole process being computer-controlled. Photosetting is of very high quality and has largely superseded movable type and hot-metal setting. Different type sizes are produced by varying the magnification from a single disc

**(photo)stat** — Copy produced by a photostat machine, using a camera that generates an opaque paper negative from which a positive print is made; good for line work reduction, enlargements, etc., relatively inexpensive

**phthalocyanine** — Synthetic organic pigments of extreme permanence

**phthalocyanine blue (phthalo blue; thalo blue)** — Pigment; an intense, permanent, transparent blue, close to Prussian blue. *See* **colour chart.** Trade names include Winsor Blue and Monestial Blue

**phthalocyanine green (phthalo green; thalo green)** — Pigment; an intense, transparent,

permanent green. Trade names include Winsor
Green and Monestial Green

**pica** — A printer's unit of measurement equal to 12
points (4mm or ⅙ in), used in page printing for
line width, depth of columns, paragraphs, etc.

**pica ruler** — A ruler marked with agate and mm or
inches on one side and picas and mm or inches
on the other, used by printers and in commercial
art

pica ruler (inches)

**Picasso, Pablo** — 1881-1973, born in Spain,
settled in France, he had much influence on
twentieth-century art. His early work was realistic.
He then helped formulate cubism and later other
modes of nonobjective art. He was a painter,
sculptor, printmaker, and ceramist

**pictograph** — Picture writing, expressing an idea
with picture symbols, as in primitive writing

**picture frame** — A moulding or other border,
usually wood or metal, that surrounds a picture

**picture plane** — The imaginary plane, like a sheet
of glass, at right angle to the viewer's line of
vision, on which the picture is projected

**picture varnish** — A final varnish used on oil
paintings to protect them and give a uniform
finish. *See* **damar**

**piece mould** — A rigid mould made in pieces,
used for casting sculpture

**pietà** (Italian, *pity*) — A work of art showing Mary
mourning the dead Christ, a recurring theme in
devotional art

**pietra dura** — A stone mosaic using semiprecious
stones

**pigment** — The dry, powdered colouring agent in
a paint that is mixed with a medium to form tube
colours or sticks

**Pablo Picasso** *The
Three Dancers*

**pigment yellow** — Pigment; Hansa yellow, both transparent and opaque, permanent; close to cadmium yellow, pale on the colour chart

**piling** — In printing, a buildup of ink on the plate, rollers, or blankets, causing a poor print

**pine-soot black** — Pigment; Chinese carbon lampblack, name obsolete

**Pink Pearl eraser** — Trade name for a good all-purpose eraser, pink in colour

**pin registration** — The use of holes and special pins on copy, film, plates, and presses, for exact alignment

**pinstripe** — A very fine stripe, especially on a fabric

**pinx** — (Latin, *pinxit, he painted it*) Credit on a print after the name of the one who painted it; may also indicate *he designed it*

**Piper, John** — 1903-    , English-born artist concentrating on landscapes who believes in the importance of drawing but works in most media including engraving and stained-glass design (in Coventry Cathedral). Piper's early work was largely conventional landscape, but he developed an individual style in France in the 1930s under the influence of Braque and other leading abstract artists

**Pisarro, Camille** — 1830-1903, mainstay of the Impressionist movement, featuring in all its eight exhibitions (1874-1886) and the Salon des Refusés of 1863 as well as having work regularly accepted by the Salon of the Académie des Beaux Arts

**pitcher** — In stone carving, a large, heavy implement similar to a chisel, used with a hammer to remove big pieces of stone in the early stages of carving

**Pittura Metafisica** — (Italian, *metaphysical picture*) An art style in Italy about 1918-1921. *See* **magic realism; metaphysical painting**

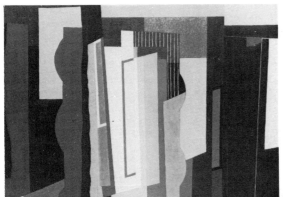

**John Piper**
*Abstract 1*

145

**plaid** — In textile design, a pattern in which lines and colours crisscross. *See* **tartan**

**plane** — A two-dimensional flat or level surface, as one surface of a cube

**planographic printing** — A printing procedure in which the printing surface attracts printing ink and is on the same level as the nonprinting surface, unlike *intaglio* or *relief* procedures. Lithography, callotype, and aquatone are included in this category of printing

**plaque** — An engraved, painted, or otherwise decorated piece of wood, metal, etc. for hanging on a wall

**plaquette** — A small version of a plaque

**plaster cast** — A mould of plaster used for reproducing sculpture

**plaster of Paris** — A gypsum plaster that dries into a solid when mixed with water, used for casting sculpture and ceramics

**plaster print** — 1. A relief print made from an inked plaster plate. 2. A print made by casting plaster on an inked intaglio plate

**plastic** — A polymerized product; a nonmetallic, synthetic compound in various forms, capable of being shaped, made pliable, or hardened

**plastic arts** — Arts that use vision, space, and physical materials, such as painting, sculpture, ceramics, and architecture

**plastic cutter** — A cutting device used to score and cut plastic, lightweight copper foil, brass, and aluminium

**Plasticine** — Trade name of a non-toxic and non-setting modelling material, mainly used in schools

**plasticizer** — An additive for paint, varnish, etc. to give it elasticity

**plate** — 1. In graphics, a smooth surface applied to copper, zinc, or steel for etching, or to metal, plastic, or wood for printing. In photography, a prepared surface usually applied to glass. 2. A special illustration bound into a book

**plate finish** — A smooth finish

**platemaker** — In graphics, the person or machine that does the platemaking in a printing process

**plate mark** — In printmaking, the mark of the edges of the plate that are left on the paper

**plate oil** — A form of linseed oil, mixed with etching ink to make it more manageable

146

**plein air/en plein air** — (French, *open air*) Term applied since about 1850 to artists who paint scenes outdoors directly from observation

**pleinairistes** — A group of Impressionists who painted *en plein air*; included are Monet, Pissaro, Renoir, Sisley, and others

**Plessy's green** — Pigment; a variety of chromium oxide green, name obsolete

**Plexiglas** — *See* **acrylic sheets**

**plus** — A piece of wood inserted in a woodcut in order to rework an area

**plumbago** — graphite

**ply** — pertains to layers of paper, to indicate weight and thickness

**pochoir** — (French, *stencil*) The use of stencils to produce and colour fine prints by hand

**point** — 1. A unit of measurement of type, ·35146mm. 2. In carving, a pointed tool, available in different sizes, used with a mallet to remove waste stone

**point of entry** — The likely place of eye entry into a picture; often varies from viewer to viewer

**point of sight** — *See* **centre of vision**

**point of station** — *See* **station point**

**pointillism** — System of painting devised by Georges Seurat and Paul Signac (which they preferred to call 'divisionism'), relying on the optical mixing of minute dots of colour. Although the technique grew out of Impressionism, it could not achieve the spontanaeity generally associated with the movement

**polishing** — In lithography, putting a fine grain on the stone with a grinding stone

**political cartoon** — A satirical or humorous drawing on a political subject often accompanied by abbreviated written material

**polka dot** — In textile design, a dotted pattern of either small or large dots

**Pollock, Jackson** — 1912-1956, an American who is considered an abstract expressionist. His works are known for their huge size and dripped and splattered paint. The work is non-objective.

**polyurethane brayer** — In graphics, similar to a composition roller, but firmer

**Pompeian blue** — Pigment; Egyptian or cobalt blue; name obsolete

**Pompeian red** — Pigment; Tuscan red; a form of Indian red; a red oxide; name obsolete

**Jackson Pollock**
*Yellow Islands*

**Pompidou Centre** — (*Le Centre National D'Art Et De Culture Georges Pompidou*). Massively controversial national art centre in Paris, one of the most provocative pieces of modern architecture. It is nevertheless a major feat of technological and aesthetic engineering and provides an important base for arts of all kinds

**pop art** — Also called new realism and neo-Dada; a movement of the 1950s utilizing as art such articles as soup cans, comic strips, and other mass-produced, found, or ready-made objects. This so-called 'Coke culture' art rejects any distinction between good and bad taste; artists include Warhol, Rauschenberg, and Lichtenstein

**pop colours** — Bright chrome colours, high intensity colours

**poppy seed oil** — A medium made from poppy seeds, used for thinning oil paints

**portable easel** — A lightweight, easily carried, folding easel

**portfolio** — 1. A portable case for carrying papers, drawings, etc. 2. The drawings, paintings, or photos of artwork in a portfolio that are presented to interested parties for review in the course of seeking employment or school acceptance

**portrait** — A head-and-shoulder drawing or painting of a person, loosely meaning three-quarter or full length

pop art by Roy Lichtenstein (*Wham*)

**portrait shape** — A rectangular picture shape used in a vertical position, the most common picture shape for a portrait, although many successful portraits are in a horizontal shape

**pose** — 1. The stand or position a model assumes and holds while the artist works. 2. The position the artist gives a figure in a picture

**positive space** — The area containing the subject matter in a composition

**positive tint or screen** — Dots or texture pattern on a white background; a term usually used in commercial art

**poster** — Any illustration and/or lettering publicly displayed to advertise a service, product, or event

**poster board** — A smooth-finished paperboard used for signs and posters, available in several colours; also called *show card*

**poster colours** — Inexpensive opaque watercolour paints used for posters and commercial art; also called *show card colours*

**post-Impressionism** — A term generally relating to the paintings of four artists, Cézanne, Van Gogh, Gauguin, and Seurat, from about 1875 to 1900. They accepted the Impressionists' use of light with bright colours and conspicuous paint handling, but rejected the casual compositional structure of the Impressionists

**post modern art** — 1980s art indicative of humanism and things of our visible world

**pounce** — 1. A fine powder of chalk or charcoal contained in a small bag and used in pouncing. 2. A powder used to condition a surface for inking. *See* **pouncing**

**pouncing** — 1. A means of transferring a drawing in which a perforating or tracing wheel or needle is used to prick small holes in the lines of a drawing, and a pouncing bag is tapped over the holes and transfers the design. 2. When applying paint to a picture, a tapping motion with a brush, sponge, or cloth

**pouncing bag** — A cloth bag filled with pounce. *See also* **pouncing**

**pounce wheel** — A tracing or perforating wheel. *See also* **pouncing**

**Poussinistes** — Seventeenth- and eighteenth-century followers of Poussin, who felt drawing was superior in importance to colour in painting;

pounce wheel

one of the leading advocates was Charles Lerun. *See also* **Rubenism**

**powder colours** — Opaque watercolours available in powder form, to which water is added as the binder; available in a variety of nontoxic colours

**powdered charcoal** — charcoal in powder form used for pouncing bags

**powdered tempera colours** — Tempera colours available in a powdered form to which water is added to make show card paint

**Pozzuoli blue** — Pigment; another name for Egyptian or cobalt blue

**Pozzuoli red** — Pigment; a red earth used in frescos

**Prang colour wheel** — A colour wheel that deals with the mixing of colours. The three primaries of yellow, red, and blue are used; the secondaries are made from the primaries, and the intermediaries are derived from the colours on either side, as yellow and orange make the intermediary of yellow-orange. Researched by Louis Prang (1824-1909). *See* **colour wheel**

**pre-Columbian art** — Early art from the Americas, prior to the landing of Columbus

**prehistoric art** — Anything relating to art earlier than about 3000 BC. Some prehistoric art exists that was done more than 25,000 years ago, such as incised drawings preserved on cave walls

**Pre-Raphaelite Brotherhood** — Literary and artistic movement of the late nineteenth century whose progenitors sought to bring a realism to their work in reaction to what they saw as sentiment and degeneration in contemporary art. Its chief members included Dante Gabriel Rossetti, William Holman Hunt, John Everett Millais, Ford Maddox Brown and Edward Burne-Jones. *See also* **New English Art Club**

**presentation** — A sketch or layout shown to a client to suggest a projected design or illustration plan

**press printing** — *See* **printing press**

**press, block-printing** — A hand press used for block printing

**pressboard** — A strong, durable, high-gloss paperboard, often used as a cover stock

**press, dry-mounting** — *See* **dry-mounting press**

**press etching** — A press made especially for intaglio printing, which includes etching, drypoint, aquatint, and engraving. The ink fills the incised lines below the surface of the plate and the pressure of the press forces the paper to contact the ink

**press, lithograph** — A press made for printmaking from litho stones or plates

**press type** — *See* **pressure-sensitive letters**

**pressure-sensitive letters** — 1. Dry-transfer letters and symbols easily applied to paper by burnishing; available in different sizes, colours, and typefaces. 2. Permanent vinyl plastic letters and symbols that are available for glass, metal, wood, leather, and outdoor use

**presto-seal film** — A self-sealing protective film for artwork, maps, and blueprints

**primary colours (artists')** — Red, yellow, and blue

**primary colours (printing inks)** — Magenta, cyan, and yellow

**prime** — To prepare a canvas or panel for painting by covering it with a glue-like paint, such as gesso. The primer penetrates the surface and prepares the support so that paint does not seep through the backing

**primed canvas** — Canvas that has one or two coats of gesso or other primer

**primer** — The glue or size, such as gesso, used to prepare a canvas or panel

**primitive art** — 1. Native art of such cultures as African, Eskimo, American Indian, etc., usually associated with daily life or with religious rites. 2. Works produced by an artist who has not received or absorbed professional art training or has not been influenced by others' work. *See also* **naïve painting**

**primrose yellow** — Pigment; a pale yellow close to cadmium yellow pale on the colour chart

**print** — 1. An impression pulled from an original plate, stone, block, screen, or negative, prepared solely by the artist; in collagraphy, engraving, etching, drypoint, aquatint, mezzo-tint, and silkscreen. 2. In textile design, a floral or geometric design as opposed to plaids or stripes. 3. A positive made from a photograph negative

**printer's ink** — Ink made and used specifically for printing presses

**printer's proof** — *See* **bon à tirer**

**printing press** — A hand- or power-operated machine that prints impressions on paper and other suitable materials. *See* **offset reproduction; press, block-printing; press, etching; press, lithographic**

**print rack** — a rack used to exhibit prints, drawings, watercolours, etc.

**prismatic colour** — *See* **iridescence**

**Prismacolour pencils** — Trade name for a type of coloured pencils

**process art** — Art of the 1960s and 1970s, based on the idea that the artist's product is less important than the process that brought it into being; related to minimal art

**process black** — Pigment; contains no blue and so will reproduce at its full value

**process colour printing** — Using yellow, magenta, cyan, and black, full-colour representations are made of paints or photos; each colour is separated with camera filters and processed onto a separate printing plate

**process colours** — 1. In commercial four-colour printing, yellow, magenta (red), cyan (blue), and black. 2. Standardized ink printing colours. 3. Commercial silk-screen colours

**process plates** — In reproduction, a set of plates made in halftone to produce different colours, usually black, yellow, magenta, and cyan

**process white** — Pigment; an opaque white paint used for corrections on artwork

**production manager** — At advertising agencies, publishers, etc., the person responsible for scheduling and ordering printing, paper, binding, etc.

**profile** — The side view of a subject

**progressive proofs/progs** — A set of separate proofs from each successive colour run of a multicolour print for checking colour

**projection principle** — The phenomenon whereby the imagination is able to create form from any amorphous elements, such as clouds, ink blots, etc.

**proof** — In graphic arts, a preliminary print that is examined for perfection before final printing is done

**proportion** — The mathematical relation of things

to the whole, the harmonious relationship between the parts of a form

**proportional dividers** — An instrument for transferring measurements to make enlargements or reductions of an original drawing/illustration

**prototype** — The first of its kind; an original work of art, usually intended for reproduction or copying

**protractor** — A calibrated semicircular or circular instrument used to measure or construct angles

**protrude** — To jut out or extend beyond the borders

**provenance** — The history of a work of art, its origin and collectors; records kept to help assure authenticity and forestall forgery

**Prussian blue** — Pigment; intense, transparent blue, permanent

**Prussian brown** — Pigment; iron brown; Indian red in its unburned state; permanent but seldom used

**Prussian green** — Pigment; Brunswick green, a chrome green, fugitive

**Prussian red** — Pigment; a light red oxide, permanent

**psychedelic art** — Distortions of visual perception taking the form of exaggerated colour and movement associated with hallucinogenic drugs; include swirls that resemble *art nouveau*

**psychedelic colours** — The bright fluorescent colours seen in psychedelic art

**puce** — Pigment; a purple colour with a decided brown influence

**puddle** — 1. In watercolour, a small pool of water or colour either on the palette or on the paper. 2. In tole painting, to add medium to paint to achieve the required consistency

**pull** — 1. In graphic arts, to make a print and 'pull' from the press. 2. In a picture, the tension generated by the juxtaposition of lines, values, shapes, colours, in the composition

**pull together** — To unify elements in a picture to make the work more effective

**pumice powder** — A lightweight powdered porous volcanic rock used as an abrasive and as a polish

**pure tube colour** — Pigment, straight from the tube

**Purism** — A 1918 protest against cubism by Amédé Ozenfant and Le Corbusier, who sought to restore representational construction by means of stressing purified outlines and machine-like qualities of forms

**purist** — 1. An artist who adheres to set principles; for example, one who does not mix mediums in the same picture, such as transparent watercolour and opaque watercolour. 2. Followers of Purism

**purple lake** — Pigment; a purple somewhat bluer than manganese violet on the colour chart, moderately permanent, gouache

**purple madder (alizarin)** — Pigment; a blend of alizarin lake and violet organic lake somewhat bluer than magenta, moderately durable

**pusher blanket** — In intaglio printing, the top or upper blanket on the press

**pushpins/push points** — 1. Tacks similar to drawing pins, but with a longer point and a top-hat style head. 2. A metal device that is pushed into the back of a frame (the moulding) to hold the glass, picture, and backing in place

pushpin

**push-pull technique** — A method of drawing and painting in which parts of a form are left out and parts are pulled back in; also said of a 'push-pull' type of brush or drawing stroke. *See also* **lost and found**

**push-pull values** — Seen in a decorative form of art in which the light source is not consistent; the artist strives for balance in values rather than realism. *See also* **shifting planes**

**putto** — In art, a male child as a cherub

**put to bed** — Said of a publication when all material is ready to be printed

**putty colour** — Pigment; an off-tan, greyish mixture considered a neutral

**putty eraser** — A soft eraser similar to a kneaded eraser, but more flexible

**putty rubber** — a kneaded eraser

**PVA** — Polyvinyl acetate. Resin adhesive which is chemically inert; also used as a base for acrylic colours

# Q

**Q-Tip** — American. Generally sold in the UK as cotton buds

**quadrille paper** — Paper printed with a grid of lines that act as a drawing or writing aid

**quarter drop** — In textile design, the motif dropped a quarter down from the first motif

**quatrefoil** (French, *quatre feuille, four-leaved*) — A motif made up of four leaves, seen in Gothic tracery

**quenching** — The method of hardening metal by plunging it into water or oil while it is red hot

**quercitron lake** — Pigment; a yellow lake, fugitive

**quickies** — Rapid little sketches done as exercises or to visualize picture concepts

**quiet area** — An area in a composition that is less busy in line, colour, texture, etc. than other areas

**quill** — A large bird's feather cut to be used a pen

**quill pen** — *See* **crow quill pen**

**quilted pattern** — In textile design, a stitched design imitating quilting

**quinacridone red** — Pigment; a rosy red, durable, acrylic

**quinacridone violet** — Pigment; a red violet, durable, acrylic

**quire** — Twenty-five sheets of paper, or $^1/_{20}$ of a ream

**quoins** — Little steel triangular wedges used to lock type and plates in chases for the press

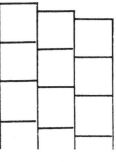

quarter drop

quatrefoil window design

155

# R

**R.A.** — Royal Academician, a member of the Royal Academy of Arts, London

**rabbitskin glue** — Glue used as a size or binder; sold in solid form, granules, or sheets

**radial balance** — Accomplished by forms or elements designed as a wheel around a main subject

**radiation lines** — Lines that emit from a common point, but radiate in different directions. *See* **radial balance**

radial balance

**radius bone** — A long bone parallel to the ulna bone in the forearm; it alone connects to the wrist

**rag** — Paper made exclusively from cloth; if only partial, the percentage of rag is stated on the label

**railroad board** — An American term for a smooth six-ply board, available in many colours, that can be used on both sides for posters, lettering, etc.

**rainbow printing** — In graphics, rolling several colours simultaneously onto a plate or stone from a single roller, and blending the edges

**raising preparation** — A nonflowing paste used for raised or embossed effects before gilt is applied; may become tacky in humid conditions but holds its form when dry

**Rapidograph** — Trade name of a reservoir-supplied technical drawing pen with a tube-like nib supplied in precise sizes. Often applied generically to all pens of this type

**rasp** — A tool with a rough texture like a file, used for rough shaping wood, stone, plaster, and clay

rasp

**raw colour** — Colour straight from the tube, with no mixing or adulterations

**raw sienna** — Pigment; a natural earth, deeper than yellow ochre, permanent

**raw umber** — Pigment; a natural earth, a cool brown, permanent

**rayonnism** — (Called lutschism in Russia) A Russian offshoot of cubism, led by Mikhail Larionov (1881-1964), who was interested in the forms created when intersecting rays of light hit a subject

**R.B.A.** — The Royal Society of British Artists

**ready-made** — A found object used in collage, junk sculpture, etc. which is exhibited as it is, as an aesthetic object

**realgar** — Pigment; a reddish-orange colour, toxic, obsolete

**realism** — 1. A way of painting nature without distortion. 2. The philosophy of painting, led by Courbet, centred on unidealized, everyday subject matter

**realistic** — Said of a work of art striving to resemble reality or portray a likeness with a strong resemblance to the sitter

**ream** — Now five hundred sheets of paper, but originally 480

**receding** — Appearing to go back or away from the observer, as in an illusion of a space or line in a picture

**receding colours** — Cool colours – blue, green, and violet – that seem to move back, in comparison with warm colours – yellow, red, and orange – that appear to come forward or advance

**rectangle** — A four-sided plane figure that has four 90-degree angles

**rectified petroleum** — A good-quality petroleum spirit used to thin oils and clean brushes

**rectified turpentine** — A pure form of turpentine (double-distilled) used by artists to clean oil brushes, and as a medium for oil and alkyd paints

**rectilinear** — Made of straight lines

**recto** — Right-hand page. *See also* **verso**

**red lead** — Pigment; an opaque, heavy Indian red colour used industrially

**red ochre** — Pigment; a form of Venetian red, originally a native earth

**red oxide** — Pigment; a red earth colour; Indian red made with a bluish or red undertone somewhat redder than Mars violet; opaque and permanent

**red sable** — *See* **sable/red sable brush**

**reducer** — In printmaking, a medium added primarily to dilute thick ink so it will print more easily

**reducing glass** — A double-concave lens used to see how artwork looks when reduced in size

**reduction printing** — In printmaking, for registration purposes, the largest colour areas are printed first, then the next sizes in sequence, and finally the smallest areas

**reductivism** — A procedure for reducing, diminishing or simplifying, with fewer lines, less colour, etc.

reducing glass

**reed pen** — Now only the bamboo pen, usually sharpened at both ends and used for ink drawings

**reference file** — *See* **clip file**

**reflected light** — Light is 'bent' or 'thrown back' on something; for example, if you paint a silver pitcher which is placed on a red cloth, some red will probably be apparent in the pitcher. This red is called a reflected colour

**reflex printing** — A copy method in which a sensitized film or paper is placed face down on the material to be copied; light passes through the base of the sensitized film and is reflected from the light and dark portion of the original back to the emulsion

**Regional Arts Associations** — Regional bodies under the auspices of the Arts Council concerned with the promotion of the arts in their own region

**registration marks** — Marks that indicate where overlays or plates are to be aligned

**Reichenau school** — A German school of manuscript illuminators, about 965-1025, noted for its huge gold letters that often took up a whole page

**Reims school** — A French school of manuscript illuminators during the Carolingian era, eighth to eleventh centuries

**relief** — A variation of elevation in sculpture; a raised effect ranging from low (bas-relief or basso rilievo) to high (alto rilievo)

**relief etching** — A procedure in which large areas of a plate are etched away and the design is left standing so it can be surface-printed

**relief printing** — In printmaking, a means of printing design or type that stands above the surface of the printing block; woodcuts and rubber stamps print by relief methods

**religious art** — Art pertaining to religion, as the Buddha, Christ, the Virgin Mary, etc.

**relining** — In restoring an old painting, the process of mounting it on a new canvas support

**Rembrandt, Harmensz, van Rijn** — 1606-1669, Dutch, printmaker and painter. His works, which focus on landscapes, history, people, and portraits, are well known for their chiaroscuro technique. A series of self-portraits covering a period of forty years show his deep concern for expression and control of values. Rembrandt is considered among the most important painters of all time.

**Renaissance art** — Fourteenth-, fifteenth-, and sixteenth-century art in Western Europe characterized by the revival of classical design and concern for humanistic values; artists included Michelangelo, Raphael, da Vinci, and many more

**Renaissance fold** — In folded cloth, where all folds and ends are rounded

**render** — 1. The process of drawing or painting a given subject. 2. To make a detailed drawing, usually enhanced with watercolour, of an architectural project

**Renoir, Pierre-Auguste** — 1841-1919 – Renoir's early paintings were accepted by the Salons of 1864 and 1865, but shortly after this he became influenced by the Impressionists, and Gustave Courbet in particular. He worked frequently with Claude Monet and contributed to the major Impressionist exhibitions of 1874, 1876, 1877 and 1882. He did not entirely lose contact with the artistic establishment, however, and also exhibited at the Salon during this period

**repeat glass** — An optical instrument used by textile designers, made of four lenses through which a design appears to be repeated four times

**repeat pattern** — A pattern occurring several times in a design

**replica** — A copy or reproduction of a work of art, especially when made by the same artist who created the original work

**Pierre Auguste Renoir** *Regatta at Argenteuil*

159

**repoussé** — In metalwork, a technique of hammering, scratching, or pressing metal on either side to create a design

**representational art** — Artwork that purports to represent what is seen; also called *objective art*

**repro** — Common abbreviation of **reproduction**

**reproduction** — A copy of an original work of art made by someone other than the artist, usually by mechanical means and most often for commercial use

**reproduction proofs/repros** — Clean, sharp proofs, usually of type, on a coated paper, used as copy for photographic reproduction

**reproduction right** — The right to maintain control of the reproduction of artwork or other copyrighted material

**repro type** — A high-quality reproduction type used for pasteups on mechanicals

**rescale** — To enlarge or reduce artwork so the material will fit into a given space in a page layout; usually figured in percentages, calibrated for the engraver's copying camera

**resensitize** — To treat and prepare a lithographic stone so it can be used again; to treat a metal plate so it can be worked again

**resin ground** — A ground used when making an aquatint by dusting it on the plate and heating the plate, causing the ground to stick to the surface. The covering acts as an acid resistant that is necessary in creating the tonal effects in the aquatint

**resist** — A substance (such as wax) which protects a surface from receiving dyes, inks or pigments

**restoration/restoring** — Bringing a work of art as nearly as possible to its original condition; includes cleaning, repairing, mending, remounting, restretching, and sometimes, retouching

**restricted palette** — *See* **limited palette**

**retardant** — An additive to a paint medium to delay the drying time, such as oil of cloves, oil of lavender, and others

**rétirage** — (French, *pulling again*) In graphics, the pulling of a second print without reinking the plate

**retouch greys** — A series of opaque watercolour paints, white through graduated greys to black, used to retouch photos and artwork

**retouching** — 1. Making corrections on artwork. 2. Eliminating or altering parts of a photograph

**retouching varnish** — A diluted liquid or spray varnish used between applications of oil paint to restore the wet look to mat colours for easier colour matching; also utilized as a gloss coat on a finished painting until the final varnish is applied

**retouching white** — An opaque white paint used to cover unwanted areas in pictures and to make corrections

**retrospective** — A review of a large body of work produced during an artist's lifetime

**retroussage** — In printmaking, a method of leaving a trace of ink on the surface of an intaglio plate; the process makes the value of the incised lines richer

**reverse** — 1. In textile design, to flop over a design. 2. In commercial art, to change negative to positive or positive to negative, or to flop the picture to change its direction

**reversed copy** — White type on a dark background

**reversed perspective** — In opposition to mechanical perspective; objects in the front of a picture are smaller than those farther way

**reverse etching** — An etching procedure in which an intaglio plate is surface-inked and printed like a woodblock

**reverse image** — An image in which lines and areas normally black become white, and vice versa

**reverse print** — In textile design, a print in which the light areas are made dark and the dark areas light

**Reynolds, Sir Joshua** — 1723-1791, the first President of the Royal Academy (1768), who set the style for English portraiture for many decades. Author of *Discourses on Painting*, a study of Raphael, Correggio, Rubens, Rembrandt and Titian

**Sir Joshua Reynolds** *Self-portrait*

161

**rhodamine** — A synthetic dyestuff used for making red lake pigments

**rhomb/rhomboid/rhombus** — A four-sided figure with all sides equal and opposite sides parallel, but two angles are acute and the other two angles are obtuse

**rib(s)** — 1. A series of curved bones encasing the chest cavity in humans and animals, extending from the spine to or toward the breastbone. 2. Certain structural support members of ships, buildings, etc.

**rib cage** — The confined area made up of the ribs

**rice paper** (Japanese) — A lightweight paper made in different textures, sizes, weights, and colours; can be used for watercolours, inks, and printing

**rich** — Said of paint with intense colour, strong values, and/or a thick application

**riffler** — A particular style of curved rasp. *See also* **rasp**

**rigger** — A long, pointed, usually sable brush used to paint long lines, branches on trees, and fine details

**Rinman's green** — Pigment; cobalt green; name obsolete

**rocker** — A textured tool used in mezzotint to prepare the surface on the plate; also called a *cradle*

**rococo** — A delicate eighteenth-century style of art and decoration with a concern for the trivial rather than the significant; colourful and capricious, closely linked historically with the fashionable reign of Louis XV of France. Artists include Watteau, Boucher, Fragonard, and Tiepolo

**Rodin, Auguste** — 1840-1917, a French romantic sculptor who was influenced by the work of Michelangelo. One of the leading sculptors of the late nineteenth and early twentieth centuries. Two of his most famous works are *The Thinker* and *The Kiss*

**R.O.I.** — The Royal Society of Oil Painters

**roller** — *See* **brayer**

**roller art** — A means of painting with a roller/brayer technique that involves bouncing, twisting, scraping, or any other means of laying paint on a surface with a roller; unique effects can be created that are difficult to achieve by other means

**Auguste Rodin**
*The Kiss*

**roller printing** — *See* **direct printing**

**roll-up** — The process of inking a plate or stone with a roller

**roman** — 1. A general term used to describe any typeface with serifs. 2. Any upright typeface, as distinguished from the slanting italic

**Romanesque** — A transitional style of European art from the ninth to the twelfth centuries, preceding Gothic art. Primarily for and of the church, its most notable art contributions were in architecture and stone-sculpture adornments

**Roman key** — *See* **Greek key**

**Roman ochre** — Pigment; a variety of ochre, name obsolete

**Roman stripes** — In textile design, bright and usually wide vertical stripes

**romanticism** — An emotional, often idealized means of expression. Romanticism in art, notable in the nineteenth century, is usually thought of as in basic opposition to the classical

**Romayne medallions** — Profile portraits used as design in Gothic art

**rose carthame** — Pigment; an orange red, moderately permanent, gouache

**rose doré** — Pigment; a variety of rose madder, inclined to scarlet in oils, in watercolours an organic quinacridone, durable

**rose madder** — Pigment; madder lake, a transparent red; similar to alizarin crimson but weaker; moderately durable

**rose malmaison** — Pigment; a reddish rose close to thalo red rose on the colour chart, fugitive, gouache

**Rosenstiehl's green** — Pigment; manganese green, name obsolete

**rose pink** — Pigment; a weak pink made from brazilwood, fugitive

**rose Tyrien** — Pigment; a rose somewhat redder than magenta, fugitive, gouache

**rosin** — A brownish or yellowish resin derived from pine trees, used in aquatint

**rotary press** — A press with two cylinders, one of which rotates the paper while the other prints on it; large continuous rolls of paper are used

**rotogravure** — A photomechanical intaglio printing process with a velvety or soft quality that makes for excellent halftone effects

**rotten lines** — In etching, lines that are uneven or interrupted, caused by uneven needle pressure

**rottenstone** — A soft, decomposed limestone used in powder form for cleaning and polishing photographs for retouching

**Rouault, Georges** — 1871-1958, French painter and printmaker; the expressive dark lines and vivid colours in his paintings were developed from his experience in a stained-glass workshop. Rouault exhibited with the original Fauves

**rough** — A quick, incomplete sketch to express an idea

**rough stipple** — A heavy texture on reproduction board

**roulette** — A tool with a sharply pointed, revolving cylinder at the end of the handle, used to make dotted lines on a plate for intaglio printing

**round** — A pointed brush available in sable, synthetic, and bristle

**roundel** — In design, a semicircular recess, as a rounded window or niche

**Royal Academy of Arts** — The premier art society in the UK

**royal** — *See* **watercolour paper sizes**

**royal blue** — Pigment; a colour similar to cobalt blue

roulette

**Georges Roualt**
*The Three Judges*

**royal green** — Pigment; chrome green, a mixture of Prussian blue and chrome yellow

**royal red** — Pigment; a bright red lake, fugitive

**royal yellow** — Pigment; king's yellow, an artificial arsenic trisulphide, toxic and obsolete

**royalty** — A percentage paid to an artist by a publisher for each copy of the artist's work that is sold

**R.S.A.** — The Royal Scottish Academy

**R.S.M.A.** — The Royal Society of Marine Artists

**rubber brayer** — In graphics, a soft rubber roller used for inking in etching, block printing, etc. *See also* **brayer**

**rubber cement** — A paper-mounting compound that dries quickly; excess is easily removed by rubbing after it is dry. May stain surface in time and is not recommended for mounting art of permanent value

**rubbing** — A design or pattern transferred from a tombstone or other surface to a slightly damp paper laid on the surface; a flat piece of chalk, charcoal, or pencil is rubbed over the surface until the design is transferred

**rubbing ink** — In lithography, a rectangular cake of ink, applied by rubbing a finger across the ink and then onto the stone

**'rub-down'** — A transfer of an original design to another paper or surface

**Rubenism/Rubenistes** — Following the style of Rubens. The late seventeenth- and eighteenth-century artists involved felt colour in painting to be more important than draftsmanship. Watteau was one of the leading artists. *See also* **Poussinistes**

**Rubens brown** — Pigment; a form of Vandyke brown; name obsolete

**Rubens madder** — Pigment; alizarin brown, obsolete

**Rubens, Peter Paul** — 1577-1640, a Flemish painter in the high baroque style. A superb draftsman, he is known for his luminous flesh tones and flamboyant compositions. Rubens was without doubt the outstanding painter of his day.

**rub-up** — In lithography, the process of rubbing the stone with a sponge saturated with thinned litho ink and then with a sponge saturated with a gum solution and water, to bring up the drawing

**Rubylith** — A transparent ruby-coloured masking film used in making mechanicals and in film processes of photolithography

**ruby masking film** — A red light-safe masking film used in the preparation of artwork for photography, silk screen, etc.

**rufous** — Pigment; a rust colour similar to a medium burnt sienna

**ruling pen** — A drawing instrument made of two parallel blades that are adjustable to regulate the size of the point and amount of ink

**rumpling** — Bumps or wrinkles formed in paper, usually from too much moisture

**run** — The edition, or number of prints pulled in lithography, etching, etc.

**run-around** — A composition where the text is indented or formed to accommodate an illustration

**running head** — In a book or magazine, the heading repeated at the top of consecutive pages

**running motif** — A design repeated many times in a row

**runs** — Wet paints that drip or dribble; sometimes allowed purposely, for effect

**rust** — Pigment; a reddish burnt sienna colour

**R.W.S.** — The Royal Society of Painters in Watercolours

ruling pen

# S

**sabeline brush** — A dyed ox-hair brush designed to serve as a substitute for sable; useful, relatively inexpensive, used mainly with waterbased paints

**sable/red sable brush** — A brush made of kolinsky, which is a semiaquatic Siberian mink. The hairs hold their shape well and cling together when wet; the brush has good 'spring' and comes to a fine point. Most manufacturers reserve the name Kolinsky for their top range of brushes

**sacred subject** — pertaining to religious art or symbols

**sacrum** — A triangular bone that forms the posterior section of the pelvis

**safety** — Although art is generally regarded as a safe and sedentary occupation, certain materials and practices can be hazardous. All petroleum-based products are inflammable; some pigments, particularly the leads, chromes and cadmiums, are poisonous; most solvents are more or less toxic. Most manufacturers print a warning and identify such products clearly in their catalogues and on packaging. These warnings should be heeded. It is in general good practice to work in a well-ventilated room, to avoid pointing and moistening brushes on the tongue and to re-cap all bottles after use. Always ensure that easels, especially the heavy studio variety, are securely tightened and stable before use and that floors are kept clear of obstructions. In the heat of creativity, movements can become vigorous and this is when accidents happen. When using specialist equipment, such as for sculpting or welding, always read and understand the instructions before starting work

**safflower** — Pigment; a red lake, fugitive and obsolete

167

**saffron** — Pigment; a bright yellow, fugitive and obsolete

**S.A.G.A.** — Society of American Graphic Artists

**saibokuga** — (Japanese) An ink painting using the traditional black with colour

**St Ives school** — A group of painters based in St Ives, Cornwall, originated by Barbara Hepworth and Ben Nicolson. All members are highly individual, although their style tends towards abstract landscape

**salamander** — A restorative used on oil paintings

**salmon** — Pigment; a coral pink mixture, the colour of salmon

**Salon** — 1. The annual exhibition of the Académie des Beaux Arts, representing nineteenth-century French establishment taste. 2. A regular social/ philosophical meeting of artists, usually in the house of a patron

**Salon des Réfusés** — An exhibition held in 1863 under the orders of Napoleon III to show the very high number of works turned down by the official French Academy. It included Cézanne, Manet, Pisarro and Whistler, but public reaction confirmed the official view and the experiment was not repeated

**salt aquatint** — Aquatint made by sprinkling salt on a hot, already grounded plate to create a different texture

**sample** — A picture shown to an art director as an example of the artist's proficiency

**sampler** — In textile design, various designs in small squares or rectangles, grouped together in one pattern

**sand** — 1. Very fine, gritty particles of rock used as an additive to paint to create texture. 2. Pigment; a very light brown or tan colour, considered a neutral

St Ives school – David Bomberg (*Tregor and Trefoff*)

**sandaraca** — A varnish resign; term originally used indiscriminately for orpiment, realgar, cinnabar, lead oxide yellow, and the red earths

**sandboard** — A fine or rough sand-surface product used mainly to sharpen pencils and pastels

**sandcasting** — A method of laying mosaics. Also, a mould for a casting made with molten metal

**sanded finish** — 1. A finish obtained by the use of sandpaper to smooth usually relatively soft surfaces such as wood, gesso, etc. 2. A paper (often pastel paper) with a rough finish like sandpaper

**sand ground** — 1. An aquatint ground preparation whereby sandpaper is placed face down on a printing plate which has a resist surface, then both are run through the press to produce a texture in the ground. 2. Sand sprinkled on wet oil or acrylic paint as a texture. 3. Sandpaper glued to a support for direct painting or pastel rendition

**sand painting** — (American Indian) 1. A picture composed on the ground with coloured sands, usually for a ritual purpose, such as marriage or healing. 2. A facsimile of the same on canvas or panel

**sandpaper** — A heavy paper coated on one side with an abrasive, used to smooth or shape wood and other surfaces; used sometimes in artwork for a textural effect. Available in textures from light to heavy

**sandpaper aquatint** — See **sand ground**

**sandpaper block** — A pad of small sandpaper sheets

**sanguine** — A reddish crayon long used for drawing and toning; often referred to as a conté crayon, from the French manufacturer's name

**sans serif** — having no serifs, as in gothic type

**san sui** — (Chinese/Japanese) Mountain and water, meaning a landscape

**sap green** — Pigment; a transparent earth green, permanent

**sapwood** — The lighter, soft wood found between the bark and the heartwood, used in woodcarving

**satin finish** — A moderately shiny finish, not as luminous as a gloss finish

**saturated** — Thoroughly wet so that no more liquid can be absorbed

Sans serif

Serif type

**saturation** — 1. The degree of vividness of a hue, from its concentration; used synonymously with *chroma*. 2. In a solution, the material's limit of solubility

**satyr** — In design, a woodland god with ears, legs, and horns of a goat

**scale** — 1. The dimensions of an artwork relative to those of the original. 2. To enlarge or reduce (scale up or scale down) artwork or photographs for reproduction without changing the original proportions

**scaleograph** — An instrument used to scale photographs and illustrations

**scale ruler** — A ruler with different scales printed on the sides, available in divisions of tenths and twelfths

**scan** — 1. To check or quickly study something, as to scan a blueprint. 2. A computer method of making colour separations to be used in printing

**scapula** — A shoulder blade; a large, flattish, triangular bone forming the back part of the shoulder

**scarlet** — Pigment; a strong, vivid red colour

**scarlet lake** — Pigment; a bright orangish red lake, permanent

**scarlet vermilion** — Pigment; an orange red, permanent

**Sceptre** — Trade name of a range of synthetic oil and watercolour brushes

**schablone** — The use of a stencil to colour prints

**Scheele's green** — Pigment; same as emerald green, toxic, obsolete

**Schnitzer's green** — Pigment; a form of chromium oxide green, name obsolete

**school of Paris** — *See* **Paris, school of**

**schrottblatt** — *See* **criblée**

**Schweinfurt green** — Pigment; emerald green, toxic, obsolete

**score** — 1. To mark or lightly cut a line, not cutting all the way through. 2. A printing term meaning a blank impression on the inside fold of a signature, made with a blank hard tool, to locate the fold and prevent surface damage to certain heavy stocks

**scotchstone** — A fine abrasive used to wear away a surface

**scraper** — In printmaking, a tool with a sharp blade, used to remove the burr and to smooth areas

scraper

scratchboard by
Cecile Curtis

**scraperboard** — *See* **scratchboard**

**scrap file** — *See* **clip file**

**scraping down** — A technique for oils and acrylics in which a palette knife is drawn across the wet paint, pressing the paint into the canvas and at the same time softening the hard edges; on dry paint a slightly different effect is accomplished

**scratchboard** — An ink drawing method using a cardboard sheet that is coated with a clay finish and covered with drawing ink; special cutting tools are used to scratch in the drawing, which resembles wood engraving. Makes excellent reproductions

**scratchboard tools** — Small knives about the size of pen tips are used as cutting or scratching tools, some with multiple points for drawing several parallel lines at once, as for crosshatching

multiple line
scratchboard tool

**scratch foam board** — A foam-coated board on which a drawing is pressed or scratched, which can then be used as a printing plate with either oil- or water-based printing inks

**screen** — 1. In textile design, a colour separation device. For instance, in three separations on white, screen no. 1 is the white and screens 2, 3, and 4 are the colours. 2. Various textured adhesive-backed shading sheets used in design, usually for art to be reproduced. 3. The process of making a half-tone illustration by breaking the image up into fine dots by superimposing a screen

**screen opener** — For silk screen, a spray used to open a screen that has dried ink

**screen printing (hand and machine)** — In textile design, hand screen printing is known as silk screen; machine screen printing is about the same process, but performed mechanically. *See also* **silk screen**

**scribble** — Lines interwoven or intermixed in a fast, unplanned manner

**scribble drawing** — A quick-gesture drawing in which the pencil does not leave the surface of the paper

**scriber** — A pointed tool for marking wood, metal, and other surfaces

**scrim** — In intaglio, a heavy, coarse cloth used to wipe the plate

**scrimshaw** — Whalebone and ivory decorations carved by sailors in the nineteenth century

**script** — Lettering that imitates handwriting; also, the handwriting style called cursive (flowing)

**script brush** — A brush with extra-long red sable hairs that come to a fine point, used for script lettering, scroll work in design, and for fine details

**scrive** — A hollow burin with a 'V' shape, used in sculpture

**scroll** — (Japanese) *See* **makimono; kakemono**

**scroll pattern** — In design, a rolling design resembling the beginning of a spiral, almost immediately reversed

**scrubbing** — A means of applying paint with a brush in a scrubbing motion

**scruffing** — 1. Drawing or blocking in a quick, loose drawing. 2. Roughing up a surface area in a painting, usually with brush strokes. 3. Dry-brushing colour over a rough surface, allowing the underneath colour to show through

**sculpture** — The art of three-dimensional or relief carving and modelling

**sculptured design** — In textile design, a pattern indicating two or more levels in the pile, for carpeting or fabric. The pile is actually cut long and short or the design is painted to resemble that effect

**sculpture in the round** — Free-standing sculpture, completed on all sides

**scum** — In lithography, the grease on non-image areas of the stone or plate; a film of ink printing where it should not print

**scumble** — To lay a light, semitransparent colour on a surface already painted with another colour, to unify or soften the area and create a textural quality. Usually accomplished with a dry-brush or with a rag or finger

**S curve** — Design in the shape of an S

**seal** — (oriental) A stamp on an artwork of the artist's given name, a family name, the name of his home or household, the date of his birth, a poetic phrase, or a pictorial symbol. Also, a collector may stamp his seal on the artwork. Sometimes called a *chop mark*

**seal print** — A blind-embossed print

**search lines** — *See* **pentimenti**

**seascape** — A view of the ocean and/or the surroundings as composed in a picture

**secco** — (Italian, *dry*) A mural painting procedure using colours ground in a binder such as casein, and applied to dried lime plaster; less permanent than fresco, which is applied to wet plaster

**secondary colours** — Orange, green, and violet, made from mixing the primaries: red and yellow make orange, blue and yellow make green, and red and blue make violet

**section d'or** — (French, *golden mean/golden section*) *See* **golden mean/golden section**

**Sellotape** — Trade name for a clear adhesive tape

**semi-abstract art** — Art that depicts a subject in a stylized or partially abstract manner

**separation** — *See* **colour separation**

**sepia** — A brown-coloured pigment originally made from cuttlefish, also a sepia ink; now a mixture of burnt sienna and lamp black, permanent

**sequence** — In cartooning, a series of panels that relate to each other, to tell a story or series of events

**serifs** — The small cross-lines or embellishments at the termination of the main stems of roman letter forms

**serigraphy** — *See* **silk screen**

**serrated** — Having toothlike or notched projections

**set-in** — In woodcarving, to outline the design with stop-cuts prior to removing unwanted wood. *See* **stop-cut**

**set palette** — A limited palette

**setup** — Articles arranged in a still life

**Seurat, Georges** — 1859-1891, best known as the creator of pointillism (he preferred to call it divisionism). This style was debated as either the logical conclusion of Impressionism in its methodical use of colour or as a break with the free, open-air execution of the movement

**sfumato** — (Italian, *smoke*) An imperceptible transition of gradual change in colour or value

173

**Georges Seurat** *Le Bec du Hoc, Grandcamp*

**sgraffito** — Decoration made by scratching through a layer to reveal a different colour underneath. Now applied to pottery, it was earlier a Renaissance procedure using stucco and stained glass. *See* **graffiti** and **graffito**

**shade** — A degree of colour obtained by adding black to a hue

**shading** — Suggesting various shadow values in a drawing or painting by gradation of tone

**shading film** — *See* **shading sheets**

**shading sheets** — In commercial art, transparent acetate sheets with an imprinted pattern of dots, used by overlaying wherever a tone or texture is desired

**shadow** — The darkest area of a subject; that area that is away from direct illumination. *See also* **cast shadow**

**shape** — Configuration, form

**shaping claw** — In stone carving, a chisel with teeth that produce serrated gouges, used in the early shaping stages of a sculpture

**sharpening stone** — A Carborundum stone used to sharpen cutting and carving tools

**sheet-fed** — Describes a printing press that prints on flat sheets of paper rather than rolls

**sheeting** — A light cotton canvas used as a painting support

**shellac** — A thin varnish made from flake shellac (resin) and denatured alcohol, used as a size over rabbitskin glue ground, but must be completely covered with pigment for best results. Also used as a blockout for silk screen

**shifting planes** — Images drawn or painted on various planes other than what are observable

174

from a single station point. Cubist art is often based on shifting planes

**ship curve, adjustable** — *See* **curve ruler**

**shocking pink** — Pigment; a brilliant pink, a mixture of a bright red and a touch of white

**short ink** — Buttery thick ink that does not flow well

**shoulder blade** — *See* **scapula**

**show cards** — Indoor posters for temporary announcements

**show-card board** — A smooth, dull-finished cardboard used for posters; takes many mediums and is available in a variety of colours

show-card brushes

**show-card brush** — A lettering brush, square-tipped (usually sable), available in many sizes

**show-card colours** — *See* **poster colours**

**shuan kou** — (Chinese, *double outline*) *See* **kou le**

**Siberian charcoal** — Compressed charcoal

**siccative** — *See* **drier**

**Sienese school** — Fourteenth-century Italian artists located at Siena, painting in the Byzantine and Gothic styles; Duccio and Simone were the prominent artists

**sienna** — Pigment; *See* **burnt sienna; raw sienna**

**sighting** — A means of seeing and mentally measuring the relationships of angles, shapes, spaces, etc., and applying them to a drawing or painting

**sight line** — In a picture, an imaginary line from the eye of a figure, indicating the direction of his glance

**signature** — 1. The artist's name or initial on artwork. 2. In printing and binding, the grouping of pages according to the folding of the paper as it comes from the press; usually printing signatures consist of 16 or 32 pages

**sign cloth** — A specially primed cloth used for signs and display art, available in sizes to 127cm x 44m

**signet** — 1. A small seal used as a design, as on a signet ring. 2. An official seal or stamp

**sil** — Pigment; ochre, an obsolete Roman name

**silhouette** — A flat shape in profile, usually in one value

**silhouette paper** — A smooth paper, dull black on one side and white on the other, used for making silhouettes

**silhouetting** — In commercial art, a means of separating an element from the rest of the picture for printing by painting a white area around the subject to isolate it from other areas (usually in a photograph). The film stripper can then more easily produce the plates necessary for the desired effect

**silicoil brush washer** — A jar containing silicone with a wire coil at the bottom, to facilitate cleaning oil paint from brushes

**silk screen** (serigraphy) — A stencil-printing process where paint or ink is forced with a squeegee through a silk, organdy, or other screen onto the paper or textile below, the area not to be painted being previously stopped out

silk screen printer

**silk-screen frame** — In the silk-screen process, a wooden frame that has silk or other material stretched over it and is hinged for pulling proofs

**silver leaf** — Silver used like gold leaf in medieval paintings; tarnishes easily

**silverpoint** — A method of drawing with a silver point on a specially prepared paper, leaving a delicate grey line that becomes darker and warmer with age. *See also* **metal point**

**silverpoint tool** — A tool that holds a rod of silver used to draw on silverpoint paper

**silver white** — Pigment; synonymous with flake white. *See* **white**

**simplify** — To make a design or picture less complicated

**simultaneism** — *See* **orphism**

**simultaneous contrast** — *See* **pointillism**

**simultaneous representation** — In a picture, the depiction of a person or thing in more than one view; some pictures incorporate two or more eye levels. *See also* **universal perspective**

**simultaneous submissions** — Artwork, such as cartoons, submitted to more than one prospective buyer at a time

**singe** — To burn lightly the edges of paper or board. To burn lightly the fibres that are loose and sticking up on a stretched raw canvas to prevent the absorption of moisture

**single-panel cartoon** — A single-picture cartoon, often with caption or balloon-enclosed comment

**single-primed** — Having one application of gesso

**single-stroke brush** — *See* **one-stroke brush**

**sinking in** — Dull areas of an oil painting resulting from some of the medium being absorbed into the ground. Usually remedied by the application of retouching varnish

**sinopia/sinope/sinoper** — 1. The Roman name for red iron oxide. 2. In fresco painting, a red ochre underpainting

**sirens** — Mythological sea nymphs whose singing lured mariners to destruction on the rocks of their islands; may appear in artwork, especially fountain sculpture

**Sisley, Alfred** — 1839-1899, Impressionist painter of English parentage whose style compares with that of his contemporary, Claude Monet. He achieved little recognition during his lifetime

**sitter** — The subject of a portrait

**sitting** — The period of time the model poses for the artist who is painting a portrait

**size/sizing** — A gelatinous substance used as a glaze or filler on canvas, panels, and paper

**sizing catcher** — In intaglio, the thin bottom blanket next to the dampened paper, used to absorb the sizing

**sketch** — A quick drawing or painting, freely done, often purely suggestive and incomplete

**sketchbook or sketch pad** — A book or pad of paper especially for sketching, available in various shapes, styles, and sizes

**sketch box** — Any box that carries sketching equipment

**sketching easel** — *See* **easel**

**skew** — To twist on an oblique angle; to distort

**skew chisel** — A chisel used in woodcarving

**sky blue** — Pigment; a bright blue close to cerulean

**sky brush** — *See* **oval wash brush**

**slab** — A heavy piece of marble, porcelain, or plate glass used for grinding pigments or for other studio purposes

**slant tiles** — On a watercolour palette, colour containers that are on a slight slant so the watercolour paint stays within its wells

**slate black** — Pigment; powdered slate of a greyish colour with poor opacity

**sleeve** — A container or cover; a plastic pocket designed to hold items such as transparencies or negatives

**slick** — Very smooth; said of paintings that are

skew chisel

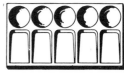

slant palette

177

handled deftly or where the paint quality has the look of creamy consistency

**slick stock** — Paper with a fine, smooth finish

**slipsheet** — Blank sheet of paper used to separate newly printed pages while drying, or wherever one thing is to be isolated from another in stacking

**slipsheet mounting method** — Used when mounting paper, tissue, photos, etc. Use rubber cement on both papers to be mounted together. Let dry. Place a tracing paper over the base paper, leaving about 2.5cm of the cement showing at the top. Mount the top paper on the 2.5cm of rubber cement, lining up all corners. Then slip the tracing paper out from the bottom. Press the top paper down, working out any air bubbles

**slipsheet alternative method** — Use rubber cement on both papers that are to be mounted together. Let them dry. Place two tracing papers (one overlapping the other at the middle) onto the bottom paper which has rubber cement on it. Place the artwork on top exactly where you want it, then pull the bottom tracing paper out a little at a time, pressing the artwork down at the middle while working out the air bubbles. Then remove the other tracing paper the same way

**slugs** — 1. In typesetting, leads that are more than six points high, used for spacing. 2. Pieces of cast metal type produced by a hot-metal setting machine

**small caps** — Capital letters the size of lowercase letters in a given point size

**smaragd green** — Pigment; viridian, hydrated chromium hydroxide, name obsolete

**smock** — A long, jacket-type covering worn to protect an artist's clothing when working

**smoking** — In etching, the use of a candle to darken or smoke a hard ground on a plate

**snake slip** — An abrasive in stick form used to clean scraper marks off litho plates around the margins

**snapline** — A piece of string coated with chalk, which is extended between two points, pulled back, and snapped against a surface, marking a straight chalk line; sometime used in mural painting

**snow white** — Pigment; zinc oxide, an obsolete name

STYLE represents

**soaking the paper** — In watercolour, placing the paper in a tray or tub of water for a period of time as a preliminary step for stretching or as a wash-off procedure

**soapstone** — In sculpture, a soft, easy-to-carve stone, available in a few different colours

**socialist realism** — Official style of art in the Soviet Union, socialist in theme and realist in form, not to be confused with *social realism*

**social realism** — A twentieth-century movement in painting dealing directly and critically with social, political, and economic issues. Some nineteenth-century painters, such as Daumier and Courbet, were forerunners of this movement

**soft ground** — An etching ground that is part tallow, is tacky and greasy

**soft-ground etching** — An etching technique using soft ground, producing a soft quality to the lines similar to a crayon effect. When a paper or textile is laid on the plate and a pencil or stylus is used to copy the design, various effects can be achieved by the ground adhering to the paper under the strokes and by the impression of the paper or textile on the ground

**solder** — A fusible alloy, such as tin and lead, used to join metal pieces

**solferino** — Pigment; a reddish mauve lake bluer than cobalt violet, fugitive, obsolete

**solids** — Forms having three-dimensional mass in any shape and volume; not liquids or gases

**Solomon's Seal** — Two equilateral triangles overlapping, indicating the union of body and soul; the Star of David

Solomon's seal

**solvent** — A substance capable of dissolving another substance, as benzine, kerosene, turpentine, alcohol, etc.

**solvent-resistant tape** — In silk screen, a tape used inside a frame to eliminate seepage

**sotto in sù** (Italian, *from below upwards*) — A realistic painting style of illusionism used on ceilings of churches and public buildings; also called *frog perspective*

**space** — 1. The unoccupied area in a painting. 2. The interval within a boundary as positive or negative space. 3. Two-dimensional space is the picture plane. 4. Three-dimensional space possesses height, width, and depth

**space arts** — *See* **plastic arts**

179

**spacing** — In lettering, adjusting the letters so they flow together properly and aesthetically

**Spanish black** — Pigment; charcoal made from cork; obsolete

**Spanish brown** — Pigment; burnt umber, name obsolete

**Spanish red** — Pigment; a bluish shade of native iron oxide, comparable to Indian red, permanent

**Spanish white** — Pigment; bismuth white, obsolete

**spatter/splatter** — A painting technique in which a finger or knife is used with a stiff brush (toothbrush) that has pigment on it, creating an uneven spotted pattern; or, a loaded brush is struck on the hand or a ruler. May also be achieved with an airbrush

**spectrum** — 1. A band of colours, as seen in a rainbow or through a prism. 2. A broad range of colours

**spectrum red** — Pigment; a colour close to cadmium red medium on the colour wheel, gouache

**spectrum violet** — Pigment; a blue violet close to Prussian blue, fugitive, gouache

**spectrum yellow** — Pigment; a colour close to cadmium yellow medium on the colour chart, permanent, gouache

**Speedball pen** — Trade name of a penholder and many different-sized nibs, used for hand lettering and for drawing

**speed lines** — See **action lines**

**Spencer, Sir Stanley** — 1891-1959, English painter of landscape and domestic scenes, particularly associated with the Surrey village of Cookham. Much of Spencer's work is both religious and erotic in content

splatter techniques

Speedball pens

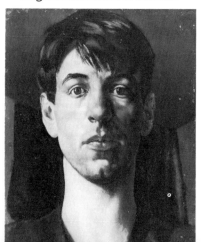

**Sir Stanley Spencer**
*Self-portrait*

**sphere** — A globular form in which all points on the surface are equidistant from the centre; one of the basic forms used in construction drawing

**sphinx** — From ancient Egypt, a stone image of a reclining lion with a human head

**spine** — 1. The backbone; the column of vertebrae extending from the cranium to the coccyx. 2. The backbone of a bound book

**spire gothic** — *See* **gothic type**

**spit bite** — Saliva applied to a plate to define an area and keep the acid from running

**spitsticker** — *See* **elliptic graver**

**splash print** — In textile design, colour splashed or dropped in such a way that a fairly large design is created

**splay** — The opening or spreading outward of a brush

splay

**split complement** — The use of the colours on each side of a complementary colour

**split planes** — *See* **fractured planes**

**sponge technique** — 1. To moisten a sponge with water and colour and lay a wash. 2. To daub a sponge in colour and then on paper or canvas, creating a texture

**spot design** — A design used as a single motif

**spot drawing** — A single small drawing used for illustration

**spotlight** — A portable studio light used to light models, still life, etc; designed to concentrate a spot of light in a small area

**spray gun** — *See* **airbrush**

**Spraymount** — Aerosol adhesive useful for mounting large areas of artwork, also available in forms which allow for repositioning. Produces a fine spray which is harmful if inhaled

**spread** — 1. A layout design that covers an entire page. 2. A two-page spread that encompasses two facing pages

**spring** — The bounce or manoeuvrability of the hairs in a brush

**spring clamp** — A device used to grip paper to a board or other surface; also called a *spring clip*

**springwood** — In woodcarving, the softer wood layers in the tree ring pattern; the growth during the spring season

**squared up** — 1. Said of a corner being checked for a 90° angle. 2. An illustration which is reproduced with its background, rather than cut out

**squeegee** — In silk screening, the tool used to force the ink or paint through the screen; usually consists of a rubber blade mounted in a wooden handle, similar to that used to wash windows

**squiggles** — Any curlicues, scrolls, or embellishments added to a design

**S/S** — (same size) In printing, a mark for the printer indicating the reproduction is to be the same size as the original

**S-scroll** — A design in the shape of an S

**stabile** — Sculpture that is stationary, does not move like a mobile

**stabilizer** — Ingredient in artist's pigments to make them easy to brush and keep the oil from separating

**staff artist** — An employee of an agency, store, business, or publisher, who works on salary as an artist

**stain** — 1. A dye that has no bulk, dissolves completely. 2. To put a thin colour over a canvas or panel. 3. In oils, colour plus turpentine, and in water media, colour plus water

**stained glass** — Coloured glass used to make picture windows, usually for public buildings and churches; also popular for home decoration in windows, wall plaques, lamps, etc.

**stand oil** — *See* **linseed oil**

**staple gun** — A tool used to hold and dispense staples, useful when stretching canvas

**Star of David** — *See* **Solomon's seal**

**stat** — *See* **photostat**

**static** — Said of certain artwork, meaning fixed, conservative, without aesthetic energy

**station point** — In perspective, the point of the artist's eye at which sight lines begin in relation to the picture plane; the point at which the artist views the scene in creating the picture

**statue** — A carved or modelled figure of a person, animal, or thing, in any size

**steel brush** — A flexible brush (pen) used for lettering, made of steel

**steel facing** — In printing, an added steel layer deposited on the surface of a copper plate, allowing a greater number of prints to be pulled from the plate

**stele** — An upright pillar or slab of stone with a design and/or inscription

**stencil** — Any material that is cut out to mask certain areas and allow a colouring medium to be applied to the open areas

**stencil brush** — A round brush with short, square-cut bristles that is used for stencil work

**stencil paper** — A heavy, often oiled, paper that will withstand rough treatment and can easily be cut to a clean edge

**stencil printing** — Making copies of a design from a stencil by silk screen or other stencil method

stencil brush

**stereotype** — A metal printing plate cast from a papier-mâché matrix or mat that has been made from a page of metal type

**sternomastoid** — A muscle originating behind each ear, moving forward and down each side of the neck, forming a *V* shape in the front of the neck

**sternum** — The breastbone, a bone that is between the cartilages of the upper seven ribs

**stet** (Latin, *let it stand*) — A proofreader's mark meaning 'do not change as marked', used on corrected work that has been countermanded

**stick figures** — Stick-like lines drawn into simplistic figures

**Stijl, De** — *See* **De Stijl**

**stil-de-grain** — Pigment; Dutch pink

**still** — In animated cartoons, a single cartoon as opposed to a series of cartoons making action; also, a 'still' photo from a movie film

**still life** — Inanimate objects such as flowers and fruit, arranged as a model for a composition to be painted, photographed, etc.; also, the finished work

**stipple** — A texture made up of tiny dots; to fleck or speckle an area of a painting usually with a contrasting colour

**stipple engraving** — Using fine dots as part of an engraving

**stipple print** — *See* **stipple engraving**

**stock** — The paper used for a printing, specified by the production manager or art director

**stone** — In lithographic printmaking, the flat block on which the drawing is made

**stone carving** — Engraving or cutting into stone or cutting away stone to create sculpture

**stone green** — Pigment; green earth, an obsolete name

**stop-cut** — In woodcarving, a vertical cut into a surface to outline and to prevent accidental splitting while removing excess wood

**stop-out** — 1. In intaglio printing, a substance that prevents the plate from being bitten, or etched. 2. A substance used in silk screen to prevent the paint from penetrating any non-printing areas not blocked out by the stencil

**story boards** — Small sketches, diagrams, or photographs made in panels to suggest the sequence of action and dialogue for movies, TV ads, etc.

**story man** — In animated cartooning, one who draws a series of sketches pertaining to the story or tale

**St. Plate** — A light-sensitive plate used in photolithography and photointaglio printing

**straightedge** — A ruler or T-square; any straight bar used for ruling, cutting, etc

**straight on** — Directly in front; directly at eye level

**strapwork** — Designs made up of intertwined straplike lines. *See* **arabesque**

**straw** — Pigment; a neutral mixture resembling the colour of straw

**strawboard** — A rough, heavy board, usually brown in colour, used for mounting, backing or as a cutting-board base

**street art** — Murals on buildings, outdoor sculpture, street displays, public art happenings

**street furniture** — Anything pertaining to a street, such as lampposts, signs, benches, etc.

**strength** — (in art) 1. The saturation of a colour. 2. The impact of a work of art

**stretched canvas** — Canvas that is fastened to stretcher strips and ready to prepare for a painting

**stretcher pliers** — A pincer-type tool with wide gripping jaws used to tighten and stretch canvas when fixing it to stretcher strips

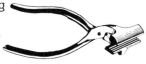

stretcher pliers

**stretchers** — The strips on which the canvas is stretched; commonly made of wood and available in a variety of lengths. The interchangeable slotted ends make for easy assembly

**strie** — (French, *groove*) In textile design, fabric that has a fine, irregular streak or stripe made by a slight variance in colour of the warp

**strike** — In chip carving, to make stop-cuts

**strike-off** — In textile design, a sample of cloth showing the design and colours, used by decorators

**string-and-wire art** — String and wire stretched on a frame, making a design or picture

**stripe** — 1. Cartoon drawings in a series of panels suggesting a story sequence, usually with captions. 2. To remove the varnish from an oil painting

**strip-in** — A piece of artwork, film, type, or the like, which has been removed from one surface and taped in place on another; usually relates to the plate-making process in printing

**stripe** — In textile design, a long band of colour that may or may not contain a pattern. Can be straight or wavy, horizontal, vertical, or oblique

**strip frame** — A narrow border frame made of strips of wood or metal attached to the edge of the canvas stretchers or other support. Quick and inexpensive, available in a variety of sizes

**striping tool** — A tool that draws straight or curved lines in any colour; has a glass fountain for poster paint, Japan colours, lacquer, etc.

**stripping** — 1. Removal of photo emulsion from its backing, so it can be assembled on another support. 2. Artwork that has been taken off or stripped from a heavier support

**strobe light** — An electronic flash or speed light used in photography

**strong** — In art, said of work that has an impact, is not weak or trite

**strong colour** — 1. Intense colour or high chroma. 2. In watercolour, a pigment that is hard to remove from the paper once it is painted, such as Prussian blue

**strontium white** — Pigment; strontium sulphate, replaced with *blanc fixe*

**strontium yellow** — Pigment; a lemon yellow, permanent

**struck off** — Pulled or printed – said of an edition of prints

**student-grade** — Grade of artist's colours and other materials, not of the finest quality, but serviceable for most purposes

**studio** — A room or building in which the artist works and keeps his equipment

**studio easel** — *See* **easel**

**study** — A drawing or painting of a section or of a whole composition, usually detailed more carefully than a sketch

**stump** — A cigar-shaped roll of heavy paper with a point on each end, used to refine pencil, charcoal, and pastel drawings

**style** — The artist's individual manner of working. The identifying characteristics of a particular period, group, or movement

**stylize** — To modify natural forms and make a representation in a preset style or manner

**stylus** — 1. A pointed instrument used to work on scratchboard and other coated surfaces. 2. A tool for engraving

**subhead** — A secondary headline or title

**subject** — The most important figure, object, or area in a composition

**subjective** — Originating within the artist, rather than a reporting of what is seen (objective)

**subjective colour** — Colour the artist chooses without regard for the real or original colour of an observed object

**subject matter** — What the artist renders, such as still life, landscape or seascape, figures, portraits, etc.

**subordinate element** — Anything of lesser importance than the primary element in an artwork

**subtractive colour mixing** — This form of colour mixing relies on the selective reflection of the elements of white light and is the main way in which colour is perceived in a painting. Each layer of applied pigment absorbs some parts of the visible spectrum and what remain are the constituents of colour produced. It is important to appreciate that, at each stage, the amount of light reflected is reduced and that over-mixing, for example, can diminish brilliance by producing a muddy, dark result. *See also* **additive colour mixing**

**subway art** — Graffiti taken to a high level; best exemplified on the New York Underground (subway)

**sugar bite** — *See* **lift-ground etching**

**sugar paper** — A British term referring to a plain wrapping paper sometimes used for drawing

**suiboku** — (Japanese) A traditional ink painting on silk or paper

**'suicide'** — In graphic arts, a reduction and stencil method using only one block for the entire print; one colour is cut and printed and then cut away, preparing the block for the next colour. There is no second chance, thus the term 'suicide'

**suite** — A group of original prints, usually related in subject matter, often used in portfolio form, with a colophon

**sulphur tint** — In intaglio, made by oil spread on a plate and sulphur dusted over it, creating a lightly bitten or washed-tone effect

**sumi** — Japanese brush painting with ink and/or watercolours

**sumi-e** — (Japanese, *black ink picture*) A black-ink picture

**sumi ink** — A mixture of carbon and glue pressed into a block. This block pressed and ground on a suzuri stone with a bit of water will create the 'ink'

fourteenth-century Japanese sumi-e drawing

**summerwood** — In woodcarving, the hardwooded layers in the tree ring pattern; growth during summer and dry seasons

**Sunday painter** — A term applied to amateur artists who pursue painting for pleasure

**sun-thickened oil** — *See* **linseed oil**

**supercalendering** — A machine process that produces a glossy surface on paper

**superrealism** — *See* **magic realism; surrealism**

**support** — 1. The foundation upon which a painting is made, such as canvas, panel, metal, wood, etc. 2. The 'backing' on which paper is mounted

**suprematism** — A Russian movement, founded by Kazimir Malevich about 1913, that was derived from cubism. It encompassed nonobjective, geometric forms, using simple colour combinations such as white on white or variations of black and white. Had much effect on the following generation of artists

**surface paper** — A frisket used for corrections on pen and ink and technical drawings. A scalpel is used to scrape away unwanted areas, then it is redrawn

**surface printing** — A type of printmaking in which ink or colour is applied directly to the plate, then the paper laid onto it and rolled or daubed

**surface-rolled** — A plate inked on the surface rather than in the grooves or cut-out areas

**sur le motif** — A term that refers to working in front of the subject, indoors and outdoors

**surprint** — A combination of line and halftone from two separate negatives, merged to produce one printing plate

**Surrealism** — Major art movement of the mid twentieth century, deriving from Dadaism, in which form is secondary to the symbolic power of the image. Its main exponents include Paul Klee, Max Ernst, Marcel Duchamp, Joan Miró, Salvador Dali and Man Ray. The major Surrealist exhibition was held in Paris in 1925

**suzuri** — (Japanese) An ink grinding stone used to grind minute particles from a sumi ink block to make sumi ink

**swash** — A flourish or extended serif on a Roman letter

swash letters

**'sweat box'** — In animated cartooning, the projection room

**Swedish green** — Pigment; cobalt green, a bluish green, opaque, not commonly used

**sweetener** — *See* **badger blender**

**swing** — The movement of the body or clothing on the body

**swipe file** — *See* **clip file**

**symbol** — A sign, figure, design, pattern, motif, signet, or colour used to represent something or somebody by association

**symbolism** — The art of depicting a hidden meaning, using symbols

**symbolist painting** — An attitude more than an art movement around 1890, when artists such as Redon, Moreau, and others promoted the idea of using symbolic, enigmatic dream fantasies to represent the emotions, such as love, hate, fear, etc.

**symmetrical** — Formal in balance, with elements of equal or near-equal weight on either side of a real or implied centre fulcrum

**Syn** — (Greek, *together*) A group of German artists formed in 1964 to reveal art beyond hard-edge painting or action painting. Artists involved included Bernd Berner and Rolf-Gunter Dienst

**synchronism** — *See* **orphism**

**synthetic** — Artificially produced

**synthetic brushes** — Brushes made from materials other than hair and bristle, such as nylon, polyester, etc., used mostly with acrylics

**synthetic canvas** — Artificial fibres made into a canvas for painting

**synthétism** — Same as cloisonnisme

# T

**tableau painting** — (French) A painting which is produced in an unexpected or dramatic way; for example: a layered glass painting; three, four, or five layers of glass with a portion of a picture painted on each glass, placed one on top of the other, creating a three-dimensional picture

**table easel** — *See* **easel**

**tabouret** — A stand to hold an artist's palette, and accessories; drawers and compartments are underneath for supplies

**taches** — Effective touches of impasto paint

**tachisme** — (French, *tacher*, to *stain* or *blot*) An offshoot in the 1950s of abstract expressionism, closely associated with activism. An unplanned pattern of splotches and dabs of paint, the emotional impact of which results from the outburst of the artist's spirit while working; exponents of this approach: Jean Atlan, Camille Bryen, Alfred Wols, Georges Mathieu, and others

tabouret

**tacking iron** — A tool heated by electricity, used to tack pictures, photographs, or papers to cardboard by a dry mounting procedure

**tackle box** — A compartmented box of a kind most frequently sold for storing fishing tackle, but equally useful for artists' materials

**tacky** — 1. Sticky, neither really wet nor dry; in graphics, describes the stickiness of ink or the pull of the ink against a surface. 2. Slang word used to describe poor quality or over-sentimentalized work

**tailpiece** — An illustration used at the end of a page or end of a book

**talc** — A fine-grained mineral used as a filler, sometimes called *French chalk*

**talent** — A natural gift or ability of superior quality

**tan** — Pigment; a very light brown mixture, considered a neutral

**tangent** — Touching or meeting, as of lines or forms

**tanka** — (Tibetan) A religious painting mounted on brocade cloth, used as a processional banner

**t'ao-t'tieh** — In design, a heraldic animal mask. *See* **devil's mask**

**tapestry** — In textile design, 1. a scenic fabric wall hanging, originally used for insulation and warmth as well as decoration. 2. A colourful, durable fabric

**tarlatan** — A strong, white absorbent cloth used for wiping inked plates

**tarsus** — The broad portion of the foot including the ankle, heel, and instep

**tartan** — In textile design, a plaid pattern, worn especially by Scots, each clan having its own pattern and colours

**taste** — Discrimination; in art, often relates to the artist's choice of colours, values, subjects, etc.

**Tate Gallery** — Major London art gallery specializing in contemporary British art. In October 1889, Henry Tate of Streatham offered to give his collection of pictures to the National Gallery at a time when there was pressure for a national collection representing native art. After long negotiation with the government of the day, his offer was accepted and the new gallery was built on the site of the old Millbank prison. *See also* **National Gallery**

**Tatlinism** — A constructivist art style named from one of the earliest constructivists. *See* **constructivism**

**Tattersall** — In textile design, a large plaid design at one time used on blankets worn by horses at the auction rooms in London, where the auction market was owned by a man named Tattersall

**tau** — *See* **tree of life**

**taupe** — A brownish grey mixture, considered a neutral

**tear sheet** — A published page showing an artist's illustrations, designs, photographs, or other artwork, or a copy of that page

**technical pen** — A drawing pen with a fine point and an ink supply cartridge; available in different point sizes. Brand names include Rapidograph, Mars, Faber-Castelli, Martin/Stano, K&E, and Unitech

**technique** — The method of using a medium or tool by an artist, or the particular method of an artist; closely linked to style

**tectiform** — A term applied to certain abstract forms/signs which accompany paleolithic wall engravings

**tectonic** — In sculptural forms, relating to the simple mass rather than extended shapes and forms

**tempera** — Originally a pigment ground with egg emulsion, properly called egg tempera, that dries hard and quickly and is very permanent. While egg tempera is still used, in general, the term refers to gouache, poster colours, and other opaque watercolours

**temperature** — In colour, the relative 'warmth' or 'coolness', warm colours being in the red-yellow range and cool colours in the green-violet range

**template** — A plastic or metal guide for drawing circles, squares, triangles, and other shapes and symbols

**Ten, the** — Ten American artists who exhibited together in 1898 and thereafter – Frank W. Benson, Joseph R. DeCamp, Thomas W. Dewing, Childe Hassam, Willard L. Metcalf, Robert Reid, Edward Simmons, Edward C. Tarbell, John H. Twachtman, and J. Alden Weir; after Twachtman died in 1902, William M. Chase became a member. All were influenced by French Impressionism

**ten chi jim** — (Chinese, *heaven, earth, and man*) A Buddhist concept in all art; in a painting, refers to the three elements: main subject, complementary addition, and auxiliary details

**tenebrism** — (Italian, *tenebroso, dark* and *gloomy*) The emphasis is on chiaroscuro to achieve dark, dramatic effects, the picture often being illuminated by a streak of light. The approach is reminiscent of the style made famous by Caravaggio; Georges de LaTour is often referred to as the great French tenebrist

**tension** — In composition, the visual feeling of strain or pull, the dynamic relationship between any of the elements

**tension points** — In fashion design, any point where there is stress on cloth: the elbow, knee, thigh, crotch, etc.

192

**tent stripe** — In design, an obvious wide stripe

**terra cotta** — Pigment; a reddish colour that imitates red clay

**terra merita** — 1. Pigment; a yellow lake, fugitive and obsolete. 2. In sculpture and pottery a hard, fired, unglazed clay

**terra ombre** — Pigment; raw umber, name obsolete

**terra rosa** — Pigment; a native earth tinctured with sesquioxide of iron somewhat close to burnt sienna, permanent

**terra verte** — Pigment; a green earth, permanent

**tertiary colours** — In contemporary usage, the intermediate colours are considered tertiaries: yellow orange, red orange, red violet, blue violet, blue green, and yellow green. In early colour theory, the mixture of the secondary colours created a tertiary, as green mixed with orange, orange mixed with violet, and violet mixed with green

**tesserae** — The tiles, glass, pebbles, etc. used to make a mosaic

**tetrads** — Colour harmonics based on four colours; using every fourth colour. The tetrads on the Prang colour wheel are yellow orange, red, blue violet and green; orange, red violet, blue and yellow green; red orange, violet, blue green and yellow

**text** — A typeface group, also referred to as *old English* and *black letter*

**textile colours** — Permanent colours made especially for painting directly on textiles

**texture** — In artworks, the quality of a surface or the representation of a surface such as smooth, rough, jagged, etc.

**textured design** — In textile design, texture actually woven into fabric, or a painted design simulating texture

**thalo blue** — *See* **phthalocyanine blue**

**thalo green** — *See* **phthalocyanine green**

**thalo red rose** — Pigment; a trade name for a synthetic quinacridone red; permanent

**theme** — The most important idea or subject in a composition; the subject for a work of art, sometimes with a number of phases or variations. For example, Cézanne used La Montagne Sainte-Victoire as a theme for many of his paintings

**Thenard's blue** — Pigment; a true cobalt blue, name obsolete

**theorem painting** — An early American decorative art using stencils and oil paint on velvet cloth

**theory** — 1. A statement of accepted principles. 2. A hypothesis yet to be proved

**thermography** — Process for making raised printing used for business cards, letterheads, etc. Made with ordinary type, but while the ink is still wet a special resinous powder is sprinkled on it; it is then heated, and the fused resin rises to produce the raised lettering, giving a general appearance of engraving

**thick and thin** — 1. The weight of a line, its graphic quality. 2. The weight of the paint, thick paint as opposed to thin paint

**thigh** — The part of the leg between the hip and the knee

**thin** — Oil colour diluted with turpentine rather than an oil medium; it creates a mat finish; also called 'lean'

**thinner** — A liquid used to reduce the thickness of a pigment, as water for watercolours, gouache, acrylics, and casein, and turpentine for oils

**thio violet** — Pigment; thioindigo, an intense purple with a red undertone close to manganese violet, permanent

**thirsty brush** — a watercolour term meaning a brush that has been wet and then squeezed dry. If then touched into a wet area, it will pick up moisture

**thorax** — The chest; the area betwen the arms, below the neck, and above the diaphragm

**three-dimensional** — Showing height, width, and depth

**three-point perspective** — Representations drawn in perspective so as to show height, width, and depth; necessary when the scene is seen either from a 'bird's-eye view' or a 'worm's-eye view'

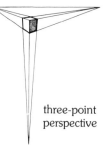

three-point perspective

**T.H. Saunders paper** — An acid-free mould-made watercolour paper suitable for general use

**thumbnail sketch** — A rough, very small sketch

**thumbtack** — American term for a drawing pin

**tibia** — A long bone occupying the front and inner side of the lower leg

**'tickling up'** — Making small, fussy adjustments on artwork

**tie, a** — In stencil printing, the bar or bridge that holds an island to the remainder of the stencil

**tie in** — To pull elements together so they make more design unity

**tight** — Said of a drawing or rendering that is exact, carefully detailed through the use of small brushes or other precise tools

**tight hand** — The ability to draw or paint with precision

**tile** — A slab of fired clay with a smooth finish, used in mosaics and in covering floors and walls. Designs are often painted on large tiles, which are then glazed

**tin leaf** — Used in the Middle Ages in place of silver leaf because it did not tarnish; also used with yellow colour or yellow varnish as a top coat, to imitate gold leaf

**tinsel painting** — The craft of painting on glass with transparent oil paints backed with aluminium foil; sometimes called *crystal painting*

**tint** — White with a small amount of colour added. The more colour added, the stronger the tint

**tintype** — In photography, the process of developing a direct positive image on a lightweight metal plate, popular until the late nineteenth century; also called *ferrotype*

**tip-in** — 1. An illustration printed separately and inserted into a book by using paste at the top of the illustration, the rest hanging free. 2. The insertion of a full-page illustration or plate, printed separately on smoother or heavier stock than the rest of the book

**tissue overlay** — A transparent paper used to keep artwork clean, for instructions, and for making corrections

**tissue paper** — A thin translucent paper used in different colours for crafts and decorations

**titanium white** — *See* **white**

**tjanting needle** — A tool used to apply liquid wax to cloth for batik

**toile de Jouy** — In textile design, a one-colour design depicting scenes pertinent to the eighteenth century or oriental scenes

**tole** — Painted tinware; a decorative folk art of painting on tin trays, lamps, and other household items with designs, borders, etc.

**toluidine red** — A red synthetic toner

**tonalists** — A term applied to some artists in the period from 1880-1910, who tried to capture realistic qualities in nature. Inness, La-Farge, and Whistler were among the artists in this group

**tonality** — The emphasis of values in a picture; tonality can also incorporate colour and how it is considered. For instance, all earth colours in a low key would be a subdued tonality; likewise a bright tonality could be the whole range of values, colours, and intensities

**tondo** — A painting in circular form, or a sculptured medallion

**tone** — The relative lightness or darkness in a picture; its value quality either in colour or black and white, its predominant value suggesting the key

**toned ground** — 1. A glaze or wash of thinned, transparent colour laid over a canvas, panel, or paper to prepare it for painting; turpentine is used with oils for thinning and water with water-base paints. 2. Colour mixed into the gesso when preparing a gesso ground

**toner** — 1. In silkscreen, a concentrated ink mixed with a colour to make it transparent; not to be used alone. 2. A synthetic organic colour in a highly concentrated form that is stronger than a lake

**tonking** — A process of using blotting paper to remove excess oil paint from an area while still leaving pigment in the hollows of the canvas. The name is derived from Henry Tonker, a professor at the Slade Art School in England

**tooth** — The texture of a paper, canvas, or other ground, that helps to hold the paint

**top tone** — *See* **mass tone**

**tormented** — Said of artwork that has been overworked

**torso** — The trunk of the body made up of the chest and shoulders, the waist, and the pelvis area

**tortillon** — A rolled heavy paper stump, pointed on one end, used to soften and tone pencil, charcoal, and pastel drawings. Similar to a stump

**Tosa school** — Japanese school of painting in the fifteenth to late seventeenth centuries, started by Tosa Motomitsu; the main subjects were court scenes, nobles, and ceremonies of the court

tortillons

**totem** — In design, an animal, plant, or natural object used as an emblem for a clan

**totem pole** — A carved pole made up of totemic symbols, telling a story of the tribe; usually relates to Indians of the Northwest

**totentanz** — *See* **dance of death**

**touch** — A term sometimes applied to the quality of a work, including the brush strokes, colour, etc.; some paintings are said to have a soft, hard, airy touch, etc.

**toxic** — poisonous

**Toulouse-Lautrec, Henri Marie Raymond de** — 1864-1901, turned to painting after an accident stunting his growth forced him to abandon his favourite pursuits of riding and shooting. He began with sporting subjects but between 1885-1895 he was based in Montmartre and produced his best work, showing the performers and habitués of the Moulin Rouge. His style was strongly influenced by the similar subjects of Degas

**tracery** — In design, curved and/or foliated design, common in Gothic art

**tracing box** — A box with a glass top, having a light inside, used for tracing

**tracing cloth** — A thin, sturdy, starched, transparent cotton cloth that is used for ink tracing; available in rolls

**tracing paper** — Transparent paper used over a drawing in order to copy (trace) it; also used for layout and planning work

**tracing wheel** — *See* **pouncing**

**traditional** — Conforming to established procedures and principles handed down from the past

**trail/traile/trayle** — A running carved design of a continuous vine

**transfer** — The conveying of a drawing from one paper to another

**transfer paper** — A carbon-, graphite-, pastel-coated paper used under an original picture to transfer the picture to its surface by pencil or other pressure

**transfer type** — *See* **pressure-sensitive letters**

**translucence** — A quality of paper or other material that allows light to pass through, but is not transparent enough to see through clearly

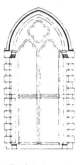

Gothic tracery

trail

**transparency** — A photographic positive film such as a colour slide; or, sheet or roll film used by commercial photographers

**transparent** — Able to be seen through; glasslike

**transparent base** — In silk screen, an extender that reduces the opaque paint to transparency; improves the screening and does not change the colour or viscosity

**transparent brown** — Pigment; burnt green earth

**transparentizing fluid** — Any of several types of fluids that can be used to make papers more transparent; often used when painting from old drawings. Available through drafting supply stores

**transparent oxide of chromium** — Pigment; viridian, a transparent dark green, permanent

**trapezius muscles** — Muscles that shape the shoulders, continue up the back of the neck, draw the head back and to the side, and rotate the scapula

**tree of life** — A symbol in the shape of a tree, usually with fruit or leaves; the Greek letter tau, a *T* is also considered the tree of life

**trefoil** — (Latin, *three-leaved*) A motif with three leaves, often found in Gothic ornamental work

**trail proofs** — In graphic arts, proofs that are pulled to work out the requirements for the choice of paper, colour, pressure, etc.

**triangle** — A three-sided drafting tool, made in several sizes and with different angles; standard are 90°/60°/30° and 90°/45°/45°

**triceps** — A large muscle running along the back of the upper arm, extending the forearm and arm

**trimetal plate** — Plate made with three layers of metal – chromium or top of copper, on a base of aluminium or stainless steel

**trim size** — The size a final printed piece will measure; the measurement to which the printed sheet will be cut

**Tripoli** — A cutting compound used to remove tiny scratches on metal

**triptych** — A panel painting in three parts, a middle section with two wings; often used for altarpieces

**trite** — Said of artwork that is ordinary, has little meaning, lacks interest and originality

**triton** — In design, a creature with the body of a man and a dolphin's tail

**trois crayons, à** — (French, *with three chalk crayons*) A drawing on toned paper, usually with black, red, and white crayons or chalk

**trompe l'oeil** — (French, *deception of the eye*) Painting rendered with photographic realism, so realistic it can fool the viewer into thinking the subjects are real rather than painted; also called *illusionism*

**trucage** — A painting forgery; a fake

**truck** — In newspaper printing, each page of type, illustrations, etc. put together on a small movable table called a *truck*, each truck holding just one page; the system is now obsolete

**truqueur** — An art forger

**'try-outs'** — In animated cartooning, series of rough animated drawings that are photographed on a film strip, then analysed or criticized

**T-square** — A drawing tool shaped like a *T* with exact 90° angles at the crossbar; used to draw accurate lines and to check squareness of art and copy, often in conjunction with a triangle

**tsuketate** — A traditional Japanese ink painting in which sumi or colour is used for the masses; no outlines are employed

**tube colours** — 1. Pigments packaged in tubes, as opposed to pans or cakes. 2. Colour straight from the tube, without additions or alterations

**tube sizes** (for paints) —

| | |
|---|---|
| no. 2 = 5 ml. | no. 14 = 37 ml. |
| no. 3 = 8 ml. | no. 20 = 60 ml. (2 oz.) |
| no. 5 = 14 ml. | no. 40 = 120 ml. |
| no. 8 = 21 ml. | |

**tube wringer** — A tool to help squeeze all the paint from a tube

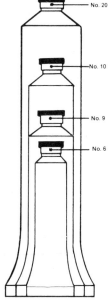

one half actual size of common tube sizes

*trompe l'oeil* by Edward Collier

**Tudor rose** — In design, five open petals in a rose shape

**Turkey brown** — Pigment; raw umber, name obsolete

**Turkey red** — Pigment; native red oxide, name obsolete

**Turkey umber** — Pigment; raw umber, name obsolete

**Turk's Florentine medium** — Trade name for an oil medium used on textiles

**'turn around'** — In textile design, same as rotate

**'turn over'** — In textile design, to flip a design

**Turner, Joseph Mallord William** — 1775-1851, although sometimes referred to as 'the English Impressionist', Turner's work has less connection with the movement than that of John Constable. His early work was in the classical mould, but he later turned to Romantic compositions and finally to the visionary, dream-like paintings for which he is best known. He left all his unsold work to the Tate Gallery

**Turner's yellow** — Pigment; an obsolete lead yellow

**turnsole** — A blue or violet dye used in medieval manuscripts

**turntable** — A revolving stand, used by sculptors

**turpentine** — A natural solvent distilled from pine trees, used as a thinner with oils and alkyds and for cleaning brushes

**turquoise** — Pigment; a greenish blue or bluish green colour

**turquoise blue** — Pigment; a blue with a green undertone, moderately permanent, gouache

**Tuscan red** — Pigment; a red oxide plus alizarin crimson, used industrially

**tusche** — A fluid used to paint the design in lithography and silk screening

**Joseph Mallord William Turner** *The Thames near Walton Bridge*

Tudor rose

**T.V. story-board pad** — A white visual paper with a slight transparency for sketching story-board presentations; made of little T.V. screens (about 5 × 3 in) with a panel below for comments. *See also* **story boards**

**tweed** — In textile design, a weave of two or three colours which produce a mottled colour effect, as in tweed coats or rugs

**tweezers** — A tool used to grip, move, and lift type or small papers and pictures, particularly when mounting and pasting up mechanicals

**Twenty, the** — *See* **Vingt, les**

**two-dimensional** — Flat, having only two dimensions – height and width

**two-point perspective** — The type of perspective in which objects in a picture viewed on an angle will have two vanishing points, with verticals remaining parallel to the sides of the picture plane; also called *angular perspective*

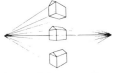

two-point perspective

**tympan** — 1. In lithography, a greased fibreboard or zinc sheet used to protect the paper and allow the scraper bar to move easily. 2. In architecture, the space between the arch and the lintel of a portal

**type** — A mechanical means of reproducing letters, such as typewriters, Linotype machines, computers, etc.

**typeface** — The style of a type letter form – italic, roman, gothic, or script; a named type style such as Caslon, Goudy, etc.

**type high** — The height of letterpress type, 23.317mm in Britain and the U.S.; also, the height of the photoengraving when blocked for printing on letterpress

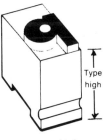

type high

**typography** — The study, practice, and art of using or designing with movable type

**Tyrian purple** — Pigment; an obsolete purple used by the Greeks and Romans

# U

**U-gouge** — A woodcutting tool, scoop-shaped like the letter *U*

U-gouge

**Ukiyo-e** — (Japanese, *floating world*) Eighteenth-century, and after, art featuring woodblock prints depicting everyday customs and habits. Inexpensive prints that attracted the attention of Europeans and sold well in Europe as well as Japan

**ulna** — The inner parallel bone to the radius bone in the forearm, placed slightly behind the radius

**ultramarine blue** — Pigment; a deep blue, transparent and permanent

**ultramarine green** — Pigment; a pale green, semitransparent, permanent

**ultramarine red** — Pigment; a pale red, semitransparent, permanent

**ultramarine violet** — Pigment; a pale violet, semitransparent, permanent

**ultramarine yellow** — Pigment; a pale yellow, semitransparent, permanent

**umber** — Pigment. *See* **burnt umber; raw umber**

**umbra** — (Latin, *shade* or *shadow*) The darkest part of a shadow on a curved surface

**Umbrian school** — Artists working in central Italy in the fifteenth and sixteenth centuries. Important artists were Perugino, Pintoricchio, and Raphael

**undercut** — In woodcarving, to cut back and beneath an exposed edge

**undercutting** — When acid gives a side-bitten effect, it is undercut

**underpainting** — The first paint applied to a picture surface, to be overpainted with other layers or glazes of paint; also called *abbozzo*

**underpainting white** — A quick-drying white oil paint used in underpainting

**undertint** — A transparent undercoat or veil, over a white ground

**undertone** — The underneath or less noticeable part of a colour, as the bluish undertone of alizarin red

**uninked intaglio** — Blind embossing from an intaglio plate

**universal perspective** — Perspective from different eye levels in the same picture

**universal quality** — In art, a quality that is not limited or dated, but creates the feeling of agelessness

**unprimed canvas** — Raw canvas or support that has no primer on it

**unsized** — Without any sizing or filler

**uppercase letters** — Capital letters

**urn** — A vase or a vase shape

**Utrecht school** — An early seventeeth-century Dutch school emulating the style of Caravaggio. The most important artists were Baburen, Honthorst, and Terbrugghen; influenced Hals and Rembrandt

# V

**value patch** — An area in a painting that has a specific value

**value scale** — The range from light to dark, including white, greys, and black; colours can be evaluated on this scale. Values are often numbered on scales of 0 to 10. In one system 0 = black and 10 = white; another system reverses the designations and has 0 for white and 10 for black. Generally, high values are considered to be light, and low values dark

**Vandyke brown** — Pigment; a dark earth brown close to burnt umber, moderately permanent

**Vandyke red** — Pigment; shades of brownish red, brown, and reddish violet; an obsolete, toxic colour

**Van Eyck, Jan** — 1390?-1441, Dutch painter whose style demonstrates the transition from the medieval to the Renaissance in its modelling and attention to detail, best exemplified in his best-known painting, *The Arnolfini Marriage*

**Van Eyck green** — Pigment; verdigris, hydrated copper acetate, obsolete

**Van Gogh, Vincent Villem** — 1853-1890, probably one of the world's best known painters as a result of events in his personal life rather than his art. His early work shows him as a capable draughtsman, but he was also a vivid and powerful user of colour in a way best described as Expressionist. Often disturbing, his work always provokes thought by its composition, execution and perspective

**vanishing point(s)** — In perspective, a point or points on the horizon at which parallel lines converge

vanishing point by Michael Woods

**vanitas** — *See* **memento mori**

**vantage point** — An advantageous point from which to view something; the position from which you view a scene

**varnish** — A protective liquid or spray coating used as a finish coat on oil paints. *See also* **retouch varnish**

**Vasarely, Victor** — A Hungarian who migrated to Paris in 1930 and devoted himself to advertising. He became an innovator of op art/vibration art, working with geometric shapes and colour combinations for optical effect

**veduta** — A painting attempting faithfully to represent a portion of a town or city

**veduta ideata** — An imaginary view of a place, realistically rendered

**vehicle** — 1. A word often used in place of *medium*. 2. The liquid that is ground with dry pigments

**veil** — *See* **undertint**

**veining tool** — A *V*-shaped tool used in wood carving to cut a broad channel

**vellum** — Originally a writing and painting surface, made from young animal hides. A fine parchment; name now given to a heavy, smooth paper used as fine stationery and a semismooth drawing paper, also called *kid finish*

**vellum cloth** — A fine cotton cloth made into a transparent tracing film

**velour paper** — A heavy paper that looks and feels like velvet, good for pastels; available in different colours

**velox** — An American term designating a screened photographic print of a continuous-tone photo, or a piece of art that can be printed in line, without halftone screening

**velvet brown** — Pigment; an obsolete name for fawn brown, which is also obsolete

**Venetian red** — Pigment; a reddish earth colour, permanent, different from burnt sienna or Indian red

**Venetian school** — Initially the workshops of St. Mark's, under the influence of Paolo Veneziano in the fourteenth century; later, more of an attitude of place than a school. In the sixteenth century it was dominated by great Venetian artists including Bellini, Canaletto, Gorgione, Guardi, Tintoretto, and Titian

**Venice red** — Pigment; Venetian red

**verdaccio** — A neutral or brownish green colour similar to raw umber, used as an outline, shading, or undercoating by Italian painters in the fourteenth century

**Verderame** — Pigment; verdigris, hydrated copper acetate, obsolete

**verdetta** — Pigment; green earth, name obsolete

**verdigris** — Pigment; a light bluish green made from hydrated copper acetate, obsolete. *See also* **patina**

**vermilion** — A bright orange red comparable to cadmium red light. Considered permanent, but if exposed to the sun for a length of time, it turns dark

**Vernet green** — Pigment; Bremen green, a form of Bremen blue which is a combination of copper hydroxide and copper carbonate; toxic and obsolete

**Verona brown** — Pigment; burnt green earth, name obsolete

**Verona green** — Pigment; green earth, name obsolete

**Veronese green** — Pigment; a pale viridian, name obsolete

**verso** — Left-hand page. *See also* **recto**

**vertebrae** — The thirty-three bones or cartilaginous segments forming the spinal column

**vert emeraude** — Pigment; viridian, a transparent green, permanent

**vertical** — Up and down, at right angles to a base line

**Vestorian blue** — Pigment; Egyptian or colbalt blue

**vibration art** — An optical sensation, partly manipulated by design and partly by colour. *See also* **op art**

**Victorian art** — Nineteenth-century style in Britain at the time of Queen Victoria; tends to be romantic, ornamental, and massive

**video art** — Video technology used as a means of expression to be seen on a television screen; Andy Warhol, among others, has recorded such images

**Vienna blue** — Pigment; an obsolete name for cobalt blue

**Vienna green** — Pigment; copper arsenate, toxic, obsolete

**Vienna lake** — Pigment; carmine, a fugitive lake

**viewfinder** — A small (about 10 × 12.5mm) cardboard frame used to isolate or frame a scene in order to locate a desired composition to be painted or sketched

**viewpoint** *See* **station point**

**vignette** — 1. An irregular shape to a picture without square edges to frame it. 2. A photograph that is prepared (usually with airbrush) so the edges fade gradually to white

**vine black** — Pigment; an inferior carbon black with a bluish undertone

**Vingt, les** — (French, *the Twenty*) A group of twenty avant-garde painters, active from 1884-1894 in Brussels, who promoted and exhibited new and unconventional art. A few of their exhibitors were Cézanne, Gauguin, Monet, Pissaro, Renoir, Seurat, and Van Gogh

**vinyl inks** — Inks used in silk screen for printing on vinyl, usually commercial; opaque but can be thinned with a special base to become transparent; toxic and flammable

**violent** — Said of strong, hard, and/or harsh artwork

**violet** — Pigment; a light purple colour

**violet carmine** — Pigment; a clear reddish violet, transparent and fugitive

**violet madder lake** — Pigment; alizarin violet, a clear transparent lake, fugitive

**violet ultramarine** — Pigment; ultramarine violet, pale, transparent, and permanent

**viridi aeris** — Pigment; a bluish green, hydrated copper acetate, obsolete

**viridian** — Pigment; a transparent dark green, permanent

**viscosity** — The degree of thickness in paint or ink

**viscosity printing** — The process of printing with two or more viscosities of ink, which may also be different colours; one roll-up will use an oily ink and the second will be drier, thus producing different textures and colours all from one plate

**visual** — In commercial art, a layout of a proposed artwork

**visual arts** — Graphics, painting, sculpture, and architecture, as opposed to the performing arts of the theatre, music, dance, opera, and writing

**visualizing paper** — A transparent paper used mostly for layouts and design work

**visual pad** — A pad of paper that has removable sheets of transparent paper

**visual weight** — The ability of a picture element to attract attention and thus assume its part in establishing visual balance

**vogue** — The prevailing style or fashion of the time

**void** — 1. An area where there is nothing happening, emptiness which needs to be filled. 2. A hole in a picture

**volume** — Bulk; mass; space occupied

**volute** — In design, a spiral form; a scroll-like ornament

**vorticism** — An art movement in England, 1912-1915, an offshoot of cubism and futurism, led by Wyndham Lewis. Simplified forms into angular, machine-like representation, abstract and often nonobjective. Prominent in the movement were Jacob Epstein, Henri Gaudier-Brzeska, William Roberts, Edward Wadsworth, and C.R. Nevinson

**voussoir** — In architecture, one of the wedge-shaped stones forming a stone arch

voluted column

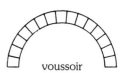

voussoir

# W

**waffle** — *See* **honeycomb**

**walk-off** — In graphic printing, the impairment or deterioration of part of an image on the plate during the printing process

**wall of Troy** — *See* **Greek key**

**wall painting** — *See* **mural**

**walling wax** — *See* **bordering wax**

**Warhol, Andy** — 1928?-1987, enigmatic American painter who first came to notice in the pop-art boom of the early 1960s. Much of his work is deliberately provocative, but his art and film-making have been surprisingly influential

**warm colours** — Colours in which red, orange, and yellow predominate

**warming the ink** — In printmaking, the act of softening the ink on a hard surface

**warp** — 1. The bend that develops in stretcher strips, frames, paper boards and hardboards, usually due to unseasoned wood or to moisture. 2. In textile design, the lengthwise or vertical yarn in weaving

**wash** — A thin, liquid application of paint in any medium, brushed on in a free-flowing manner. In oil colours, when applied over dry underpainting, it is a *glaze*

**wash out** — 1. In lithography, to wash the stone with a sponge and turpentine just before inking. 2. In water-based painting, to remove a painted area of a picture by applying water and washing out the colour as much as possible with brush or sponge

**watercolour** — Paint that uses water as the medium; categories are: traditional watercolours – transparent; gouache – opaque; casein – a

watercolours

209

casein glue pigment, opaque; acrylics – used as watercolour, transparent or opaque

**watercolour block** — A number of watercolour papers, bound on all four sides to lie flat, designed so the top sheet may be painted on, then removed singly, leaving the next sheet ready for use

**watercolour mediums** — Mainly water; two special types are available from Winsor and Newton: watercolour medium No. 1 encourages smooth application and No. 2 enriches the colours; also called *wetting agents*

**watercolour pad** — Sheets of watercolour paper bound into tablet form

**watercolour paper** — Paper made specifically for watercolours; hot pressed (HP) – smooth; cold pressed (CP) – medium texture; and not pressed (Not) – or rough (R) – heavier, rougher texture; 100 percent rag content is a superior paper

**watercolour paper sizes** — Demi, 15 × 20 in; medium, 17 × 22 in; royal, 19 × 24 in; imperial, 22 × 30 in; elephant, 23 × 28 in; double elephant, 26½ × 40 in; and antiquarian 31 × 53 in. Imperial is the most common in single sheets. Rolls of paper are also available

**watercolour paper weights** — 72 lb. – lightweight; 90 lb. – lightweight; 140 lb. – medium weight; 250 lb. – medium weight; 300 lb. – heavyweight; 400 lb. heavyweight; 555 lb. – extra-heavy weight; 1114 lb. – extra, extra-heavy weight. 72 lb., 140 lb., and 300 lb. are most popular

**watercolour pencils** — Pencils made in various colours of watercolour pigments, used for drawing, or dipped in water to create texture. When a wet brush is pulled across the coloured line a wash effect is generated

**waterleaf paper** — unsized paper

**watermark** — A translucent name or design moulded into paper during the manufacturing process; more visible when held to a light

**water mask** — In silkscreen, a block-out used as a stencil filler; it dries fast and is removed with water

**water mat gold size** — A stiff paste sizing used for illumination where gilt is applied; can become moist and tacky to accept gilt when it is warmed by breathing on it

**water-of-Ayr stone** — *See* **snake slip**

**waterscape** — A picture in which a body of water is a primary compositional element; surrounding land area, trees, boats, shacks, etc. may also be included

**wave scroll** — A running design that suggests a breaking wave

**wax coater** — A tool that applies an even coat of wax to paper, plastic, film, cardboard, etc., so it is pressure-sensitive for mounting pasteups. One type is large and stationary and another is a hand-held roller-like tool

**waxed Masa** — A waxed Japanese rice paper, used mostly by textile designers; soft but strong and translucent

**wax medium** — A concentrated wax used for encaustic painting and for preserving wood carvings, paintings, art objects, etc.

**wax painting** — *See* **encaustic**

**wax proofing** — A method of pulling a rough print from a paper covered with melted wax

**wax varnish** — A paste varnish made from beeswax and petroleum spirit; can be thinned with rectified petroleum, applied with a cloth or brush

**weak artwork** — Artwork that lacks character or strength, has no impact, is bland; often refers to timid use of values or colour in painting or to unsure drawing

**weaving** — In textile design, the process of forming a fabric on a loom by interlacing the warp and woof

**weft** — *See* **woof**

**weight** — The visual feeling of mass or heaviness in a composition; the heaviness of line, shape, size, value, colour, or texture

**weld** — A natural yellow dyestuff, practically obsolete

**welding** — Joining metal parts in metal sculpture

**wet-in-wet** — Painting additional colour into an already wet area, creating a soft, flowing effect. Usually applies only to water-based mediums

**wet palette** — A palette of colours that are still loose and workable; the paint is not dry and hard

**wetting agent** — *See* **watercolour mediums**

**Whatman** — A high-quality watercolour paper first made in 1724. Unavailable for some years, it has now been reintroduced

**James Abbot
McNeill Whistler**
*The Little White Girl:
Symphony in White
No. 2*

**wheat** — Pigment; an off-white mixture, usually
with a yellow undertone
**wheel, colour** — *See* **colour wheel**
**whiplash line** — A line prominent in art nouveau
**Whistler, James Abbott McNeill** — 1834-1903,
born in America, a painter, etcher, and portraitist
who spent most of his life abroad
**white** — Pigment: Chinese white – zinc white;
Cremnitz, Krems, or Kremnitz white – a white
lead paint, toxic; flake white – gives good
coverage, excellent drier, flexible film, has a
tendency to yellow or turn dark, toxic; lead white
– flake and Cremnitz; zinc white – brilliant, cold
white, brittle, slow-drying, permanent and
nontoxic; titanium white – opaque, gives good
coverage, nondiscolouring and nontoxic
**white-on-white** — An embossed print made with
an uninked plate. Some avant-garde artists have
dealt with white-on-white paintings. *See*
**suprematism**
**whiteout** — to use an opaque white paint to block
out unwanted areas
**white spirits** — *See* **mineral spirits**
**whiting** — A type of chalk, a natural calcium
carbonate, used as a filler in gesso and in cheaper
paints

212

**Wiener Werkstätte** — A Viennese organization of designers and craftsmen started in 1903, dedicated to certain aesthetic principles; their style is related to art nouveau

**Williamsburg collection** — In textile design, designs pertinent to America in the 1700s, based on the research of the Williamsburg, Virginia restoration

**wind chimes** — Pieces of bamboo, wood, metal, or glass hanging from a string or wire, so the air currents can move them to make sounds. *See* **mobile**

**Win-gel** — Trade name for a clear medium for oils and alkyd, to increase the gloss and transparency

**Winsor colours** — Trade name for a variety of pigments which substitute for expensive or impermanent colours in the artists' range

**Winton** — Trade name for a range of students' quality oil colours and sundries

**wipe-on plate** — In photolithography, a light-sensitive plate

**wire-end modelling tools** — Tools with many different-shaped wire ends, used to model clay, plaster, etc.

**woad** — A blue dye used in the Middle Ages

**wood-burning tool** — An electric tool with a point or interchangeable points, used to burn or incise a design on wood, leather, and other materials and sometimes to create a wormwood effect on frames

**woodcut** — In graphic arts, a relief print obtained when knives and tools are used to cut a design with the grain into wood, and the surface not cut away is printed

fifteenth-century woodcut of St Dorothy

**wood engraving** — A process in which the design is cut on the end grain of a wood block. Usually only very hard, even-grained wood such as cherry, pear, or boxwood is used. When printed, the lines are usually white against a dark ground

**Wood, Grant** — 1892-1942, American, a metal craftsman turned painter who became famous for his realistic but stilted style.

**woodless drawing pencil** — A solid stick of graphite, lacquer-coated; can be sharpened to a drawing point. Available in a variety of weights

**woof** — In textile design, the filling threads, running horizontally in weaving; also called the *weft*

**word spacing** — Increasing or decreasing the
space between words in copy or lettering

**workable eraser** — *See* **kneaded eraser**

**working proof** — In graphics, a trial proof on
which corrections and additions are indicated

**worm's-eye view** — A picture in oblique
perspective from an extremely low eye level, with
the horizon at the bottom of the picture or below it

**wove paper** — Paper with a smooth, uniform
surface, unlined in texture

**wrapping** — A so-called art form mainly associated
with the Bulgarian, Christo, consisting of
wrapping buildings, mountains, and other forms
with material such as plastic sheeting; this
procedure is called *empaquetage*

**writing brush** — *See* **calligraphy brush**

Caslon Bold with Ital
Caslon Bold with Italic

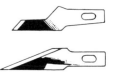

X-acto knife blades

**X-Acto knife** — Trade name for a small, sharp
knife used to cut paper, friskets, cardboard, mats,
etc., having different handles and shapes of
blades for a variety of jobs

x-height of several 48 point typefaces

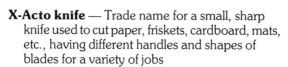

**x-height** — The height of lowercase letters; various
typefaces have different x-heights for the same
point size

**xylography** — Woodprint engraving or
woodcutting to produce a woodblock print

# Y

**Yamato-e** — The traditional painting style of Japan

**Yamato school** — A Japanese ninth-century school that lasted five centuries; the famous Kose Kanaoka painted landscapes and portraits in a pure Japanese style

**yeast black** — Pigment; a form of vine black, carbon, name obsolete

**Yellow Book style** — *See* **art nouveau**

**yellow carmine** — Pigment; a yellow lake, transparent and fugitive

**yellowing** — Discolouration of paint or paper that becomes darker from age or poor quality of product

**yellow ochre** — Pigment; a yellow earth, opaque and permanent

**yellow oxide of iron** — Pigment; a brilliant artificial yellow earth, permanent

**yellow ultramarine** — Pigment; an obsolete name for barium yellow

# Z

**Zen calligraphy** — Calligraphy executed by the Zen monks; the strokes are of a bold and pure nature

**zensho** — Zen calligraphy

**zinc chrome** — Pigment; zinc yellow

**zinc green** — Pigment; cobalt green

**zincography** — A lithographic process using zinc plates in place of stone

**zinc oxide** — Pigment; zinc white

**zinc white** — Pigment; *See* **white**

**zinc yellow** — Pigment; colour close to cadmium yellow pale on the colour chart, semiopaque, toxic, and permanent

**zinnober** — Pigment; vermilion, obsolete

**zoomorphic design** — Designs, symbols, or ornaments based on animal forms

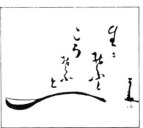

Zen calligraphy – an ancient oriental saying: whether for life or for death depends on what's in the spoon

# Noteworthy Artists of the Western World

This list in chronological order identifies artists who have made a telling contribution to Western art in the past 800 years. Many of the names are household words, known throughout the world as the giants of our culture. However, not all those listed are of equally lofty stature. Some artists are included because their approach is helpful in defining periods and establishing guideposts for schools, styles, and trends that followed.

The country or region following the artist's name is his place of origin, or the area with which he was closely associated through most of his career. The dates shown are the years of the artist's birth and death, or, if unknown, when he was active in his career.

**Code:**

c.  (circa) Approximate time; exact dates unknown
a.  The period when the artist is known to have been active; even approximate vital dates are unknown
f.  Indicates the artist was the *father* of one or more of the listed artists
s.  The *son* of another listed artist
b.  The *brother* of one or more of the listed artists
sc.  The artist is chiefly known as a sculptor
*[Brackets]* indicate the name by which the artist is usually known

Many fine examples of Western art predate the thirteenth century; however, relatively few such works can be traced to specific individuals. Many earlier masterpieces were either created by an unknown artist, or by artists working as a team, usually anonymously.

*Thirteenth century*

Nicola Pisano (Pisa, a. 1258-1278) f., sc.
Guido (Siena, a. 1260-1285)
Giovanni Pisano (Pisa, a. 1265-1314) s., sc.
Giotto (Florence, c. 1267-1337)
Cimabue (Florence, a. 1272-1302)
Cavallini (central Italy, a. 1273-1330)
Duccio (Siena, a. 1278-1318)
Simone Martini (Siena, c. 1285-1344)
Tino di Camaino (Siena, c. 1285-1337) sc.

*Fourteenth century*

Gaddi (Florence, c. 1300-1366)
Ambrogio Lorenzetti (Siena, a. 1319-1348) b.
Pietro Lorenzetti (Siena, a. 1320-1348) b.
Altichiero (northern Italy, c. 1330-1395)
Orcagna (Florence, a. 1344-1368)
Gentile Da Fabriano (central Italy, c. 1360-1427)
Hubert Van Eyck (Flanders, c. 1366-1426) b.
Bertram (Germany, a. 1367-1387)
Campin (Flanders, 1375-1444)
Jan Van Eyck (Flanders, c. 1390-1440) b.
Masolino (Florence, c. 1383-1447)
Donatello (Florence, 1386-1466) sc.
Lorenzo Monaco (Florence, a. 1388-1422)
Sassetta (Siena, c. 1392-1450)
Pisanello (northern Italy, c. 1395-1455)

Uccello (Florence, 1397-1475)
Malonel (France, a. 1396-1419)
Van der Weyden (Flanders, c. 1399-1464)

*Fifteenth century*

Fra Angelico (Florence, c. 1400-1455)
Jacopo Bellini (Venice, c. 1400-1470) f.
Multscher (Germany, a. 1400-1467)
Tommaso Giovanni Guidi [Masaccio] (Florence, c. 1401-1428)
Pol de Limbourg (France, a. 1402-1416)
Giovanni Di Paolo (Siena, c. 1403-1482)
K. Von Soest (Germany, a. 1405-1422)
Fra Filippo Lippi (Florence, c. 1406-1469)
Petrus Christus (Flanders, c. 1410-1472)
Lochner (Germany, a. 1410-1451)
Castagno (Florence, c. 1410-1457)
Domenico Veneziano (Florence, c. 1410-1461)
Vecchietta (Siena, 1412-1480)
Antonio Vivarini (Venice, c. 1415-1484)
Piero Della Francesca (central Italy, c. 1416-1492)
Fouquet (France, c. 1420-1481)
Dirck Bouts (Flanders, c. 1420-1475)
Benozzo Gozzoli (Florence, c. 1420-1497)
Andrea Bregno (central Italy, 1421-1506) sc.
Gentile Bellini (Venice, c. 1429-1507) s., b.
Francke (Germany, a. 1424-1435)
Baldovinetti (Florence, 1425-1499)

Matteo Di Giovanni (Siena, c. 1430-1495)
Giovanni Bellini (Venice, c. 1430-1516) s., b.
Antonello Da Messina (Venice, c. 1430-1479)
Cosimo Tura (northern Italy, 1430-1495)
Memling (Flanders, c. 1430-1494)
Schongauer (Germany, c. 1430-1491)
Pollaiuolo, A. (Florence, c. 1431-1498)
Mantegna (northern Italy, 1431-1506)
Lucas Moser (Germany, a. 1431-1440)
Pietro Lombardo (Italy, 1433-1515) sc.
Konard Witz (Switzerland, a. 1433-1447)
Pacher (Germany, c. 1435-1498)
Cossa (northern Italy, c. 1435-1498)
Crivelli (Venice, c. 1435-1495)
Verrocchio (Florence, 1435-1488)
Martorell (Spain, a. 1433-1453)
Melozzo da Forli (central Italy, 1438-1494)
Francesco Di Giorgio (Siena, 1439-1502)
Nan der Goes (Flanders, c. 1440-1482)
Signorelli (central Italy, c. 1441-1523)
Botticelli (Florence, c. 1444-1510)
Neroccio Di Landi (Siena, 1447-1500)
Pietro Perugino (central Italy, 1445-1523)
Hieronymus Bosch (Flanders, c. 1450-1516)
Gerald David (Flanders, c. 1450-1523)
Chirlandaio (Florence, 1449-1494)
Veit Stoss (Germany, 1450-1533) sc.
Froment (France, a. 1450-1490)
Leonardo da Vinci (Florence, 1452-1519)
Pinturicchio (northern Italy, 1454-1513)
Carpaccio (Venice, c. 1455-1526)
Filippino Lippi (Florence, 1457-1504)
Mathias Grünewald (Germany, c. 1460-1528)
Hans Holbein, The Elder (Germany, 1460-1524) f.
Massye (Flanders, c. 1466-1530)
Albrecht Dürer (Germany, 1471-1528)
Lucas Cranach (Germany, 1472-1553)
Fra Bartholommeo (Florence, 1472-1517)
Bermejo (Spain, a. 1474-1495)
Jean Clouet (France, c. 1475-1547)
Michelangelo (Florence, 1475-1564)
Sodoma (Siena, 1477-1549)
Jan Gossaert [Mabuse] (Flanders, c. 1478-1533)
Joachim Patenier [Patinir] (Flanders, c. 1478-1524)
Giorgione (Venice, 1478-1510)
Dosso Dossi (northern Italy, c. 1479-1542)
Altdorfer (Germany, c. 1480-1538)
Hans Baldung [Grien] (Germany, 1480-1545)
Palma Vecchio (Venice, 1480-1528)
Lorenzo Lotto (Venice, 1480-1556)
Raphael (central Italy, 1483-1520)
Sebastiano Del Piombo (Venice, 1485-1547)
Giulio Romano (central Italy, 1492-1546)
Andrea Del Sarto (Florence, 1486-1531)
Beccafumi (Siena, c. 1486-1551)
Titian (Venice, 1487-1576)
Rosso Fiorentino (Florence, 1494-1540)
Correggio (northern Italy, 1494-1534)
Pontormo (Florence, c. 1494-1557)
Lucas Van Leyden (Holland, 1494-1533)
Jan Van Scorel (Flanders, 1495-1562)
Hans Holbein, The Younger (Germany, 1497-1543) s.
Moretto (northern Italy, c. 1498-1555)

Maerten Van Heemskerck (Holland, 1498-1574)

*Sixteenth century*

Benvenuto Cellini (Florence, 1500-1571) sc.
Bronzino (Florence, c. 1503-1572)
Parmigianino (northern Italy, 1503-1540)
Aertsen (Holland, 1508-1575)
Morales (Spain, 1509-1586)
Jean Goujon (France, 1510-1568) sc
Jacopo Bassano (Venice, 1510-1592)
Coello (Spain, 1515-1590)
Antonis Mor [Moro] (Holland, c. 1519-1576)
Tintoretto (Venice, 1518-1594)
Moroni (northern Italy, c. 1525-1578)
Pieter Bruegel, The Elder (Flanders, c. 1525-1569) f.
Veronese (Venice, 1528-1588)
Giovanni Bologna (Italy, 1529-1608) sc.
Domenikos Theotocopoulos [El Greco] (Spain, c. 1542-1614)
Nichols Hillard (England, c. 1547-1619)
Annibale Carracci (Italy, 1560-1609)
Pietro Bernini (Italy, 1562-1629) f., sc.
Caravaggio (Italy, c. 1565-1609)
Gentileschi (Italy, c. 1565-1647)
Pieter Brueghel (Flanders, 1564-1638) s.b.
Jan Brueghel (Flanders, 1568-1625) s.b.
Guido Reni (Italy, 1575-1642)
Pietro Tacca (Florence, 1577-1640) sc.
Peter Paul Rubens (Flanders, 1577-1640)
Elsheimer (Germany, c. 1578-1610)
Frans Hals (Holland, 1580-1666)
Strozzi (Italy, 1581-1644)
Terbrugghen (Holland, c. 1588-1629)
Ribera (Spain, 1588-1652)
Antoine LeNain (France, c. 1588-1648) b.
Seghers (Holland, c. 1589-1638)
Honthorst (Holland, 1590-1656)
Guercino (Italy, 1591-1666)
Maurice LaTour (France, 1593-1652)
Jacob Jordaens (Flanders, 1593-1678)
Louis LeNain (France, 1593-1648) b.
Nicolas Poussin (France, 1594-1665)
Hubert LeSueur (France, c. 1595-1650) sc.
Pietro Da Cortona (Italy, 1596-1669)
Jan Van Goyen (Holland, 1596-1656)
Pieter Saenredam (Holland, 1597-1665)
Zurbaran (Spain, 1598-1664)
Gianlorenzo Bernini (Italy, 1598-1680) s., sc.
Van Dyck (Flanders, 1599-1641)
Velasquez (Spain, 1599-1660)

*Seventeenth century*

Claude Lorrain (France, 1600-1682)
Champaigne (France, 1602-1674)
Brouwer (Flanders, 1605-1638)
Rembrandt (Holland, 1606-1669)
Mathieu LeNain (France, 1607-1677) b.
David Teniers (Flanders, 1610-1690)
Van Ostade (Holland, 1610-1684)
Salvatore Rosa (Italy, 1615-1673)

217

Emanuel De Witte (Holland, 1617-1692)
Gerald Ter Borch (Holland, 1617-1681)
Murillo (Spain, 1617-1682)
Peter Lely (England, 1618-1680)
Charles Lebrun (France, 1619-1690)
Cuyp (Holland, 1620-1691)
Fabritus (Holland, c. 1622-1654)
Jan Steen (Holland, 1626-1679)
Francois Girardon (France, 1628-1715) sc.
Jacob Van Ruidael (Holland, c. 1628-1682)
Pieter De Hoogh (Holland, 1629-1683)
Jan Vermeer van Delft (Holland, 1632-1675)
Hobbema (Holland, 1638-1709)
Jose de Mora (Spain, 1642-1724) sc.
Kneller (England, 1646-1723)
Rigaud (France, 1659-1743)
Magnasco (Italy, 1677-1749)
Van Huysum (Holland, 1682-1749)
Watteau (France, 1684-1721)
Nattier (France, 1685-1766)
John Smibert (USA, 1688-1751)
Tiepolo (Italy, 1696-1770)
Canaletto (Italy, 1697-1768)
Hogarth (England, 1697-1764)
Chardin (France, 1699-1779)
Bouchardon (France, 1698-1762) sc.

*Eighteenth century*

Liotard (Swiss, 1702-1789)
Pietro Longli (Italy, 1702-1785)
François Boucher (France, 1703-1770)
Robert Feke (USA, c. 1705-1750)
Guardi (Italy, 1712-1793)
Richard Wilson (England, 1714-1792)
Joshua Reynolds (England, 1723-1792)
Greuze (France, 1725-1805)
Thomas Gainsborough (England, 1727-1788)
Anton Mengs (Germany, 1728-1779)
Fragonard (France, 1732-1806)
George Romney (England, 1734-1802)
John Singleton Copley (USA, 1737-1815)
Benjamin West (USA, 1737-1820)
Jean-Antoine Houdon (France, 1741-1828) sc.
Charles Wilson Peale (USA, 1741-1827) f.
Goya (Spain, 1746-1828)
Jacques-Louis David (France, 1748-1825)
Gilbert Stuart (USA, 1755-1828)
John Trumbull (USA, 1756-1843)
Henry Raeburn (England, 1756-1823)
Thomas Rowlandson (England, 1756-1827)
Antonio Canova (Italy, 1757-1822) sc.
William Blake (England, 1757-1827)
Prud'hon (France, 1758-1823)
Georges Michel (France, 1763-1843)
John Crome (England, 1768-1821)
Bertel Thorwaldsen (Denmark, 1768-1844) sc.
Thomas Lawrence (England, 1769-1830)
Gros (France, 1771-1835)
Caspar Friedrich (Germany, 1774-1840)
Phillip Otto Runge (Germany, 1777-1810)
Raphaelle Peale (USA, 1774-1825) s., b.
Thomas Girtin (England, 1775-1802)
J.M.W. Turner (England, 1775-1851)

Rembrandt Peale (USA, 1778-1860) s., b.
John Constable (England, 1776-1817)
Washington Allston (USA, 1779-1843)
Jean Auguste Ingres (France, 1780-1867)
John Sell Cotman (England, 1782-1842)
Thomas Scully (USA, 1785-1851)
John James Audubon (USA, 1785-1851)
Gericault (France, 1791-1824)
Jean-Baptiste Corot (France, 1796-1875)
Eugene Delacroix (France, 1798-1863)

*Nineteenth century*

Richard Bonnington (England, 1801-1828)
Thomas Cole (USA, 1801-1848)
Narcisse-Vergile Diaz (France, 1807-1876)
Honoré Daumier (France, 1810-1879)
George Caleb Bingham (USA, 1811-1879)
Theodore Rousseau (France, 1812-1867)
Jean Francois Millet (France, 1814-1875)
Adolf Menzel (Germany, 1815-1905)
Alfred Stevens (England, 1818-1875) sc.
Gustave Courbet (France, 1819-1877)
Johan Jongkind (Holland, 1819-1891)
Rosa Bonheur (France, 1822-1899)
Puvis De Chavannes (France, 1824-1898)
George Inness (USA, 1825-1894)
William A. Bougureau (France, 1825-1905)
Frederic E. Church (USA, 1826-1900)
W.H. Hunt (England, 1827-1910)
Jean-Baptiste Carpeaux (France, 1827-1875) sc.
Arnold Boecklin (Switzerland, 1827-1901)
Dante G. Rossetti (England, 1828-1882)
John E. Millais (England, 1829-1896)
Albert Bierstadt (USA, 1830-1902)
Camille Pissarro (France, 1830-1903)
Edouard Manet (France, 1832-1883)
Eduard Burne-Jones (England, 1833-1898)
Edgar Degas (France, 1834-1917)
James McNeill Whistler (USA, 1834-1903)
John La Farge (USA, 1835-1910)
Winslow Homer (USA, 1836-1910)
Marees (Germany, 1837-1887)
Paul Cézanne (France, 1839-1906)
Odilon Redon (France, 1840-1916)
Claude Monet (France, 1840-1926)
Auguste Rodin (France, 1840-1917) sc.
Pierre A. Renoir (France, 1841-1919)
Berthe Morisot (France, 1841-1895)
Henri Rousseau (France, 1844-1910)
Thomas Eakins (USA, 1844-1916)
Wilhelm Leibel (Germany, 1844-1900)
Mary Cassatt (USA, 1845-1926)
Albert Ryder (USA, 1847-1917)
Augustus Saint-Gaudens (USA, 1848-1907) sc.
Paul Gauguin (France, 1848-1903)
William M. Harnett (USA, 1848-1892)
William Merritt Chase (USA, 1849-1916)
Christian Rohifs (Germany, 1849-1938)
Edwin Austin Abbey (USA, 1852-1911)
Howard Pyle (USA, 1853-1911)
Vincent van Gogh (Holland, 1853-1890)
Ferdinand Holder (Switzerland, 1853-1918)
Charles Niehaus (USA, 1855-1935)

John Singer Sargent (USA, 1856-1925)
Thomas Dewing (USA, 1857-1938)
Lovis Corinth (Germany, 1858-1925)
Childe Hassam (USA, 1859-1935)
Maurice Prendergast (USA, 1859-1924)
Georges Seurat (France, 1859-1891)
James Ensor (Belgium, 1860-1949)
Anders Zorn (Sweden, 1860-1920)
Aristide Maillot (France, 1861-1944) sc.
Anna Moses [Grandma Moses] (USA, 1860-1961)
Frederic Remington (USA, 1861-1909)
Arthur Davies (USA, 1862-1928)
Frank W. Benson (USA, 1862-1951)
Gustav Klimt (Austria, 1862-1918)
Paul Signac (France, 1863-1935)
Edvard Munch (Norway, 1863-1944)
Joaquin Sorolla (Spain, 1863-1923)
Charles M. Russell (USA, 1864-1926)
Henri de Toulouse-Lautrec (France, 1864-1901)
Robert Henri (USA, 1865-1929)
Pavel Trubetskoy (Russia, 1866-1938) sc.
Wassily Kandinsky (Russia, 1866-1944)
Charles Dana Gibson (USA, 1867-1944)
Pierre Bonnard (France, 1867-1947)
George Luks (USA, 1867-1933)
Emil Nolde (Germany, 1867-1956)
Frank Brangwyn (England, 1867-1956)
Edouard Vuillard (France, 1868-1940)
Henri Matisse (France, 1869-1954)
John Marin (USA, 1870-1953)
Maxfield Parrish (USA, 1870-1966)
William Glackens (USA, 1870-1938)
Ignacio Zuloaga (Spain, 1870-1945)
John Sloan (USA, 1871-1951)
Lyonel Feinnger (USA, 1871-1956)
Georges Rouault (France, 1871-1958)
Kupka (Czech., 1871-1957)
Giacomo Balla (Italy, 1871-1958)
Aubrey Beardsley (England, 1872-1898)
Piet Mondrian (Holland, 1872-1944)
Howard Chandler Christy (USA, 1873-1952)
Ernest Lawson (USA, 1873-1939)
Joseph Christian Leyendecker (USA, 1874-1951)
Constantin Brancusi (Rumania, 1876-1957) sc.
Vlamick (France, 1876-1958)
Boardman Robinson (USA, 1876-1952)
Everett Shin (USA, 1876-1953)
Anna Hyatt Huntington (USA, 1876-1973) sc.
Marsden Hartley (USA, 1877-1943)
Dufy (France, 1877-1953)
Augustus John (England, 1878-1961)
Kasimir Malevich (Russia, 1878-1935)
Paul Klee (Switzerland, 1879-1940)
Hans Hoffman (Germany, 1880-1966)
Franz Marc (Germany, 1880-1916)
Ernst Kirchner (Germany, 1880-1938)
Andre Derain (France, 1880-1954)
Russell Flint (England, 1880-1969)
Wilhelm, Lehmbruck (Germany, 1881-1919) sc.
Fernand Léger (France, 1881-1955)
Pablo Picasso (Spain, 1881-1973)
Nicolai Fechin (Russia, 1881-1955)
Max Weber (USA, 1881-1961)
Umberto Boccioni (Italy, 1882-1916)
Elie Nadelman (USA, 1882-1940) sc.

George Bellows (USA, 1882-1925)
Rockwell Kent (USA, 1882-1971)
N.C. Wyeth (USA, 1882-1945) f.
Georges Braque (France, 1882-1963)
Edward Hopper (USA, 1882-1967)
Maurice Utrillo (France, 1883-1955)
Charles Demuth (USA, 1883-1935)
Jo Davidson (USA, 1883-1952) sc.
Charles Sheeler (USA, 1883-1965)
Max Beckmann (Germany, 1884-1950)
Guy Pène Du Bois (USA, 1884-1958)
Van Doesburg (Holland, 1883-1931)
José Orozco (Mexico, 1883-1949)
Harvey Dunn (USA, 1884-1952)
Amedeo Modigliani (Italy, 1884-1920)
Wyndham Lewis (England, 1884-1957)
Robert Delunay (France, 1885-1941)
Paul Manship (USA, 1885-1966)
Milton Avery (USA, 1885-1965)
Oshar Kokoschka (Germany, 1886-1980)
Diego Rivera (Mexico, 1886-1957)
Lajos Kassak (Hungary, 1887-1967)
Juan Gris (Spain, 1887-1927)
Jean Arp (France, 1887-1976) sc.
Marcel Duchamp (France, 1887-1968)
Marc Chagall (Russian, 1887-1981)
Georgia O'Keeffe (USA, 1887-     )
Giorgio De Chirico (Italy, 1888-1978)
John Taylor Arms (USA, 1887-1953)
Thomas Hart Benton (USA, 1889-1975)
Giorgio Morandi (Italy, 1890-1964)
Mark Tobey (USA, 1890-     )
Max Ernst (Germany, 1891-1976)
Edwin Dickinson (USA, 1891-     )
Jacques Lipschitz (Lithuania, 1891-1973) sc.
Dean Cornwell (USA, 1892-1960)
Grant Wood (USA, 1892-1941)
Harold Von Schmidt (USA, 1892-1982)
Charles Burchfield (USA, 1893-1967)
Peter Helck (USA, 1893-     )
Joan Miro (Spain, 1893-1974)
George Grosz (Germany, 1893-1959)
Stuart Davis (USA, 1894-1964)
Chaim Soutine (Lithuania, 1894-1943)
Norman Rockwell (USA, 1894-1978)
John Steuart Curry (USA, 1897-1946)
Reginald Marsh (USA, 1898-1954)
Henry Moore (England, 1898-1986) sc.
Ben Shahn (USA, 1898-1969)
Alexander Calder (USA, 1898-1976) sc.
Rufino Tamayo (Mexico, 1899-     )
Raphael Soyer (USA, 1899-     )

*Twentieth century*

Rico Lebrun (USA, 1900-1964)
Louise Nevelson (USA, 1900-     ) sc.
Alberto Giacometti (Switzerland, 1901-1966) sc
Jean Dubuffet (France, 1901-     )
Philip Evergood (USA, 1901-1973)
Barbara Hepworth (England, 1903-1975) sc.
Graham Sutherland (England, 1903-1980)
Robert Fawcett (USA, 1903-1967)
Mark Rothko (USA, 1903-1970)

Adolph Gottlieb (USA, 1903-1974)
William De Kooning (USA, 1904-    )
Peter Hurd (USA, 1904-    )
Clyfford Still (USA, 1904-1980)
Salvador Dali (Spain, 1904-    )
Isamu Noguchi (USA, 1904-    ) sc.
Arshile Gorky (USA, 1905-1948)
Al Parker (USA, 1906-    )
David Smith (USA, 1906-1965) sc.
Fairfield Porter (USA, 1907-    )
John Clymer (USA, 1907-    )
Millard Sheets (USA, 1907-    )
Feliks Topolski (England, 1907-    )
Joseph Hirsch (USA, 1910-1981)
Ben Stahl (USA, 1910-    )
Francis Bacon (England, 1909-    )
Franz Kline (USA, 1910-1962)
Will Barnet (USA, 1911-    )
Matta Echaurren (Chile, 1912-    )
Jackson Pollock (USA, 1912-1956)
Ad Reinhardt (USA, 1913-1967)
Lynn Chadwick (England, 1914-    ) sc.
Robert Motherwell (USA, 1915-    )

Jack Levine (USA, 1915-    )
Andrew Wyeth (USA, 1917-    ) s.f.
Antonio Frasconi (Uruguay, 1919-    )
Richard Diebenkorn (USA, 1922-    )
Leonard Baskin (USA, 1922-    )
Larry Rivers (USA, 1923-    )
Roy Lichtenstein (USA, 1923-    ) .
Philip Pearlstein (USA, 1924-    )
George Segal (USA, 1924-    ) sc.
Robert Rauchenberg (USA, 1925-    )
Robert Vickery (USA, 1926-    )
Robert Indiana (USA, 1928-    )
Robert Peak, (USA, 1928-    )
Andy Warhol (USA, 1928?-1987)
Jasper Johns (USA, 1930-    )
Elizabeth Frink (England, 1930-    )
Bernard Fuchs (USA, 1932-    )
Mark English (USA, 1933-    )
Frank Stella (USA, 1939-    )
Ned Jacob (USA, 1938-    )
Larry Bell (USA, 1939-    ) sc.
James Wyeth (USA, 1946-    ) s.

# Bibliography

*The Artist's Directory* Heather Waddell & Richard Layzell, London, Art Guide
    Publications n.d.
*The Artist's Handbook of Materials & Techniques* Ralph Mayer, London, Faber
    4th ed 1981
*The Artist's Studio Book* Richard Seddon, London, Frederick Muller 1983
*Catalogue of Artists' Materials*, Harrow, Winsor & Newton current ed
*Catalogue of Artists' Materials*, Bracknell, Daler-Rowney current ed
*Catalogue of Artists' Materials*, Folkestone, Conté current ed
*Colour Theory* Michael Wilcox, London, Batsford 1985
*A Concise History of Art* Germain Bazin, London, Thames & Hudson 1958
*Contemporary Artists*, London, Macmillan 2nd ed 1983
*A Dictionary of Art Terms & Techniques* Ralph Mayer, London, Black 1969
*An Illustrated Dictionary of Art Terms* Kimberley Reynolds & Richard Seddon,
    London, Ebury Press 1981
*The Impressionists* William Gaunt, London, Thames & Hudson 1970
*The Materials of the Artist* Max Doerner, London, Hart Davis 1969
*Notes on the Composition & Permanence of Artists' Colours*, Harrow, Winsor &
    Newton n.d.
*The Phaidon Companion to Art & Artists in the British Isles* Michael Jacobs &
    Malcolm Warner, Oxford, Phaidon Press 1980
*Production for the Graphic Designer* James Craig, New York, Watson-Guptill
    1974
*The Story of Art* E H Gombrich, Oxford, Phaidon Press 1950
*The Writers' & Artists' Yearbook*, London, Black annual